SIGNING
EXACT
ENGLISH

SIGNING

EXACT

ENGLISH

1980 EDITION

Foreword by Hilde Schlesinger, M.D.
Preface by Louise and Tom Spradley

Contains the vocabulary of earlier editions, revisions based on recent research and usage, and approximately one thousand additional signs.

BY
GERILEE GUSTASON
DONNA PFETZING
ESTHER ZAWOLKOW
ILLUSTRATIONS BY
CAROLYN B. NORRIS

Modern Signs Press

International Standard Book No.
      Soft Bound 0-916708-03-9
      Hard Bound 0-916708-02-0

Library of Congress Catalog No. 80-80571

Publisher
      Modern Signs Press
      P.O. Box 1181
      Los Alamitos, CA 90720

Chief Distributor
      National Association of the Deaf
      814 Thayer Avenue
      Silver Spring , MD 20910

The publisher welcomes your comments and suggestions
on this and future editions

Printed in The United States of America

ACKNOWLEDGEMENTS

Many people have contributed a great deal over the years to the signs and principles in this book. We would like to thank all the parents, teachers, interpreters, and students whose constructive suggestions have helped shape this edition.

Special thanks go to Nancy Kelly-Jones and Harley Hamilton of the Atlanta Area School for the Deaf and to Dr. Frank Caccamise of the National Technical Institute for the Deaf for their invaluable contributions.

Finally, without the patience and support of our friends, families and colleagues — David Zawolkow in particular — this volume would not have been possible.

DESIGN INNOVATION: Stephen Worley, John Heim, Carolyn Polese

TABLE OF CONTENTS

PREFACE

Tom Spradley (co-author of DEAF LIKE ME, Random House, 1978) and Louise Spradley

Each year in the United States several thousand parents are shocked by the discovery that they have a deaf child. When we learned that our infant daughter was deaf we directed all our efforts to helping her become "normal." This, we were told, meant teaching her how to lipread, talk, and use her residual hearing. We did not realize that what little speech she heard or saw on our lips did not contain the ingredients to start language growing in her mind.

Language is something that is caught, not taught, and deaf children can catch it as easily from signs as hearing children do from speech. Signing and talking are just two different indicators that language is growing in a child's mind. This fact eluded us for five years. For our daughter to be normal and catch language from us, we would have to learn to sign as clearly as we spoke.

Learning to sign seemed like an enormous task. Slowly, awkwardly, we began learning and using one sign at a time. To our delight, our daughter began to understand our signs and used them to express her own ideas. As we progressed we discovered that learning American Sign Language (ASL) was like learning a foreign language. Familiar words, when changed into signs, were often used in unfamiliar ways. Recalling the shape for each sign was difficult at first, but this problem seemed minor compared to the overall task of learning to sign, in the unfamiliar pattern of ASL, an idea we could express without a second thought in English.

When our ability to use ASL did not keep pace with our need to communicate, we took the signs we knew and, quite unconsciously, put them together in the best English possible. Finally we accepted the fact that during the time we had available to pass on language to our daughter we would not become competent signers of ASL. She would have to catch this language from deaf friends, just as she caught English from us. In time we would learn to use many of the idioms and visual characteristics that make ASL such a unique and important language. But we could not wait. We needed to communicate now.

The first edition of *Signing Exact English* provided the help we sought. In it was a vocabulary selected for use with young children, and a method of putting signs together, to match our spoken words, that allowed us to concentrate on communication, while the language we already knew guided our hands into a spontaneous flow of explanations, stories, humor, and love. And in the process our daughter began to catch our language.

There remains an urgent need for innovative strategies that will help parents play the vital role, rightfully theirs, of passing on language to their deaf children. Hopefully, help will come from current research into sign language, and enable parents and their deaf children to become bilingual, able to use both ASL and English. The authors of *Signing Exact English* have made a major contribution to this cause. English-speaking parents will find this enlarged edition a valuable resource. On its pages are the tools for making their own language visible to their deaf children. We heartily recommend this edition, and express our gratitude to the authors for their accomplishment.

FOREWORD

Hilde Schlesinger, M.D.,
Director, Center on Deafness, University of California, San Francisco;

co-author of

SOUND AND SIGN: CHILDHOOD DEAFNESS AND MENTAL HEALTH, U. California Press, 1972

For those of you -- parents, teachers and others -- who have had introductions to prior editions of this impressive work -- read no more. Undoubtedly, by now, you have gone through the many steps that lead to the exciting discovery that you can communicate with a deaf child or adult through an intricate system of movements of the body and face but more especially the hands as you continue to use spoken English. You have become an adept participant in dialogue in two modalities, through the hand and voice, through signs and words.

For those of you, however, who pick this book up for the first time -- pause awhile, and consider the following. What are the steps that have led to your interest in this book? A recent encounter? A novel experience? A successful (or unsuccessful) communication? A frequent reason is that of a recent encounter with an individual, who due to an impairment in the sense of hearing, depends to a large extent on his or her eyes for the acquisition or understanding of language. To meet an individual who acquires and uses language in a way unfamiliar to you leads to a novel experience.

Novel experiences can be exciting and rewarding or sad and fear-provoking. Most novel experiences combine all of these feelings to some extent. When the novel experience is related to the powerful human need to communicate, the feelings can become intense. Communication -- dialogue between human beings -- can and does occur in a variety of ways that are essential to our well being: the eyes through sight, the body through touch can convey a variety of meanings. Most human communication, however, is accompanied by or initiated through a very complex human achievement -- the language of the society wherein the child was born. A language can be seen as a system of symbols used with certain rules by which people have come to abide. The symbols and their rules of usage become the vehicle for dialogue between people. Yet there are other important features of

dialogue-shared interests: shared focus, shared social rules, and shared functions of language are numerous and subject to considerable research and debate. There appears to be some general agreement that a number of thought processes and concepts can develop fully without language, that some are promoted by language, and that still others require language for full development.

Language provides freedom from the "here and now," ability to anticipate the future, to recall the past, to describe objects and events beyond the field of vision, to develop solutions to some problems, to share or maybe even to develop imagination and cultural products of imagination such as stories and songs. In addition, language enhances the ability to understand the complex relationships between people and the feelings of other people. Although almost all members of the human species develop competence in the language of a culture, they differ markedly in the way in which they use language. Some use it more freely to comment on or ask questions about the world, the relationships between objects, between people, between feelings and action, between cause and effect. Others are more taciturn and tend to use language (despite full competence in its usage) less frequently for the functions mentioned above. Yet other individuals use language at great length and with much fervor and skill primarily for special areas of human endeavors such as sports, mechanics, hobbies, etc.

The Deaf Child and Dialogue

Despite the fact that acquisition of language is a complex phenomenon, most children learn it easily and playfully and by age five have achieved a nearly adult level of linguistic competence. Children do not acquire language primarily through imitation of adults. First, they are the creators of a language that has childrenese words and childrenese rules. This exciting process of first creating a language and then somehow adopting the adult version of the language of society is also subject to much research and debate. It does appear, however, that human beings are pre-programmed to develop a viable means of communication and that a certain amount of exposure to a specific language is a prerequisite for competence. For many years there existed massive confusion between speech and language. Because most of our linguistic interchanges occur through speech, language and speech were seen as identical, and yet speech is only one of the ways that can be used by the participants in a dialogue.

Under previous conditions deaf children, although continuously "exposed" to language through speech, could benefit only minimally or perhaps not at all from this exposure. The language they saw on the lips of the people around them was extremely limited because only 40 percent of the English language can be seen on the lips. In earlier times, deaf children learned neither language nor speech playfully and easily from their parents, nor did most of them become proficient in the language or speech of their hearing parents. In earlier times, deaf children of hearing parents learned the language of the deaf community -- American Sign Language -- from their peers and from the few deaf adults permitted to be in contact with them. They learned English with great difficulty and with unimpressive results.

Even in those earlier times, deaf children of deaf parents learned the language of their parents easily, playfully, and with great proficiency. The language of the deaf parents was either American Sign Language, a language in its own right with a word order and syntax **different from English (See the Introduction), or** Manual English. The language of the deaf parents was expressed through symbols made by the hands with or without the use of voice. This early parent-child dialogue resulted in clear-cut psychological and academic advantages for the deaf child of deaf parents. Exciting changes have taken place in the recent past of deaf children and their hearing parents due in large part to the existence of this volume and its prior editions. Hearing parents observing the advantages that deaf children of deaf parents had throughout their lives wanted to share in the process that led to these advantages.

The process is similar and yet different in crucial ways. Deaf and hearing parents both can use the hands to express the symbols of language. Most deaf parents, however, have a language system readily available to them, with their deaf children. Although some deaf parents may choose to use American Sign Language with their children, others may choose to sign English and still others may want their children to know both and to alternate their usage.

Most hearing parents initially feel more comfortable in using an English version of sign language than in using ASL. This is because learning a new modality is easier than learning a completely new language, or perhaps they feel more comfortable because they want their children to know the language that they themselves know best, or perhaps they feel more comfortable because they can combine the sign and the spoken word.

Dialogue and the Deaf Infant

Our experience indicates that the most ideal situation for the deaf infant and its hearing parents include the following: early diagnosis, accurate audiological evaluation, appropriate consistent amplification, and appropriate emotional support during the time of the diagnostic crisis. None of the above can be obtained from this volume. You, who want to engage in a dialogue with a deaf infant most optimally, will need to seek out the most competent professionals in your area. But while taking those steps, you can become engrossed in this book. You can seek out the vocabulary items that you want to share with your infant, repeat them to your infant, and teach them to your parents and your friends to use with your infant.

The period before the exciting moment when the infant returns the first sign to you will seem interminable, but it will come. All infants -- even hearing ones learning sign language -- will reproduce signs before they can reproduce spoken words. The ease with which the deaf infant acquires language depends in a large part on the early introduction of signs, the comfort and competency of the parents learning the new modality, the attitudes and competencies of the infant's teacher. The ease with which the deaf infant will learn the use of speech depends to a large extent on the residual hearing, the efficacy of the hearing aids and a combined use of sign and word.

You who start with the deaf infant have a distinct advantage. You can keep ahead of your infant in your acquisition of S.E.E. signs. You will experience the excitement of early language acquisition and of early dialogues. You will be spared the frustration of delayed language onset. Nevertheless, you must experience some of the pain and frustration of having a deaf infant: learning a new modality of English, meeting numerous professionals, resolving conflicting advice. It won't always be easy, but it will be easier than it was ten years ago. The deaf children we know who started S.E.E. signs about ten years ago are doing well. They learned English as their first language from their parents. They are using it in dialogues with their parents, their peers and their teachers. They are conducting their dialogues in a combination of signs and speech and they are doing well in school.

Children and parents who come upon S.E.E. signs in the early childhood years can benefit almost as well as the infants, *if* they begin to use signs before they have experienced a massive feeling of failure in communication and before they have been labelled failures by teachers and other professionals.

This book is useful for deaf children of all ages, but older children will usually have had experiences of failure with language and dialogue. Some may have developed an aversion to human communication, some may have developed a very personal system of communication, still others may have acquired American Sign Language as their first language. The feelings and language style of these youngsters must be respected before we require their acceptance of another language we want them to learn.

It is my hope that all these groups of deaf children will acquire the skills that will enable them to communicate happily and competently with a wide variety of people, and that they do not come to believe that one means or mode of communication should be used to exclude the possibility of any other.

INTRODUCTION
To the Revised Edition

The present edition of *Signing Exact English* includes both some revisions of previously published signs and the addition of new sign vocabulary. Over the past several years there has been a great expansion of research on sign language and simultaneous communication (the use of signs and spoken communication together). Much more is now known about receptive and expressive features of various types of sign language, and about the structural, grammatical, and production features of American Sign Language (ASL). This research information, plus comments and suggestions from users in the field, has been taken into account in the development of this revised edition.

We are aware that revision, or change of any previously published sign book, leads to complications and confusion for the users of the book. However, we felt we would be remiss if we did not make every effort to adjust the signs published here according to two different criteria: what has proved most feasible in use, and what is consistent with American Sign Language features without sacrificing Signing Exact English principles. While ASL and English are two quite distinct languages, and the overlap can never be complete, we wish to stay as close as possible to signs and principles or features used in ASL, while at the same time representing English as clearly and completely as possible. By respecting and considering both ASL and English, we believe we can better facilitate the learning of a first and a second language by native users of both ASL and of English, and in so doing aid in bridging the gap between users of these two languages. It must be remembered, also, that these *are* two different languages, and that this is *not* a text of American Sign Language.

Besides the recent increase in research on signs, there has been great growth in the reported use of Total Communication in schools around the country, with roughly two-thirds of all classes for the hearing impaired reporting the use of signs and fingerspelling in addition to speech, speechreading, amplification, visual aids, and the like. Among those programs, texts of sign systems designed to present English predominate (see Jordan, Gustason, and Rosen, 1976

and 1979). Given the fact that roughly ninety per cent of the parents of hearing impaired children are hearing (the majority of whom speak English as their own native language), and that the greatest amount of change has occurred in public school programs which have had limited contact with ASL, this predominance of manual English texts is understandable. This has in some cases led to the development of signs for words which are not listed in present texts which are awkward or offensive to users of ASL. For this reason, and because we are aware that we have not included in this book all the words for which individuals may desire signs, we are including in this edition some guidelines and suggestions for sign development based on principles uncovered through research on American Sign Language. Our general recommendation is that other sign books and native deaf signers in the local community be consulted before a new sign is developed, and that fingerspelling be considered a viable alternative in some circumstances. The problem here is, of course, to avoid irresponsible, uncoordinated creation of new signs by too many individuals in the child's environment. It is always necessary to guard against the danger of assuming that because a child knows a sign s/he can spell, read, or write the word s/he is signing. The transfer to spelling and print is no more automatic for manual or signed English than for spoken English.

As with our past editions, the signs in this book are presented as suggestions. This means that if we have modified a sign in the present text, and users are comfortable with the previous sign, they should feel no compulsion to change.

Variations in signs exist around the country. For instance, there are two major ways to sign "the," one used mostly in the West and the other in the East. In some instances we decided to include such variations in this book, which means that users will need to choose which version they prefer. This choice should, of course, be dependent on what is used in the geographical area concerned.

We considered, but decided against, attempting to identify for each sign whether it exists in ASL or is a newly invented sign, whether it is used in the East or the West, and the like. Obviously this could become quite cumbersome, and many signs are difficult to so identify. A number of "new" signs have found their way into ASL usage, and "Western" signs to the East, and vice versa. Accordingly, signs are presented here without any attempts at such identification. It should be pointed out, however, that in the original book roughly three-quarters of the signs were either borrowed from ASL or based on an ASL sign with the addition of an initial. Such borrowed signs are used to represent only one English word in Signing Exact English; for instance the sign for "girl" is the same in this book and in ASL, but while the sign for "run" in this book is borrowed from ASL, ASL has many other ways to sign "run" depending on the idea being conveyed, and there is no one-for-one correspondence between signs in this book and ASL.

There are some features of sign production, such as location or place where the sign is made, and size or intensity of the sign, which can and should reflect the concept or message being signed. For instance, the sign for "bow" as presented in this book should be signed in various places and various sizes depending on if one is speaking of a bow tie, a bow in one's hair, a rainbow, a bow and arrow, and the like. This kind of creative signing does not come from a strict adherence to a single picture and description of a sign, but is important in effectively using this kind of communication. Accordingly, we have pointed out some ideas for creative signing and have identified with a star some of the signs which can thus be expanded. While this is most applicable to multiple meaning words, it may also be used in an adverbial or adjectival sense. One should not sign "very big" with quite small movements -- unless one is being sarcastic -- or talk about "walking fast" with very slow hand movements.

Finally, some pictures have been changed in an attempt to improve their clarity, as in placement or direction of arrows, without any actual change in the sign itself.

To aid in instruction and learning, printed word groups for families of signs that are related both in meaning and in formation have been provided at the end of the book. Within the book, members of a given sign family are identified by placing the "head of the family" in parentheses following each sign description. For instance, the description for the sign "group" is followed by the head of the family (CLASS), the description for the sign "author" is followed by its head (WRITE), and so on. In cases of two-sign families, these signs are cross-referenced. Family heads appear with a ♕ in the book.

The signers pictured in this book are all right handed. Therefore, if only one hand is used or moves in the production of a sign, this is always the right hand unless otherwise indicated. Left-handed persons should, of course, reverse these pictures and sign with the left hand.

It is our hope that the updating and revisions discussed above will add to the clarity and helpfulness of the book, and we welcome responses from users. Language and communication are dynamic, and Signing Exact English is open to continuing development as more is learned about the use of sign language both alone and with speech.

To maximize the amount of visual language input and contribute to the child's feeling of self-worth, it is important to sign everything that is said in the child's presence, whether or not the communication is addressed to the child. This aids incidental learning. Also, it does not take advantage of the child's lack of hearing to discuss in his or her presence what would not be discussed in the presence of a hearing child. While we are aware that this is difficult for the beginner signer, the payoff in language development, self-concept, awareness of the world, and sophistication is well worth the cost.

Communication, vital though it is to the teaching-learning process, is not the only requisite. Obviously, good teaching and good parenting involve much more.

Why Signing Exact English Was Developed

In January, 1969, a group of deaf individuals, parents of deaf children, children of deaf parents, teachers of the deaf, interpreters, and program administrators met in southern California to discuss appropriate, effective ways to represent English in a gestural mode. From this group developed three published systems, originally similar but now quite different: Seeing Essential English (SEE 1), Linguistics of Visual English (LOVE), and Signing Exact English (SEE 2).

As was pointed out in the winter 1974-75 issue of Gallaudet Today: *The main concern of the original group was the consistent, logical, rational, and practical development of signs to represent as specifically as possible the basic essentials of the English language. This concern sprang from the experience of all present with the poor English skills of many deaf students, and the desire for an easier, more successful way of developing mastery of English in a far greater number of such students. (Gustason, 1975)*

The educational retardation of deaf students has been well documented over the years, and has caused deep and widespread concern. In 1965, the Secretary of Health, Education, and Welfare's Advisory Committee on Education of the Deaf stated in the Babbidge report that

. . . the American people have no reason to be satisfied with their limited success in educating deaf children and preparing them for full participation in our society. . . the average graduate of a public residential school for the deaf. . . has an eighth grade education. (Babbidge, 1965)

Many studies over the past sixty years have reported the low English language skills of hearing-impaired students, with reading and English scores reported for older deaf students hovering around the level attained by fourth and fifth grade hearing children. In Wrightstone's 1963 survey, 88% of 1075 deaf students aged 15½ and above scored below grade level 4.9 in reading. Boatner (1965) and McClure (1966) classified roughly one third of deaf students sixteen and older as functionally illiterate, or unable to read well enough to cope with ordinary circumstances in life. These findings were not new. In 1918, a fill-in-the-blanks English test given to 1098 hearing-impaired students showed the average for fourth grade hearing children to be higher than the average for any grade level of the deaf. (Pintner, 1918)

Yet research has shown that the intelligence range for hearing-impaired persons, with no other disability, is the same as in the hearing population. (Vernon, 1969). Given this level of intellectual ability among the hearing impaired, their low test scores in reading and English structure take on a new dimension, and it is not surprising that little correlation has been found between intelligence and such test scores.

At the same time that such studies were pointing out the normal intelligence range of hearing-impaired students and their problems with English, other researchers were studying normal language development in hearing children. Children exposed to English, they reported, mastered much of the structure of that language, including basic sentence patterns and inflections, by about age three. Language structures are fairly stable by age six, and extremely difficult to modify after the age of puberty. Between two and three years of age, children make a great jump in the use of prepositions, demonstratives, auxiliaries, articles, conjunctions, possessive and personal pronouns, and the tense, plural, and possessive markings. (See, for instance, Braine, 1963; Brown & Bellugi, 1964; Cazden, 1968; Weir, 1962; Labov, 1965; Penfield, 1964; Moskowitz, 1978). What hearing children learn is the language of their environment, be it French, Chinese, standard American English, the English of Great Britain, or whatever language they perceive. Many children in Europe learn two or more languages with little or no formal instruction. Adults who know only one language, on the other hand, often experience great difficulty trying to learn a different language.

Studies focusing on the English problems of hearing-impaired children identified specific areas of weakness. These weaknesses included omission of necessary words or incorrect use of words. Sentence structures were simple and rigid, with those of 17-year-old hearing-impaired students comparable to eight-year-old hearing children. Lexical, or dictionary, meanings were learned more easily than structural meanings, and deducing the meaning of words from context was not a common skill. While studies with hearing children indicated consistent sequences of structures mastered in English language development, no such sequences appeared in the English skills of deaf children; what was learned first was what was taught first in school, and this varied from school to school. Hearing impaired students used fewer adverbs, auxiliaries and conjunctions than hearing children. (See Myklebust, 1964; Heider and Heider, 1940; Hart and Rosenstein, 1964; Cooper, 1965; Simmons, 1962, as examples.) Many of these problems, especially discomfort with the idiomatic nature of many American English word meanings, are experienced by native speakers of other languages attempting to learn English, and indicate the difficulty of learning this complex language when the optimal language-learning years of childhood are past.

These problems are not surprising when it is remembered that input must precede output, that this input is most beneficial when it takes place during the critical language learning years before age six, and that the hearing-impaired child's perception of English is often very imperfect, depending on the communication mode.

Even a partial hearing loss cuts off some of the auditory input, and hard-of-hearing children have very real problems learning English. For the profoundly deaf child, the problem can be even more serious. Since 40% to 60% of the sounds of English look like some other sound on the lips (as in the old examples of pan, ban, man), it is not surprising that even the best speechreaders with a ready command of English must use educated guesswork and knowledge of the topic and the language to fill the gaps. The problem of speechreading for infants is compounded when it is remembered that

young children do not ordinarily differentiate the parts of what they perceive, especially if the stimuli are unfamiliar or have no meaning for them. They perceive largely in terms of context. (Mussen, 1963)

Although three-year-old hearing children, as noted above, are well on their way to mastery of tenses and function words,

. . . in lipreading. . . the child does not perceive every word in an utterance, but rather, catches the key words, or even only the root parts of words (e.g. BOY instead of BOYS, WALK instead of WALKED). The words that are ignored are words that are not understood, as well as the function words (e.g. TO, AT, THE, FOR) that tie the communication together. (Hart and Rosenstein, 1964)

Similarly, -ing and -ed are difficult to speechread. It is not surprising, then, that some older deaf students who have learned that -ed is used for the past and -ing for a present action believe that the movie was interested because they saw it yesterday, while they are interesting in TV because they are watching it now. It should be noted, also, that while hard-of-hearing children may pick up more vocabulary, many of these structural affixes are as difficult to hear as they are to speechread, and such students often have difficulty with -s, -ed, and the like.

Obviously dependence on speechreading as a means of providing clear and unambiguous English input is a very dangerous dependence. What was needed was some way to make use of an unimpaired input channel, a more visual mode of representing English.

Fingerspelling, or forming words by spelling the letters of the alphabet on the hand, is larger and easier to perceive than speechreading. However, there is still the perception problem for very young children, since the child's eyes do not fully mature until age eight (hence the use of large print in primary story books). Moreover, skilled adult fingerspellers normally spell at a 300-letter-per-minute rate (Bornstein, 1965), while the average speaking rate ranges from 120 to 270 words per minute (Calvert and Silverman, 1975). If the average word length is calculated at five letters, this would mean spelling 600 to 1350 letters per minute. Using fingerspelling and speech together would thus mean either the speech rhythm would be distorted or letters would be left out or distorted in the fingerspelling.

Speech alone is obviously the easiest mode for hearing persons to use with a hearing-impaired child, but it is too often unsatisfactory in terms of the amount of information the child is able to perceive. Fingerspelling, while relatively easy to learn (26 letters are, after all, not that many) is not easy to learn to use well, and still presents perception problems for a very young child as well as production problems if the parent or teacher wishes to speak simultaneously. (See Caccamise, Hatfield, and Brewer, 1978, for further discussion of research and problems with the use of fingerspelling alone and in combination with speech.)

Signs present larger, more easily perceived and discriminated symbols in communication than either speech or fingerspelling for young hearing-impaired children. With early visual input of signs, it is not surprising that deaf children of signing deaf parents, able to communicate from infancy, have been shown to enter school with an advantage over deaf children of hearing parents, and have tended to maintain this advantage throughout school.

However, it must be remembered that American Sign Language (ASL), which is used by many deaf adults, is a language in its own right and not a visual representation of English. Children who learn ASL as their native language from their parents have been shown to develop better English skills than those who were not exposed to sign language, while children of deaf parents who signed to them from infancy in English, mastered English to an even greater degree. (See Brasel and Quigley, 1975, for a report of such research.)

This introduces another factor, since adults who know only one language often have some difficulty mastering a second one. For parents, the problem of becoming fluent during the early language-learning years is a very real problem. Accordingly, it may be simpler for most hearing parents of deaf children to begin with a form of signing in English than to attempt to become fluent in a foreign language (ASL) during what is for many parents a psychologically trying period of adjustment to their child's deafness.

The important issue is that comfortable parent-child communication be established as early as possible in a language readily available to the parents and a mode clearly perceivable by the child. If the parents know and use ASL with their child, English is still needed at some point for maximal function in our society, and should be taught in a clearly perceivable mode.

Research to date has focused on the receptive abilities of older deaf students rather than younger, but has shown consistently that understanding is greater with the use of simultaneous communication (speech, spelling, and signs used in combination) than with the use of speech alone, signs alone, spelling alone, or spelling and speech without signs (See Caccamise and Johnson, 1978, for a summary of such research). While there are, of course, individual differences, the rule seems to be that the larger the number of modes used, the greater the chances for reception and understanding. A summary of research on the effect of the use of signs on English and on oral/aural communication skills finds not only that signs can assist in the development of English, but that they may facilitate the development of speech, speechreading, and listening skills. If attention is not given these oral/aural skills, they may not develop, but if such attention is given, the use of signs is not a detriment. (See Caccamise, Hatfield, and Brewer, 1978; Weiss, McIntyre, Goodwin, and Moores, 1975 and 1978, for more discussion of this research.)

Some individuals have expressed concern that the use of all modes and the inclusion of manual English signs for word-endings may overload the child. While we need much more research on language acquisition with hearing-impaired children, some studies are beginning to appear. Research with deaf children of deaf parents acquiring ASL as their native language has shown that these children are quite similar to hearing children in terms of increasing length of utterance and in their progressive mastery of structures of language. While studies of language acquisition by deaf children whose parents use manual English signs is still limited, the appropriate use of signed markers for past tense, plurals, and -ing has been reported in children at age three (Schlesinger and Meadow, 1972). Anecdotal reports of profoundly deaf children whose parents and teachers consistently used manual English indicates that children with no disability other than hearing loss have the capability for acquiring such markers. One study of preschoolers using manual communication reported that what the mother used at home had greater influence than what the teacher used at school, and that if the mother used markers the child developed skill in using them also. The ability to use signs does not automatically transfer to the ability to read and write, and there has been some question whether indeed signing English would result in better reading and writing skills. This is a legitimate question in need of much more research. Early evidence indicates that while the transfer is not automatic, children exposed to manually represented English in the early years are much better able to make that transfer than those who are not. Children profoundly deaf from birth have been reported reading at second grade level before the age of five, and writing clear, error-free, idiomatic English at ages ten to twelve. While these are individual reports, and many questions remain about the level of parent involvement and fluency needed, and the psychological-sociological impact on the parent-child relationship, the evidence is that, given a mode comfortable to parent and child, transmission of the parents' native language to the child is quite possible. (See Schlesinger, 1978, for a discussion of the bimodal acquisition of language.)

This stress on the importance of exposing the child in all modalities to English if we wish him to acquire the language easily must not be interpreted as a rejection of American Sign Language (Gustason, Pfetzing, and Zawolkow, 1974). There are many ways in which these two languages can and should go hand-in-hand for a fuller educational and developmental experience for hearing-impaired children. Ideally, we would like to see teachers and parents comfortable with both ASL and English, who could combine and otherwise utilize the two types of signing both in and out of the classroom in a variety of ways to enrich the communication experiences of students. Our goal is for hearing-impaired children to become truly bilingual, at ease in both ASL and English. How best to accomplish this is still an open question, and again we solicit constructive suggestions from users. We consider Signing Exact English a means of manual expression for those who are speaking English while they sign, and an introduction to the richness and variety of signs for parents of young deaf children. We also consider it a teaching tool for use with students who know ASL and are learning English as a second language. We would like to see the best of both languages in as many hands as possible. (See Caccamise and Gustason, 1979, Caccamise and Johnson, 1978, and Gustason and Rosen, 1975, for further discussion of the roles of both ASL and English in the education and general development of hearing impaired children, and communication with the deaf adult.)

Signing Exact English, (SEE 2), is NOT a replacement for ASL and is meant for use by parents of young children and by teachers of English. Persons working with deaf adults should understand that SEE 2 is not widely used among adults, although "new" signs crop up in common usage. The study of ASL is important not only for those desiring to work with adult deaf persons, but for parents and teachers. ASL is a rich and expressive language, worth studying for its own sake, and many of its principles should be put to good use in using Signing Exact English. While there is still a shortage of trained teachers of both ASL and SEE 2, those who wish to learn either are encourged to learn as much as possible about the other. Incomplete understanding raises the possibility of misunderstanding and personal/psychological/sociological problems--for parents, for teachers, and for the child.

Because we wish to see such problems minimized, we encourge a study of and acceptance of both ASL and manual English. In the following pages we list important principles of SEE 2, suggestions to follow in the development of additional signs, and some points to remember for clear, effective signing. In these, we have attempted to combine our knowledge of ASL and English to develop a sign system that can assist deaf and hard-of-hearing children in their development of English language skills. We present both theoretical principles and practical usage suggestions for the system. We recognize the dynamic nature of language and communication, and that any communication form must accommodate its users. Few language rules are strict, and exceptions to rules can be found in all languages. We are aware that some of the signs in this book may not seem consistent with the principles listed, but these exceptions are based on users, whose skills in language usage continue to go ahead of the knowledge of educators and linguists as to how languages may be used most effectively in various modalities (alone and in combination) for maximum communication and language development.

Important Principles of Signing Exact English

1. The most important principle in Signing Exact English is that ENGLISH SHOULD BE SIGNED IN A MANNER THAT IS AS CONSISTENT AS POSSIBLE WITH HOW IT IS SPOKEN OR WRITTEN IN ORDER TO CONSTITUTE A LANGUAGE INPUT FOR THE DEAF CHILD THAT WILL RESULT IN HIS MASTERY OF ENGLISH. This means, for instance, that idioms such as "dry up," "cut it out," "stop horsing around" would be signed as those exact words, rather than as "quiet" or "stop" or "finish." It also means that inflections or markers must be shown, such as talk*s*, talk*ed*, talk*ing*, govern*ment*.

2. A second important principle is that A SIGN SHOULD BE TRANSLATABLE TO ONLY ONE ENGLISH EQUIVALENT. Initialized signs contribute a great deal here, providing such synonyms as HURT, PAIN, ACHE, and so on. But this principle also means that only one sign should be used for such English words as RUN, which has a number of different meanings and a number of different translations in ASL.

These two principles have led to a number of problems and jokes. How does one sign "I *saw* you yesterday" or "he *left* home last week"? Is the sign for *saw* the same as in sawing wood, and the sign for *left* the same as the opposite of right? For that matter, what of right, rite, and write? In an attempt to come to terms with these problems, more principles were developed. Words are considered in three groups: 1) Basic, 2) Compound, and 3) Complex.

3. "BASIC WORDS" ARE WORDS THAT CAN HAVE NO MORE TAKEN AWAY AND STILL FORM A COMPLETE WORD (GIRL, TALK, THE, the noun SAW, etc.) for these basic words, the three-point criteria of sound, spelling, and meaning is utilized. If any two of these three factors are the same, the same sign is used. This covers multiple-meaning words such as RUN, which would have the same sign in:

The boys will *run*. The motor will *run*. Your nose will *run*. These are all signed differently in ASL. (See the following "points to remember for expressive signing" for suggestions on combining ASL principles with English words in such cases.)

To take a different example, a different sign would be used for WIND in

The *wind* is blowing. I must *wind* my watch.

In this case only the spelling is the same; sound and meaning both differ, and since two of the three factors are different a different sign is used. In the case of RUN, spelling and sound are the same, and meaning varies; since two of the three factors are the same, the same basic sign is used.

4. "COMPLEX WORDS" ARE DEFINED AS BASIC WORDS WITH THE ADDITION OF AN AFFIX OR INFLECTION: GIRLS, TALKED, the past tense verb SAW. Once such an addition has been made the combination is no longer considered a basic word. Accordingly, the past tense of SEE is added to produce the verb SAW, which is *not* the same as either the noun SAW or the verb to SAW (which would have past tense added to produce SAWED). An affix is added in signs if it is added in speech or writing, regardless of the part of speech. The suffix -s, for instance, is used both for regular plurals (GIRLS, SAWS) and the third person singular of verbs (RUNS, SEES, SAWS).

5. COMPOUND WORDS ARE TWO OR MORE BASIC WORDS PUT TOGETHER. IF THE MEANING OF THE WORDS SEPARATELY IS CONSISTENT WITH THE MEANING OF THE WORDS TOGETHER, THEN AND *ONLY THEN* ARE THEY SIGNED AS THE COMPONENT WORDS. Thus UNDERLINE would be signed UNDER-LINE but UNDERSTAND, having no relation to the meaning of the words UNDER and STAND, would have a separate sign and would *not* be signed UNDER-STAND.

6. WHEN A SIGN ALREADY EXISTS IN ASL THAT IS CLEAR, UNAMBIGUOUS, AND COMMONLY TRANSLATES TO ONE ENGLISH WORD, THIS SIGN IS RETAINED. As pointed out previously, the sign for GIRL is the same in ASL and in this book. This is clearest with single meaning words. With multiple meaning words, while the sign may fit one ASL way of signing the word, ASL may have other signs for different meanings. This is handled by Principle 3 above. Principle 6 explains why signs are presented in this book for compound or complex words such as CARELESS, MISUNDERSTAND, BASEBALL, CAN'T, that could, by following the principles above, be signed CARE-LESS, MIS-UNDERSTAND, BASE-BALL, CAN-N'T. A single sign is borrowed from ASL when ease and economy of movement are possible with no loss of clear, unambiguous English. It is our hope that users will choose the way they prefer of signing such words, while understanding that others may choose a different way of signing it.

7. WHEN THE FIRST LETTER IS ADDED TO A BASIC SIGN TO CREATE SYNONYMS, THE BASIC SIGN IS RETAINED WHEREVER POSSIBLE AS THE MOST COMMONLY USED WORD. For instance, the basic sign for MAKE is retained for that word, while the sign is made with C-hands for CREATE, and P-hands for PRODUCE. In some cases, as with GUARD, PROTECT, DEFEND, users have experienced difficulty remembering which is the uninitialized sign since all three words are used relatively equally; hence all three are initialized.

8. WHEN MORE THAN ONE MARKER IS ADDED TO A WORD, MIDDLE MARKERS MAY BE DROPPED *IF* THERE IS NO SACRIFICE OF CLARITY. For instance, the past tense sign is added to BREAK to produce BROKE, but BROKEN may be signed as BREAK plus the past participle or -EN. Similarly, EXAM may be joined by -INE for EXAMINE, but EXAMINATION may be signed as EXAM plus -TION. Such dropping of the middle markers serves to keep the flow of the sign smooth and efficient, while retaining the identifying marker which shows what word is used. Dropping is not done if confusion might result; for instance, WILL plus N'T creates WON'T, WILL plus -D or past participle marker plus N'T creates WOULDN'T. Dropping the middle marker in this case would confuse the two words.

9. WHILE FOLLOWING THE ABOVE PRINCIPLES, RESPECT NEEDS TO BE SHOWN FOR CHARACTERISTICS OF VISUAL-GESTURAL COMMUNICATION. While sign languages vary just as do spoken languages, and what is possible in one language may not appear in another, awkward or difficult movements should be avoided whenever possible. For instance, English does not use the trilled R present in other spoken languages, and some phonetic combinations are not normal in English (e.g. WUG is a possible nonsense word, but PKT is not). The same is true of ASL, where simple hand shapes (A, 5, 1) are used much more commonly than more complex hand shapes (R, P, etc.) Small differences in shape or motion should not occur far from the visual center of attention. These points are addressed further in the next section.

Suggestions for the Development of Additional Signs

Experience and common sense both tell us that when manual English is used, words are sure to crop up that have no sign in this book. When this happens, we have several recommendations.

1.   SEEK AN EXISTING SIGN. Check other sign language texts. Ask skilled signers in your community, especially deaf native signers.

2.   MODIFY AN EXISTING SIGN WITH A SIMILAR OR RELATED MEANING. Generally, this means adding the first letter of the word to a basic sign.

3.   CONSIDER FINGERSPELLING. This depends, of course, on the age and perceptual abilities of the child, and the length and frequency of use of the word in question.

4.   IF ALL ELSE FAILS, AND YOU MUST INVENT, TRY TO STAY AS CLOSE AS POSSIBLE TO ASL PRINCIPLES. We realize that many individuals using manual English are not yet familiar with ASL. In an attempt to give some guidance in this area, pertinent guidelines are summarized below. These guidelines were developed for collection, evaluation, selection, and recording of signs used in educational and work settings under the direction of Dr. Frank Caccamise of the National Technical Institute for the Deaf. The summary of these guidelines is included here with Dr. Caccamise's permission. The persons involved in developing these guidelines were for the most part concerned with college age hearing-impaired students. Most of the guidelines are, however, equally applicable when considering younger children. Those that need special consideration are noted.

There are four major components of signs: A), position, B) handshape, C) movement, and D) orientation (the direction of the palm and fingers). The guidelines discussed below are based on how these four components are combined in ASL signs, and they may be used in considering or assessing the acceptability of unacceptability of newly developed signs.

1)   THE SIGNING SPACE. Signs generally fall within an area between the top of the head and just above the waist, within a comfortable, but not fully extended, arm's reach to the sides and ahead. The center of this space is the hollow of the neck. Signs do occur outside this area, as in theatrical signing and for emphasis.

2)   THE VISUAL CENTER OF THE SIGNING SPACE is the nose-mouth area, and while many signs are made near here, they are seldom made within this center. Vision is sharpest near this center, and less sharp as you move away for the center. When reading signs people usually watch the face of the signer rather than the hands, and facial expression and lip movement are important. An effort should be made not to obstruct the mouth area when signing since this interferes with speechreading. In addition to speechreading, the mouth area should not be blocked because the face and mouth area are important for grammatical expression in ASL and can and should be effectively used in SEE 2 to enhance communication.

3)   POSITION. Signs made near the center of the signing space can use smaller movements and finer distinctions among signs than signs made further away from the visual center (e.g. APPLE, FRUIT, VEGETABLE, etc.).

4)   SYMMETRY. Signs made near the center of the signing space often use one hand, while signs made further away tend to use two hands in symmetry (e.g. HEAVEN, RUSSIA). Signs made in the neck and face area generally use one hand. Signs made below the neck generally use two hands. If both hands move, the handshapes should be the same.

5)   DOMINANCE. For two-handed signs in which only one hand moves, the non-moving or passive hand should have one of the seven neutral handshapes (1-A-S-B-C-5-0) or the same handshape as the moving hand. Ordinarily one attends to the moving hand. (Note: This need not occur when the moving hand brings attention to the non-moving hand, as in GOAL, AIM, OBJECTIVE, TARGET, COMMENCE, INITIATE, etc.)

6)   NUMBER OF HANDSHAPES PER SIGN. Most signs in ASL use only one handshape on each hand. Some signs require a slight handshape change, as in MILK or PRINT, but do not involve more than two handshapes. Accordingly, invented signs should use no more than two handshapes. (Note: Markers or inflections may be added to a sign already having two handshapes.)

7)   SIGNS INVOLVING CONTACT. Four major areas of contact in signs are the head, trunk, arm, and hand. ASL signs are systematic in that signs made with double contacts are made within the same major area (e.g. INDIAN has both contacts on the head, WE has both contacts on the trunk, etc.). Exceptions to this are signs derived from compounds, as DAUGHTER from GIRL-BABY, etc.

8)   SEMANTICALLY RELATED SIGNS. Signs which are related in meaning are often related in formation. For instance, the basic concept of a group is initialized to represent CLASS, GROUP, TEAM, and the like. (As stated previously, such related signs are grouped as "families" in this book.) This type of structural relationship should be considered in the development of new signs.

9) MOVEMENT AND WORD-TYPE: NOUN-VERB PAIRS. In ASL, some signs may have the same handshape, position, and orientation, but differ in movement, with nouns having short repeated movement and verbs having hold or continuous movement (e.g. AIRPLANE and GO-BY-AIRPLANE). (Note: This guideline may be applicable in terms of effective signing, as listed in the next section. Signing Exact English does not rely on this principle to distinguish between or among English words. See, for example, CHAIR and SIT.)

10) COMPOUNDING SIGNS. There are two kinds of compounding, lexical and grammatical. Lexical compounding refers to signs made up of several reduced signs; e.g. FRUIT in ASL may be signed APPLE-ORANGE-BANANA, etc. with shorter and assimilated movements. Grammatical compounding connects several signs to form a new one; e.g. LETTER-NUMBER for ZIPCODE, or HEART-STUDY for CARDIOLOGY. (Note: This type of compounding is clear to ASL users, and some signs derived from compounds--e.g. daughter--are used in manual English, but this guideline is at variance with the first principle of Signing Exact English, that we attempt to sign exactly the words we say. Relying on a slight difference in movement, as in Guideline 9 above, or on a compound sign, may not provide a clear, unambiguous representation of the English word as spoken/written. This is a criticism of neither ASL nor English, but a recognition of the difference between the two.)

11) ITERATIONS. This refers to the number of times a sign is repeated. Some signs in ASL are limited to one repetition (e.g. the singular form of a noun such as GIRL). Signs needing at least two repetitions do not distinguish between two or more than two repetitions.

Points to Remember for Clear, Expressive Signing

As stated previously, we believe ASL principles should be incorporated into English signs for more effective simultaneous communication. While the suggestions and guidelines listed before relate to the development of new signs, such guidelines can also be considered as an aid in production. Following are examples of this integration of principles or characteristics with SEE 2, and other points to remember in sign production.

1) Always speak when you sign, and let facial expressions and body English aid communication.

2) Affixes, and word-endings for tense, person, and the like, should not be made as signs separate from the sign for the basic word itself, but should flow from the base sign for the word. Similarly, signs for word endings should not be made with an emphasis equal to that for the sign of the basic word. Be guided by the practice of spoken English. You do not say "swing ing" or "swingING" but "SWINGing". This may be compared to syllables in spoken words: they are not pronounced as separate words, but flow into each other. Similarly, combined words (compound words) should flow together. INTO should be signed INTO, not IN TO.

3) The past tense sign does not actually need to be made over the shoulder. A backward flip of the hand at the conclusion of the sign for the verb suffices to indicate the past tense (or the addition of -d, if preferred, for regular past tenses such as WALKED).

4) When adding a suffix to a two-handed sign, keep the left hand in the position of the sign (do not drop hand) while the right hand signs the suffix. This helps indicate that the suffix is part of the word and not a separate word.

5) Raising the eyebrows and freezing the hands in the air, or holding the end position of a sign instead of letting the hands drop, are ASL techniques for indicating a question that can be answered yes or no. A slight frown is often used with "WH" questions (What, Who, Where, When, Why, How). These expressions can and should be used in conjunction with Manual English signs. A question-mark sign is only for emphasis.

6) When making a negative statement, as in "I don't think so," "She isn't here," and the like, shaking the head from side to side aids in clarifying the negative.

7) With many signs, clarity can be added by making the sign in the appropriate place. This is true not only of multiple meaning signs such as BOW tie (signed at the neck), BOW and arrow (signed in the position of a bow), and hair BOW (signed at the hair), but of signs such as PAIN (in the neck? in the side?) and BUTTERFLY or BUTTERFLIES (in the stomach?) Of course in the latter examples the entire phrase should be signed, and the sign executed in the appropriate location. In showing fear of something to your right, do not make the sign on your left.

8) When signing pronouns, if the person referred to is present, sign HE, SHE, HIM, or HER in the person's direction, or sign and point. If the person is not present, it helps to set him or her up in a specific location and orient your signs to that location when talking about him or her. When talking about more than one person, setting them up in different locations aids immeasurably in clarifying to whom you are referring. Try putting one of them on your right, the other on your left.

9) Body, eye, and hand orientation help! When signing LOOK, the motion should move toward where you want the person to look: at the sky, the floor, out the window, etc. If you are signing a dialogue between two characters, turning slightly to the left when one is speaking, and slightly to the right when the other responds, helps to indicate who is speaking. Looking up or down can indicate relative height.

10) Some verbs should show the *direction* of the action -- towards the direct object. GIVE, for example, may be signed from the giver to the receiver, as can TEACH, SHOW, TEASE, and other such verbs. When you are the receiver, these signs can begin in front of you and move towards you, in a sort of mirror image of the sign.

11) Some signs can be made more than once when you are talking about plural nouns; e.g. make the sign

for GIRL more than once before adding -s, or for BOOK two or more times before adding -s. Repeating the sign also shows an action that is ongoing, as in I AM PAINT-PAINT-PAINTING a picture or one that is very difficult, as in I AM STUDY-STUDY-STUDYING VERY HARD.

12) Some signs can vary in size. . .a big dog is not as large as a big dinosaur, and BIG can be signed accordingly.

13) Signs can also vary in intensity, or be modified in their execution. A slow, thoughtful WALK should differ from a businesslike WALK; SYMPATHY can be more or less intense as shown by the motion; I LOVE YOU can be sincere or sarcastic depending on motion and facial expression.

14) Ham it up! Use facial expression and mime to help get the message across. You will find ASL a treasure trove of graphic and expressive signs, and you will find most children are natural hams.

15) ENJOY YOUR COMMUNICATION, AND ENJOY YOUR CHILDREN.

Selected References

Babbidge, H.D. *Education of the deaf in the United States.* A report to the Secretary of Health, Education and Welfare by his Advisory Committee on Education of the Deaf. Washington, D.C.: U.S. Gov't Printing Office, 1965.

Boatner, E.B. "The need of a realistic approach to the education of the deaf." Paper given to the joint convention of California Association of Parents of Deaf and Hard of Hearing Children, California Association of Teachers of Deaf and Hard of Hearing Children, and the California Association of the Deaf, Nov. 6, 1965.

Bornstein, H. *Reading the Manual Alphabet.* Washington, D.C., Gallaudet College Press, 1965.

Braine, M.D.S. "The otogeny of English phrase structure: the first phrase," *Language*, 39:1-13, Jan-Mar 1963.

Brasel, K. and S.P. Quigley. "Influence of certain language and communication environments in early childhood on the development of language in deaf individuals." *Journal of Speech and Hearing Research*, 1977, 20, 95-107.

Brown, R. and U. Bellugi. "Three processes in the child's acquisition of syntax," *Harvard Educational Review*, 39:133-152, Spring, 1964.

Caccamise, F. and G. Gustason, eds. *Manual/Simultaneous Communication Instructional Programs in the Educational Setting.* Washington, D.C.:Gallaudet College Division of Public Services, 1979.

Caccamise, F., N. Hatfield and L. Brewer. "Manual/Simultaneous Communication Research: Results and Implications." *American Annals of the Deaf* 123:7, 803-823, November 1978.

Caccamise, F. and D. Johnson. "Simultaneous and manual communication: Their role in rehabilitation with the adult deaf." *Journal of the Academy of Rehabilitative Audiology*, 1978, 11, 105-131.

Calvert, D. and S.R. Silverman, *Speech and Deafness.* Washington, D.C.: Alexander Graham Bell Association for the Deaf, 1975.

Cazden, C.B. "The acquisition of noun and verb inflections," *Child Development*, 39:433-448, June, 1968.

Cooper, R.L. "The ability of deaf and hearing children to apply morphological rules." Unpublished doctoral dissertation, Columbia, 1965.

Gustason, G. "The languages of communication." *Deafness Annual III.* Silver Spring, Md.: Professional Rehabilitation Workers with the Adult Deaf, 1973, 83-95.

Gustason, G. "Signing Exact English," *Gallaudet Today*, vol. 5, # 2, 11-12, winter 1974-75.

Gustason, G., D. Pfetzing and E. Zawolkow. "The Rationale of Signing Exact English," *The Deaf American*, September 1974, 5-6.

Gustason, G. and R. Rosen. "Effective Sign Communication for instructional purposes: Manual English and American Sign Language." *Proceedings of the Convention of American Instructors of the Deaf*, 1975.

Hart, B.O. and J. Rosenstein. "Examining the language behavior of deaf children," *The Volta Review*, 66:679-682, 1964.

Jordan, I.K., G. Gustason, and R. Rosen, "Current Communication Trends in Programs for the Deaf." *American Annals of the Deaf*, 1976, 121:6, 527-532.

Jordan, I.K., G. Gustason, and R. Rosen. "An Update on Communication Trends at Programs for the Deaf." *American Annals of the Dear*, 1976, 121:6, 527-532.

Heider, F. and G. Heider. "Comparison of sentence structure of deaf and hearing children," *Psychological Monographs*, 1940, 52:42-103.

Labov, W. "Linguistic research on the nonstandard English of Negro children," 1965 Yearbook, New York Society for the Experimental Study of Education, pp. 110-117.

McClure, W.J. "Current problems and trends in the education of the deaf," *The Deaf American*, 1966, 8-14.

Moskowitz, Breyne Arlene. "The acquisition of language." *Scientific American*, December 1978, 92-108.

Myklebust, H.R. *Development and Disorders of Written Language:* Volume One. Picture Story Language Test. New York: Grune and Stratton, 1965.

Penfield, W. "The uncommitted cortex: The child's changing brain," *The Atlantic Monthly*, 77-81, July 1964.

Pintner, R. "The measurement of language ability and language process of deaf children," *The Volta Review*, 20:755-766, 1918.

Schlesinger, H. "The acquisition of bimodal language." in *Sign Language of the Deaf*, ed. I.M. Schlesinger and L. Namir. New York: Academic Press, 1978.

Schlesinger, H. "The acquisition of signed and spoken language" in *Deaf Children: Developmental Perspectives*, ed. *L.S.* Liben. New York: Academic Press, 1978.

Schlesinger, H. and K. Meadow. *Sound and Sign: Childhood Deafness and Mental Health*. Berkeley, Calif.: University of California Press, 1972.

Simmons, A.A. "A comparison of the type-token ratio of spoken and written language of deaf and hearing children," *The Volta Review*, 64:417-421, 1962.

Vernon, M. "Fifty years of research on the intelligence of the deaf and hard of hearing: a survey of the literature and discussion of implications," *Journal of Rehabilitation of the Deaf*, 1:1-11, 1968.

Vernon, M. "Sociological and psychological factors associated with hearing loss," *Journal of Speech and Hearing Research*, 12:541-563, 1969.

Weir, R. *Language in the Crib*. The Hague: Mouton and Company, 1962.

Weiss, K.L., C.K. McIntyre, M.W. Goodwin, and D. Moores. *Characteristics of young deaf children and intervention programs*. Research Report # 91, Research Development, and Demonstration Center in Education of Handicapped Children, University of Minnesota, Minneapolis, 1975.

Wrightstone, J.W., M.S. Aranow, and S. Muskowitz, "Developing Test Norms for the Deaf Child," *American Annals of the Deaf*, 108:311-316, 1963.

Explanation of the Text

Form of hands, position of hands, and movement -- if any -- are shown in various ways:

1. Arrows show direction and line of movement.

2. Dotted hands represent original positions.

3. Pairs of pictures (1 and 2) show movement too complex for the use of dotted original positions.

Hands are usually in the form of a letter of the alphabet or a number. Modifications are shown, such as "flat," "bent," "claw hand," and "bent hand."

Some hand-forms are difficult to represent clearly in one drawing such as those on the alphabet page. It will help you to glance at pictures in the text that use the same form, until you understand and can use that form ("parsnip" and "party" show more P-hands, for example).

Note whether movement is to be repeated. Pay special attention to whether there is touching, brushing, striking or merely an approaching motion. For a right-handed person, usually the right hand is the active hand. "Right" in the directions refers to the right of the person signing -- you. Left-handed persons may reverse hands. Do not, however, make a habit of switching from one hand to the other for movements.

Pictures of the words represented are used, when possible, to aid in understanding why the sign is made as it is (see "hippopotamus," "child," "caterpillar"), and we also feel pictures will aid the preschool child.

A ★ symbol follows a word that has two or more different meanings that should be indicated by the way the word is signed. For further explanation, see the Creative Signing pages.

A ♛ symbol follows a word that is the head of its sign-family. See the family listings at the end of the book.

Some signs are compound or complex -- that is, made with the signs for two smaller words or a word plus an affix. For example, *blackboard* would be signed as *black + board, unhappy* as *un- + happy,* or *came* as *come +*P.T. In this edition, such words appear in their alphabetical order in the text with a description of the signs for their production. When no picture of the sign is given a small figure with an arrow pointing to the description occupies the picture-space. See, for instance, *came.*

In this edition of Signing Exact English for the first time alternative signs have been included. Use the sign most comfortable for you or the sign most commonly used in your school or local area. Just as "couch," "sofa," and "davenport" mean the same piece of furniture in spoken and written English, two signs may represent the same thing in sign language. These pairs of signs are indicated by "Alt. 1" and "Alt. 2."

P.T. stands for Past Tense

P.P. stands for Past Participle

We have avoided the use of any other abbreviations in the sign descriptions.

THE PLEDGE
of ALLEGIANCE

I **pledge** **allegiance**

to **the** **flag** **of** **the**

U.S. **of** **America**

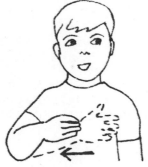    

and **to** **the** **Republic**

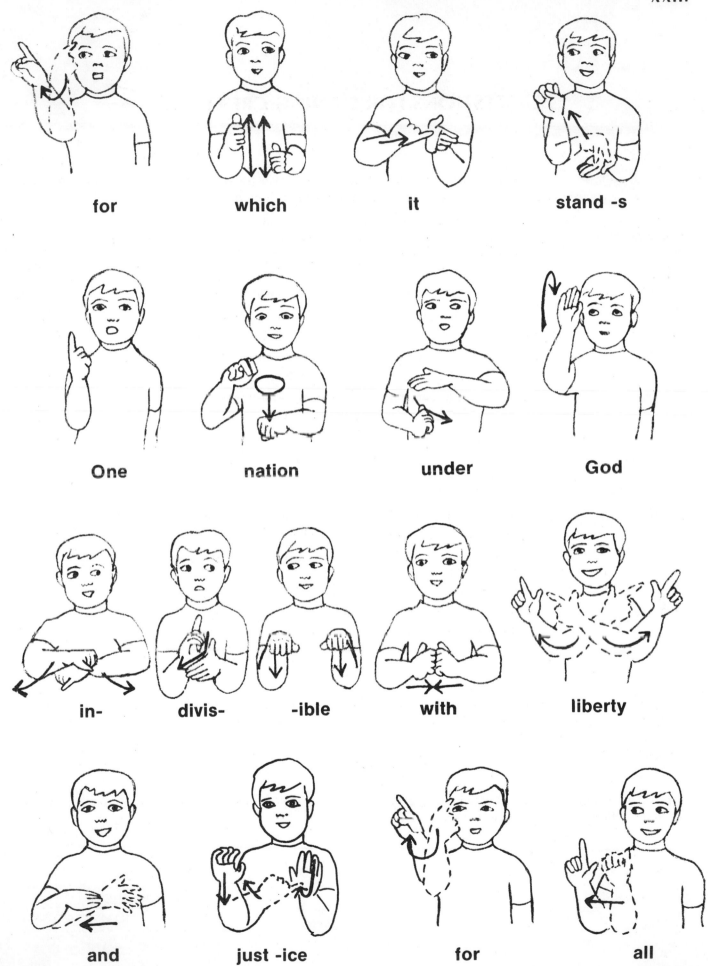

| for | which | it | stand -s |

| One | nation | under | God |

| in- | divis- | -ible | with | liberty |

| and | just -ice | for | all |

SUGGESTIONS FOR SIGNING CREATIVELY

SEE has followed a one-word, one-sign criterion in sign-selection for most words, despite their multiple meanings in English. However, the varieties of meanings have not been ignored.

When a basic sign represents various--sometimes unrelated--meanings, then, by incorporating the principles of American Sign Language, the basic sign can be altered slightly to express each separate meaning more clearly.

Pictures of three examples of creative signing are given on the facing page.

1. The sense of lasting a long time comes from continuing the moving hand for the word "last" forward after striking the other hand at the fingertips. A past time is indicated by swinging the moving hand upward and backward for a short distance.

2. The sign for "duck," can be made with the body-movement for ducking an approaching object.

3. A clawing motion represents the animal, "bear." A carrying motion, swinging slightly to the side, means to "bear" an object. To indicate endurance, close the claws into fists and minimize the swinging motion.

Further examples to illustrate possibilities for creative signing:

BARK   For a dog's bark, the sign is produced near the mouth area, with the fingers pointing outwards. For bark on a tree, the sign is produced in front of the body.

BOW   The basic sign for "bow" (long o), is made in different places to show what kind of bow is meant. At the neck for a bow-tie, in mid-air for a rainbow, vertically to outline a bow used with arrows. In the hair means a hair-ribbon bow, and on an invisible box represents gift-wrapping.

POUND   The meaning of a pound of weight is distinguished from the meaning of beating upon something, by signing "pound" with a pounding motion for the second meaning.

SOME OF THE SIGNS THAT CAN BE MADE CREATIVELY TO HELP INDICATE THE DIFFERENT MEANINGS OF THE ENGLISH WORD DESIRED ARE MARKED IN THIS BOOK BY ✸

(Note: Fingerspelling the word is a viable alternative in cases in which the signer feels very uncomfortable with the connection between sign and sense.)

LAST IN LINE

**LOLLIPOPS CAN
LAST ALL DAY**

REMEMBER LAST WEEK?

A DUCK LOVES WATER

DUCK THAT BALL!

THE BEAR IS BIG

BEAR YOUR LOAD

BEAR YOUR PAIN

THE ALPHABET

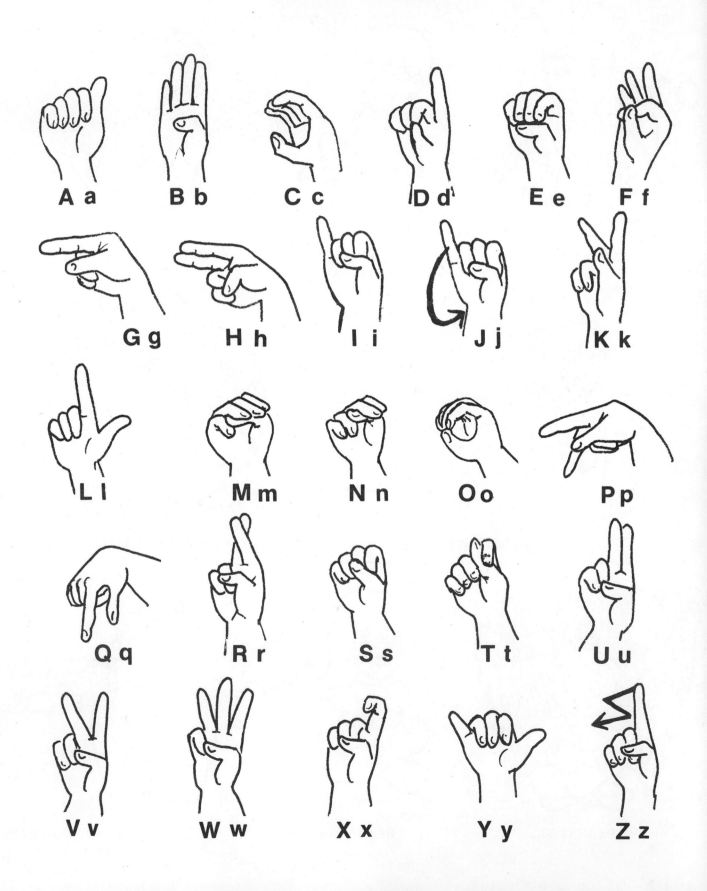

HAND-SHAPES

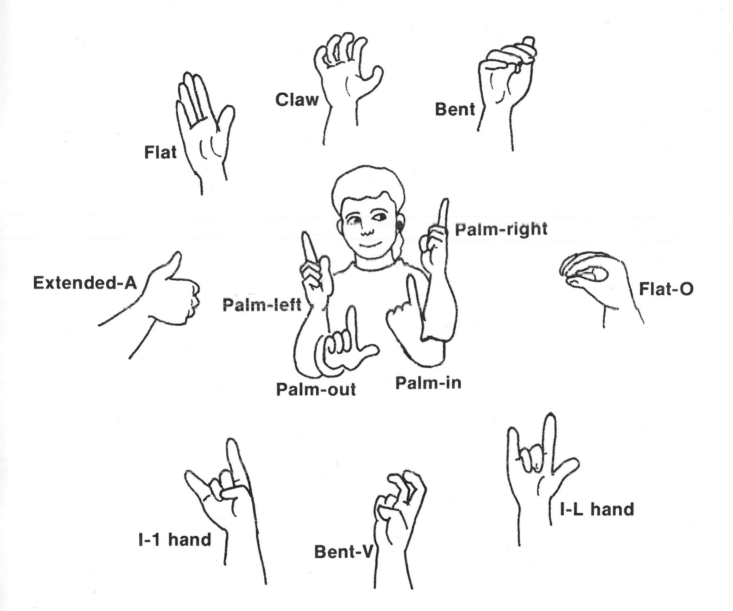

Flat

Claw

Bent

Extended-A

Palm-left

Palm-right

Flat-O

Palm-out

Palm-in

I-1 hand

Bent-V

I-L hand

NUMBERS

One (1)

Two (2)

Three (3)

Four (4)

Five (5)

Six (6)

Seven (7)

Eight (8)

Nine (9)

Ten (10)

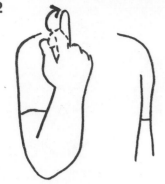

ELEVEN (11)

Index flips up twice

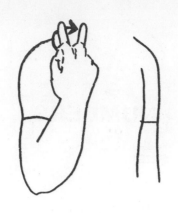

TWELVE (12)

First two fingers flip up twice

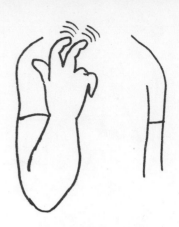

THIRTEEN (13)

First two fingers of "3" wiggle together

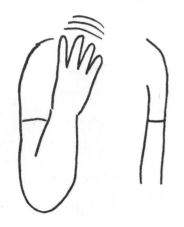

FOURTEEN (14)

"4" fingers wiggle all together

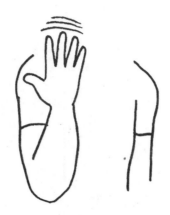

FIFTEEN (15)

Four fingers wiggle all together, thumb out

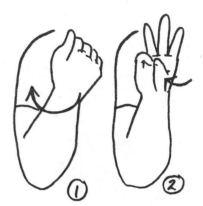

SIXTEEN

Palm-in A pivots and opens to palm-out 6

(10 + 6)

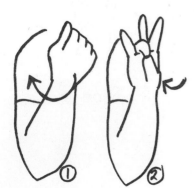

SEVENTEEN

Palm-in A pivots and opens to palm-out 7

(10 + 7)

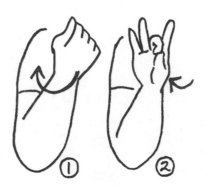

EIGHTEEN

Palm-in A pivots and opens to palm-out 8

(10 + 8)

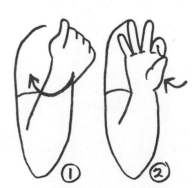

NINETEEN

Palm-in A pivots and opens to palm-out 9

(10 + 9)

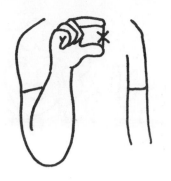

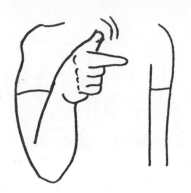

TWENTY

Index of G closes several time on thumb

TWENTY-ONE

Thumb of L wiggles, index aiming forward

TWENTY-TWO

V-hand makes two 2's

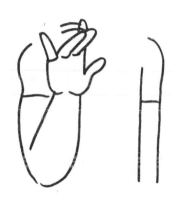

TWENTY-THREE

"L" + 3

TWENTY-FOUR

"L" + 4

TWENTY-FIVE

Middle two fingers wiggle together

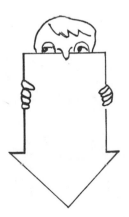

26 TO 29

"L" + 6, 7, 8, and 9

THIRTY

"3" + "0"

40, 50, 60, 70, 80, and 90

All are the numbers plus "0"

CONTRACTIONS

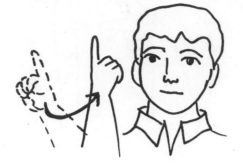

'D

Palm-out D twists inward

'LL

Palm-out L twists inward

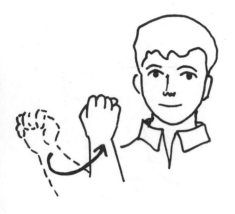

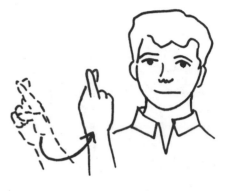

'M

Palm-out M twists inward

N'T

Palm-out N twists inward

'RE

Palm-our R twists inward

'S

Palm-out S twists inward

'VE

Palm-out V twists inward

AFFIXES

-ABLE,-IBLE

Palm-down A's drop slightly

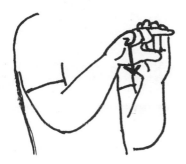

-AGE

Side of G slides down left fingers and palm

-AL

Palm-out L at end of preceeding sign

AL-,ALL-

Palm-out A slides right, changing to L

-AN, AN-

Palm-up A twists to palm-down

-ANT, -ENT

Side of T slides down left fingers and palm

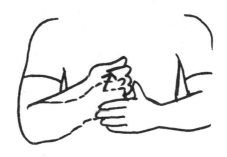

-ANTE

A-hand moves toward body from left palm

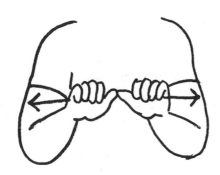

ANTI-

A-hands, thumbs touch; separate hands

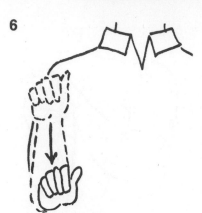

-ATE

Drop palm-out A down

DIS-

D's crossed at wrists separate sideways as in "not"

(See "NOT")

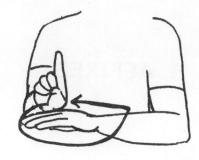

-DOM

D on back of hand circles out, left, and back along left arm

(See "GROUND")

-E

Palm-out E at end of word

-ED

(ALT. 1)

Palm of hand flips back toward shoulder

-ED

(ALT. 2)

For regular past tense (-ed), make a palm-out D at the end of the sign

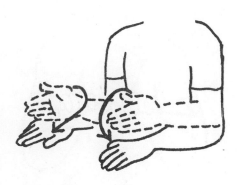

-EN

(ALT. 1)

Flat hands twist from palm-up to palms facing

-EN

(ALT. 2)

For regular past participle (-en) add N at completion of sign

-EE

Move E slightly to the right

-ENCE, -ANCE

Side of C slides down left fingers and palm

-ER, -AR, -OR

R, palm-out

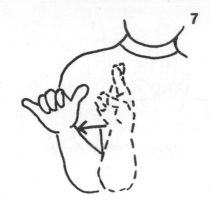

-ERY, -ORY, -ARY

Palm-out R and Y

-ESE

E moves down in a wavy motion

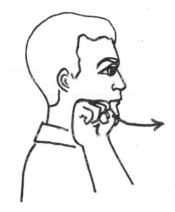

-ESS

Side of S slides along jaw forward

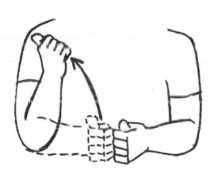

-EST

A-hands together; right A moves up

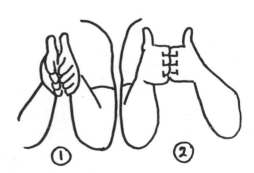

-FOLD

Palm-to-palm, keep fingertips together and bend hands back-to-back

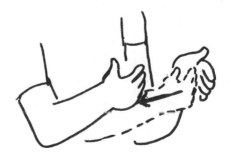

FORE-, -FORE

Bent right hand behind bent left; right moves back

-FUL, FUL-

Palm-down hand brushes inward across top of left S

-HERD

Palm-out U-hands circle horizontally to palm-in

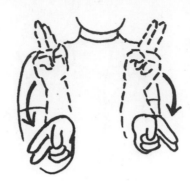

-HOOD

H-up to H-hands forward, as wrists cock

-IC

Palm-out C

-ICE

Palm-out C moves slightly down

-IFY

F's, resting right upon left, pivot as in "make"

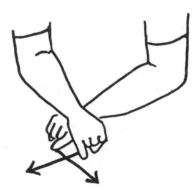

IL-, IM-, IR-, IN-

Palm-down I-hands, crossed at wrists, separate sideways
(See "NOT")

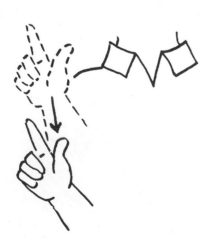

-ILE

L drops straight down

-INE

Palm-out N drops down

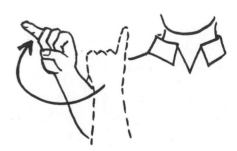

-ING

Palm-in, I-hand twists in slight downward arc to right, ending palm-out

INTER-

Little finger of I weaves among fingers of left hand

INTRA-

Little finger of I bounces between fingers of left hand

-ION, -TION, -SION

Side of S slides down fingers and palm

-ISH

I points forward and draws a wavy downward line

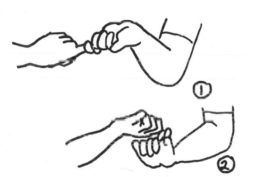

-ISM

Hook little fingers, one hand palm-up, the other palm-down, reverse

-IST

Drop I's straight down near body

(See "PERSON")

-ITE

Drop palm-out T down

-ITY, -ICITY

Thumbtip of Y slides down left fingers and palm

-IVE

Palm-out V shakes downward

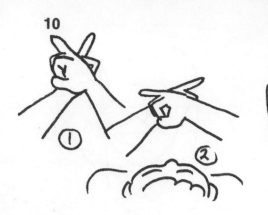

-IZE

I's, resting right on left, pivot as in "make"

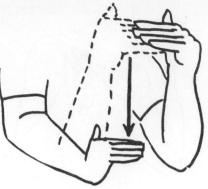

-LESS

Right bent hand under left bent hand; drop right hand downward

-LIKE

Palm-in L on chest moves forward, closing thumb and finger

-LY

(ALT. 1)

Palm-out I-L hand shakes downward

-LY

(ALT. 2)

Form L and then Y

-MENT

Side of M slides down left fingers and palm

MIS-

Palm-down M's, crossed at wrists, separate

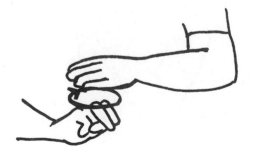

-NEATH

N circles below left palm

-NESS

Side of N slides down left fingers and palm

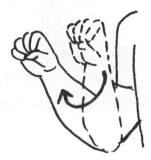

NON-

N-hands, crossed at wrists, separate to sides.

(See "NOT")

-OUS

Palm-out O draws a "U"

OVER-

Palm-down right hand circles over back of left hand

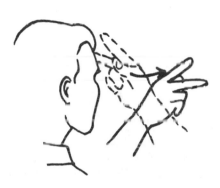

PRE-

P moves inward from left palm

(See "FORE")

POST-

P moves from back of left hand straight forward

PRO-

Middle fingertip of P on forehead twists to palm-out

(See "FOR")

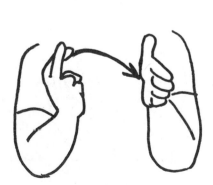

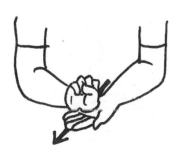

RE-

R fingertips hit left palm

-S

Palm-out S

-SHIP

Palm-out S on left palm; both move forward together

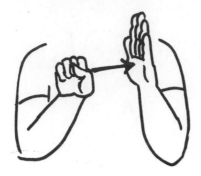

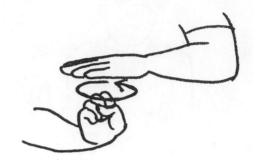

-SOME, SOME-

Side of right hand draws small arc across left palm

STEAD-, -STEAD

Side of S hits heel of left hand

SUB-

S circles under palm

(See "BASE")

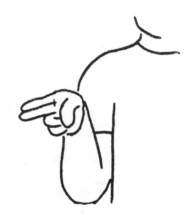

SUPER-

S circles over palm-down left hand

-T

Palm-out T

-TH

Make an H when you finish the sign for the word

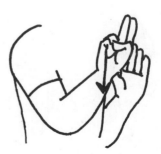

-THING

Palm-up, arc hand slightly up and down to the right

UN-

U-hands, palm-down, cross at wrists; separate sideways

(See "NOT")

-URE

Side of U slides down left fingers and palm

VICE-

Tap temple with V

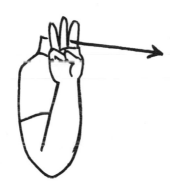

-WARD

Palm-out W moves forward

-Y

Palm-out Y

A

(Article)

Palm-out A moves slightly right

ABBREVIATE

Side of A on side of H, slide A back and forth

(See "SHORT")

ABDOMEN

A-hand, palm-in, pats abdomen

ABLE

Palm-down A's drop slightly

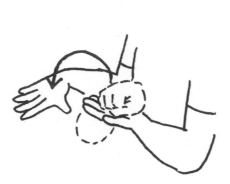

ABORT

Palm-down S on palm lifts up and throws down to open 5

(See "BARE")

ABOUT

Index finger circles the tip of left palm-in flat-O hand

ABOVE

Palm circles once over head

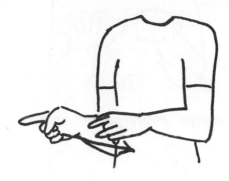

ABSENT

Right index clips bent middle finger of palm-down left hand, right to left

ABSENCE = ABSENT + ENCE

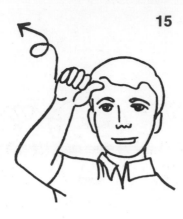

ABSTRACT

Right A-hand circles up and forward sideways from forehead

(See "IDEA")

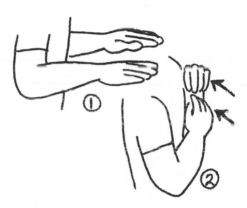

ACCEPT

Palm-down flat hands rise to flat-O's on chest, pointing toward each other

(SEE "APPROVE")

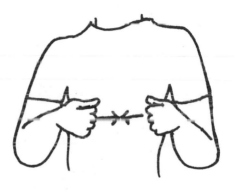

ACCIDENT

Palm-in A's at sides; hit knuckles together

ACCOMPANY

A-hands come together, palm-to-palm, and move forward

(See "WITH")

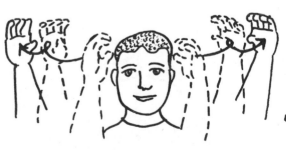

ACCOMPLISH

C-hands facing temples, twist out and up twice as palm-out C's

(See "SUCCESS")

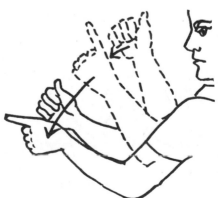

ACCUSE

A drops to hit top side of left index

ACHE

A's, with twisting motions, jerk toward each other; repeat

(See "HURT")

ACHIEVE

Palm-out, A's twist out and up twice   (See "SUCCESS")

ACQUAINT

Rest extended A-thumbs first right on left, then left on right
(See "FRIEND")

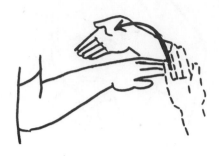

ACROSS

Right palm-left hand arcs across back of left palm-down hand

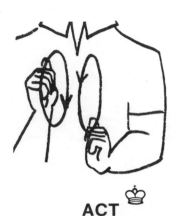

ACT ♛

Thumbs of A-hands brush alternately down chest, hands facing each other

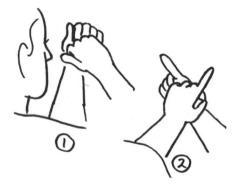

ADAPT

A-palms together, reverse position, changing to D's
(See "CHANGE")

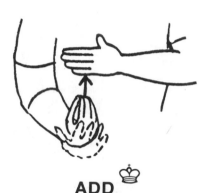

ADD ♛

5-hand to flat-O rises to touch little-finger side of palm-in left hand

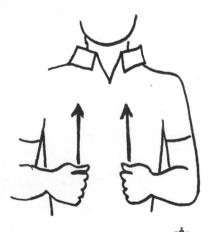

ADDRESS ♚

Palm-in A-hands move up body once

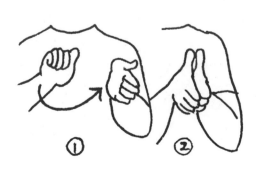

ADHESIVE

Palm-out right A flattens against flat left hand

(See "COHESIVE")

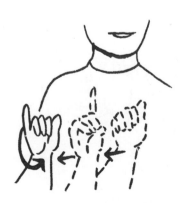

ADJECTIVE

Fingerspell A + D + J

ADJUST

A-palms together, reverse position, changing to I's
(See "CHANGE")

ADMIRE

A arcs in toward forehead down and outward
(See "GOD")

ADMIT

A-hands on chest turn over and out to palm-up open hands
ADMISSION = ADMIT + -TION
(See "CONFESS")

ADOPT

Palm-down 5's up to D's
(See "ASSUME")

ADULT

A-thumb on temple then to side of chin
(See "PARENT")

ADVANCE

Bent hands move up several levels
(See "PROMOTE")

ADVERB

Fingerspell A + D + V

ADVERTISE

Right S in front of left, right moves forward and back twice

ADVICE

Right flat-O set on back of left hand moves forward several times to palm-down 5

ADVISE 👑

Right flat-O set on back of left hand moves forward to palm-down 5; repeat

(See "ADVICE")

AFFECT

A moves forward off stationary left hand

(See "ADVICE")

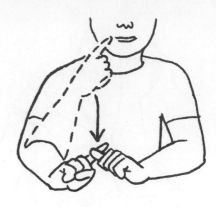

AFFIRM

Index at mouth moves down to make a cross with thumb of palm-down left A

(See "POSITIVE")

AFRAID 👑

Slightly to left, palm-out A's move downward in shaking motion

AFRICA

Palm-left A hand circles face

AFRICAN = AFRICA + -AN

AFTER

Right palm on back of left hand; right moves out

(See "POST")

AFTERNOON

Flat hand, arm resting on back of left hand, drops slightly

AGAIN

Strike heel of left hand with bent right fingertips

(See "REPEAT")

AGAINST 👑

Fingertips of flat hand hit left palm at right angles

AGE

A circles, then touches left palm

(See "HOUR")

AGENDA

Palm of A on fingers, then on heel of left hand

(See "LESSON")

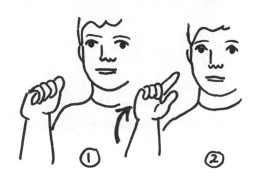

AGO

Palm-down A twists up and back over shoulder, opening to G

AGREE

Index finger touches forehead together then drops to index fingers

AHEAD

A-hands together; right arcs forward

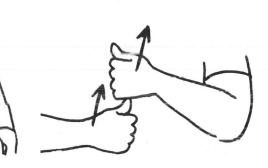

AID

Right A pushes left A upward, both palm-in

(See "HELP")

AIM

Indexes point up, right behind and slightly lower than left; right jerks down to point at left fingertip

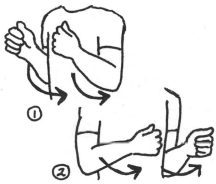

AIR

A-hands sweep from side to side twisting at wrists

(See "WIND")

AIRPLANE

L-Y hand, palm-down, flies through the air a short distance; repeat

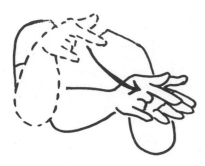

AIRPORT

L-Y hand, palm-down, lands on left hand

ALASKA

Palm-down A-hand arcs around parka hood to an open flat-hand

ALBUM

A-hands separate like a book opening

(See "BOOK")

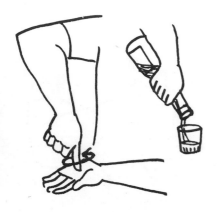

ALCOHOL

Circle tip of thumb of extended-A above palm

(See "MEDICINE")

ALERT

Palm-out A's at temples move sharply forward to palm-out L's

ALFALFA

A brushes up through C twice

(See "GRAIN")

ALGAE

Extended A-thumb makes small circle on little finger of palm-up left I-hand

ALGEBRA

A-hands, palm to palm, brush each other sideways twice

(See "ARITHMETIC")

ALIKE

Make A, slide into sign for "LIKE"

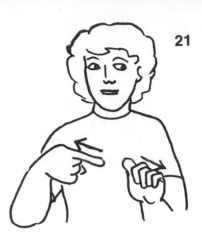

ALL

Palm-out A slides right, changing to L

ALLEGIANCE

Palm-in S pushes left L up

(See "SUPPORT")

ALLERGY

Index points at left A and both draw sharply apart

ALLERGIC = ALLERGY + -IC

(See "OPPOSE")

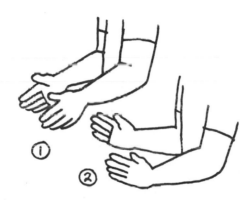

ALLIGATOR

Heels of flat hands touching, snap top "jaw" open and closed

ALLOW

Palm-to-palm hands point downward, swing upwards, still parallel

ALL RIGHT

Side of right hand slides forward across left palm, arcing slightly up

(See "LEGAL")

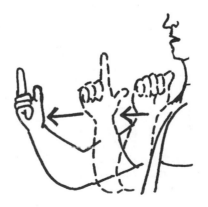

ALMOST

Stroke upwards off back of left fingers once

ALONE

Palm-out A moves slightly right, changes to L, twists to palm-in, and moves forward

ALONG

Heel of A slides up left arm to elbow

(See "LONG")

ALPHABET

A-hand moves across left 5-fingers, changing to B-hand

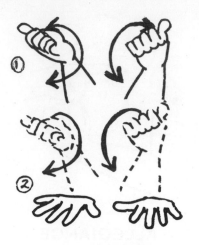

ALREADY

A-hands, palm-up, swing inward and down; repeat, ending in palm-down 5's

ALSO

AL- + SO

ALTAR

Separate and move down A-hands

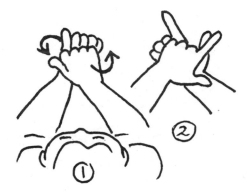

ALTER

A-palms together, reverse position, changing to L's
(See CHANGE")

ALTERNATE

A-hand from off thumb, to off tip of index

ALTERNATIVE = ALTERNATE + -IVE
(See "THEN")

ALTHOUGH

Spell A + L; then slap hands forward and back against each other alternately

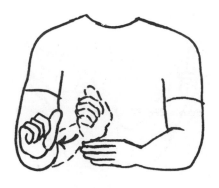

ALUMINUM

A-thumb hits down in an arc on index of B hand
(See "METAL")

ALWAYS

Palm-up index, pointing forward, circles clockwise

AM ♔

Thumbtip of A just below lips; move forward

AMAZE

Palm-out A-hands circle near eyes and flick index and thumb out

(See "SURPRISE")

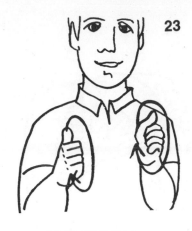

AMBITION

Thumbs of A's brush alternately up chest (Reverse of "act")

AMBITIOUS = AMBITION + -OUS

AMBULANCE

Thumb of A draws a cross on left upper arm, across then down

(See "HOSPITAL")

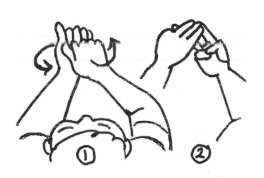

AMEND

(Alt. 1)

A-palms together, reverse position, right changing to M

(See "CHANGE")

AMEND

(Alt. 2)

Arc right hand up from beneath to grasp side of left hand (Attaching amendment)

(See "ADD")

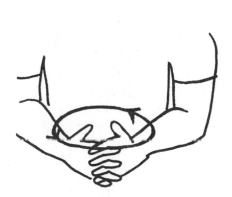

AMERICA

Mesh palm-In fingers, circle horizontally

AMERICAN = AMERICA + -AN

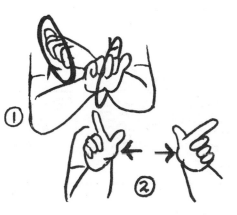

AMESLAN

(American Sign Language)

A's circle alternately and pull out to L's

AMONG

Right Index finger weaves among left fingers

AMOUNT ♔

Index side of flat hand on heel of left hand, outline amount to little-finger side of hand on left fingertips

AMUSE

Sides of A's rub in opposing circles on chest and stomach

((See "ENJOY")

AN

Palm-up A twists to palm-down

ANALYZE

Bent-V's stretch apart twice
(See "DIAGNOSE")

ANCESTOR

Palm-in flat hands circle each other back to right shoulder

ANCESTRY = ANCESTOR + -Y

ANCHOR

X-hand drops anchor in sideways arc from 3-hand

ANCIENT

Left A-thumb supporting right A, move down together in wavy motion   (See "OLD")

AND

Palm-in, 5-hand, pulls to right, closing to a flat-O

ANGEL ♔

Fingertips on shoulders swing out

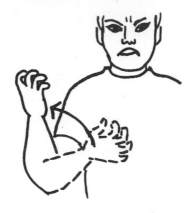

ANGER ♛

Claw arcs near chest to right.
(Can be done with two hands)

ANGRY = ANGER + -Y

ANGLE

Right index finger traces angle
of left L

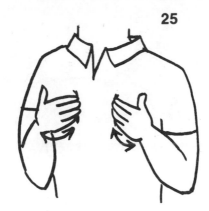

ANIMAL

Keep fingers on chest; swing
wrists toward center of body
twice

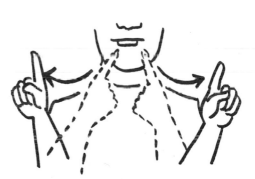

ANNOUNCE ♛

Palm-in index fingers at side of
mouth twist out and sideways
to palm-out

ANNUAL

Right hand brushes forward off
left while index flicks forward
from under thumb; repeat
several times

ANOTHER

An + Other

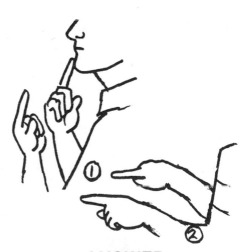

ANSWER

Right index finger on chin, left
palm-in; both hands turn palm-
down, left one ahead

(See "REPLY")

ANT ♛

A rides forward on wiggling
fingers of left hand

ANTELOPE

Extended A's curve up and
back from temples

ANTLER

A's on temples move slightly up to 5's

(See "DEER")

ANY

Palm-up A twists to palm-down A, changes to Y

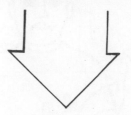

ANYBODY = ANY + BODY
ANYHOW = ANY + HOW
ANYONE = ANY + ONE
ANYTHING = ANY + THING
ANYWAY = ANY + WAY
ANYWHERE = ANY + WHERE

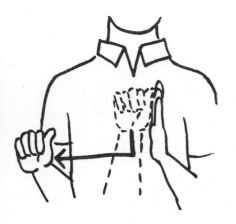

APART

Thumb-tip of palm-out A-hand moves down palm and away to side

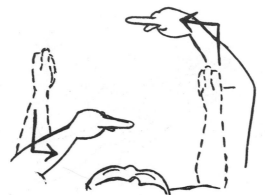

APARTMENT

Box in apartment with A-hands changing to P-hands

(See "BOX")

APATHY

Flat-O, palm-in at nose, twists out to open and fling down

(See "IGNORE")

APE

A-hand thumbs scratch sides

(See "MONKEY")

APOLOGIZE

Palm-in A circles on chest; moves down to left open palm and moves forward

APOLOGY = APOLOGIZE + -Y

(See "EXCUSE")

APOSTROPHE

X-finger makes apostrophe in the air

APPEAR

Right index rises to appear between index and middle fingers of palm-down left hand

APPEARANCE = APPEAR + -ANCE

APPETITE

A-hand palm-in moves down chest once

(See "HUNGER")

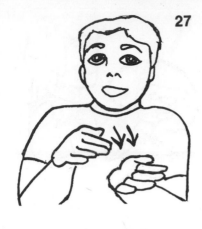

APPLAUSE

Clap several times quickly

APPLE

X twists against corner of mouth

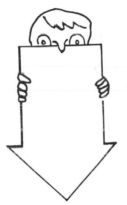

APPLICATION

Apply + -Tion

APPLY

Right V falls over left vertical index

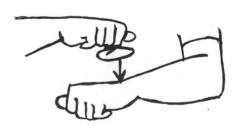

APPOINT

Right A circles over left, then drops to wrist

APPOINTMENT = APPOINT + -MENT

APPRECIATE

A on chest changes to P and circles once on chest

(See "PLEASE")

APPROACH

Bent right hand move in stages toward left palm; does not touch it

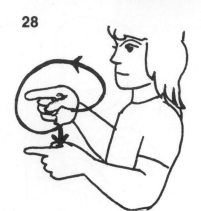

APPROPRIATE

Right index above left, both pointing forward; right makes clockwise vertical circle and drops onto left

APPROVE

A-hands, palm-down, draw back to P's on shoulders
(See "ACCEPT")

APPROXIMATE

Palm-out 5 moves in small circles

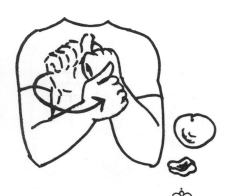

APRICOT

Right A circles left S, touching

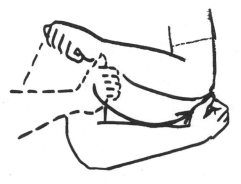

APRIL
(ALT. 1)

Right A-hand at wrist arcs down and up to touch near elbow   (See "BASKET")

APRIL
(ALT. 2)

A-hand turns calendar page outward over left flat hand
(See "CALENDAR")

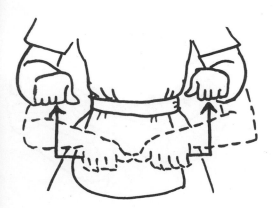

APRON

A-hands outline small apron at waist

ARCHITECT

Right A draws down vertical palm in wavy motion
(See "ART")

ARE

R, just below lips, moves forward
(See "AM")

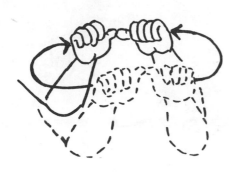

AREA

A-thumbs touch, circle in toward chest, touch again

(See "PLACE")

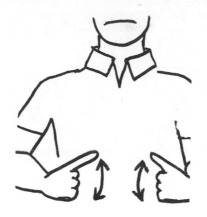

ARGUE

Palm-in index fingers move rapidly up and down from wrists

(See "HASSLE")

ARITHMETIC

Palm-in V's brush past each other sideways two or more times

ARIZONA

Touch chin twice with A-thumb, fist on left, then on right

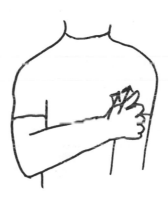

ARM

Pat arm with A

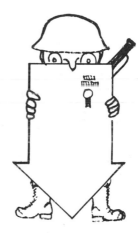

ARMY

A r m + -Y

AROUND

Palm-down A moves slightly right, changes to palm-down R and circles once, horizontally

ARRANGE

Parallel palms move right in small vertical arcs

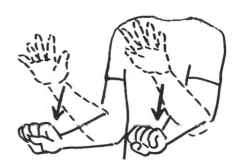

ARREST

5-hands drop downwards, closing sharply to S-hands

ARRIVE

Back of right hand arcs forward and touches left palm

(See "REACH")

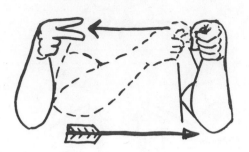

ARROW

Pull bowstring back to right V from left S

(See "CUPID")

ART

I- fingertip draws wavy line on palm

ARTIST = ART + -IST

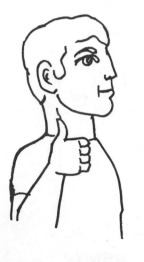

ARTERY

Extended-A thumb presses side of neck

ARTICHOKE

Hold left A-thumb and peel backward

ARTICLE

Curved index and thumb move down horizontal left palm

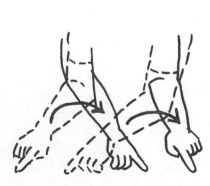

AS

Parallel indexes at right arc up and then drop, to the left

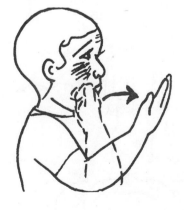

ASHAMED

A-hand, palm-out to palm-in, on cheek; A opens, fingers brushing up cheek; flat hand falls forward

ASIA

Thumbtip of A at corner of eye; hand twists forward slightly

(See "CHINA")

ASK

Palms of open hands come together and arc toward body

(See "REQUEST")

ASLEEP

A + drop 5-hand before face to flat-O, palm-in

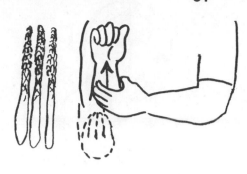

ASPARAGUS

Flat-O twists up through Left C to palm-out A

(See "GROW")

ASSASSIN

Side of A twists diagonally under left palm

ASSASSINATE = ASSASSIN + -ATE

(See "KILL")

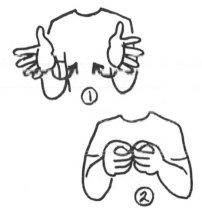

ASSEMBLE

Palm-out 5's approach, close to flat O's; touch

ASSEMBLY = ASSEMBLE + -LY

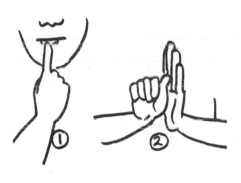

ASSIGN

Right index finger at mouth moves to palm-out A on palm

ASSIST

Left L pushes right A upward

ASSISTANCE = ASSIST + -ANCE

(See "HELP")

ASSOCIATE

Thumbs of extended A's circle each other

ASSUME

Palm-down 5's draw up to S's

(See "ADOPT")

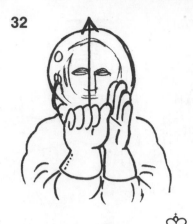

ASTRONAUT

Right A slides up palm-right flat hand and takes off

AT

Right fingertips approach and touch back of left fingers

ATE

Ate = Eat + P. T.

ATHLETE

A-hands lift weight (bar-bell) repeat

ATHLETIC = ATHLETE + -IC

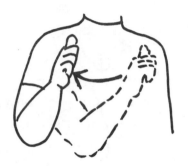

ATLANTA

Thumb of A touches left and then right shoulder

ATMOSPHERE

Right A circles left index

ATTACH

Pinch left A-hand thumb between index and thumb and draw back to left shoulder

ATTACK

Right claw hand approaches and grabs left vertical index finger

ATTEMPT

A-hands, facing each other, move forward away from body in a slight arc

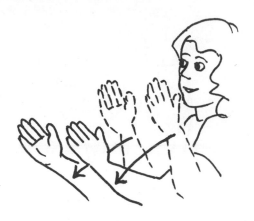

ATTEND

Vertical parallel palms drop to
point forward

ATTENTION = ATTEND + -TION

(See "CONCENTRATE")

ATTIC

A on back of hand arcs up and
makes small circle

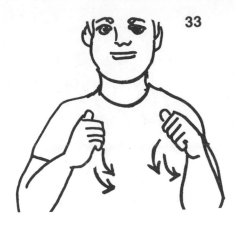

ATTIRE

A-hands brush off shoulders
two or more times

(See "DRESS")

ATTITUDE

Right A-hand circles the heart
and touches chest

(See "CHARACTER")

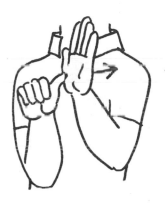

ATTRACT

(ALT.1)

Thumb of right A on palm; both
move toward body

(See "BELONG")

ATTRACT

(ALT.2)

Palm-up open hands, left
behind right, draw toward
body and close to palm-up S's

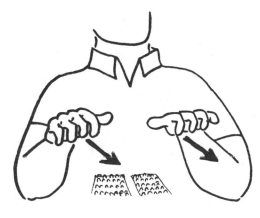

AUDIENCE

Parallel claw-hands palm-
down, move forward

AUDIO

Thumb of A touches ear, palm-
out

AUDIOGRAM

Right A slides down horizontal
left palm, then G slides across

AUDIOLOGY
A circles clockwise by right ear
AUDIOLOGIST = AUDIOLOGY + -IST

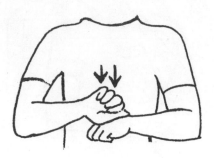

AUDITORIUM
Tap side of right A-thumb on back of left S

(See "CHURCH")

AUGUST
(ALT. 1)
A circles inward twice, touching chest

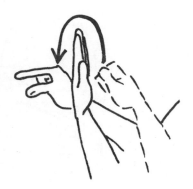

AUGUST
(ALT. 2)
Arc A to G over side of vertical hand

(See "CALENDAR")

AUNT
A-hand shakes near jaw

AUSTRALIA
Bent-B at temple twists to touch side of hand on head, palm-out

AUTHOR
Palm-down A writes across left palm

(See "WRITE")

AUTHORITY
Thumb of A-hand draws muscle on left arm

(See "STRONG")

AUTO
One A behind the other, right one moves back toward shoulder (See "CAR")

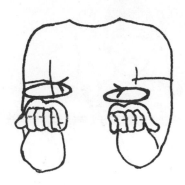

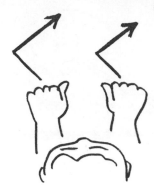

AUTUMN

Right A brushes off left elbow

(See "SEPTEMBER")

AVAIL

Palm-up A's circle slightly

AVAILABLE = AVAIL + ABLE

(See "HERE")

AVENUE

Palm-down A's move forward, zig-zagging

(See "BOULEVARD")

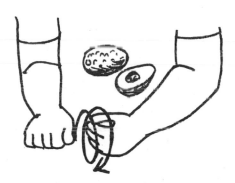

AVERAGE

Side of right flat hand crossways on side of left, rock top one slightly side to side

(See "MEDIUM")

AVOCADO

Thumb of palm-down extended A circles around palm-in flat-O, peeling

AVOID

Right A, behind left A, draws wavy motion back toward body

AWAKE

A + closed G-hand at corner of eye opens to L

AWARD

A's, right above left, arc diagonally forward to left

(See "GIFT")

AWARE

Right A at temple opens to W

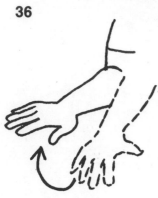

AWAY

Palm-in hand flips forward and up to palm-down

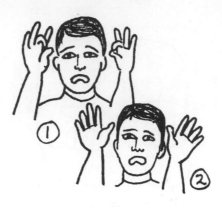

AWFUL

8's at temples flick open to 5's

AWKWARD

3-hands, palm-down, alternately move up and down

AXE ♔

Side of palm-down A chops at wrist of vertical left hand

BABBLE

Flat O's pointing forward near mouth, move forward opening and closing rapidly

BABY

Rock baby

(See "INFANT")

BACHELOR

B-hand arcs from left side of mouth to right side

BACK

Extended-A thumb jerks back over shoulder

BACKWARD = BACK + WARD

BACKGROUND

Right palm-out B, on left vertical palm, drops slightly and changes to G

BACON

H-fingertips touch and separate, waving

(See "SPAGHETTI")

BACTERIA

Heel of B circles on little finger of palm-up left I

(See "ALGAE")

BAD

Palm-in hand at mouth; twist to palm-out and throw down

BADGE

Make C's with thumbs and indexes on chest (form a badge)

BADMINTON

Hit bird twice sharply upward to right

BAG

Right B draws bag under left S

BAKE

Right B slides under left flat hand

BAKERY = BAKE + -ER + -Y

BAKERY

Bake + -ery

BALANCE

Palm-down flat hands rise and fall alternately

BALD ★

Middle finger circles on the back of left S-hand

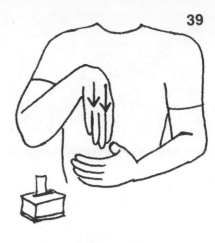

BALL
Claw-hands form ball-shape

BALLOON
S-hands at mouth open and form ball (like balloon)

BALLOT
Fingertips of B-hand stick into left C; repeat

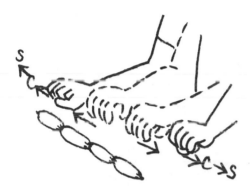

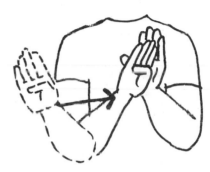

BALONEY
C-hands change to S-hands, twice, moving sideways

BALTIMORE
Shake B-tip up and down, palm-left

BAN
Side of right B strikes left palm
(See "FORBID")

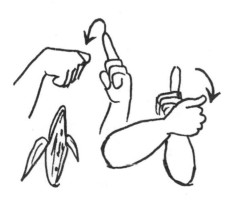

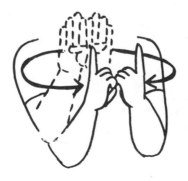

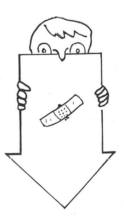

BANANA
Right thumb-tip peels left index finger more than once

BAND
Palm-out B's together, circle outward to palm-in D's together

BANDAID
Band + aid

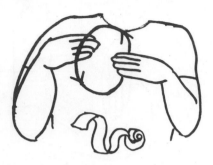

BANDAGE

Right B circles left B

BANG

Hit back of B-hand with S

(See "BUMP")

BANJO

Right hand strums banjo held by B-hand

BANK ★

Horizontal B jerks rapidly toward and away from side of left C

(See "STORE")

BANNER

Right B-hand waves in breeze with left index near wrist

(See "FLAG")

BANQUET ♔

Flat O-hands, palm-down circle alternately up to chin

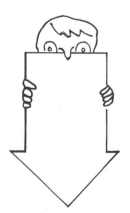

BAPTIST

Baptize + -ist

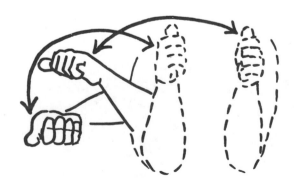

BAPTIZE

A-hands move to the right palm-up right and palm-down left, dipping person. Return to original position

BAR ♔ ★

B moves right, palm-out, off left index

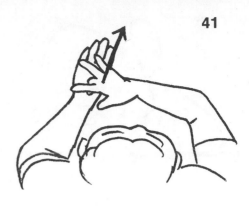

BARBER

V-hand clips hair

BARBEQUE

B + B + Q

BARE 👑

Right middle finger brushes along back of left hand and off

BARK

Bent-hands open out one above another; repeat

BARLEY

Palm-out B brushes up through left C twice
(See "GRAIN")

BARN

Palm-out B's outline barn
(See "HOUSE")

BAROMETER

Side of right B slides up and down left index
(See "THERMOMETER")

BARREL ★

Open B's outline barrel upward

BASE 👑

B circles under palm
BASIC = BASE + -IC

BASEBALL

Swing bat; repeat

BASEMENT

Basement = Base + ment

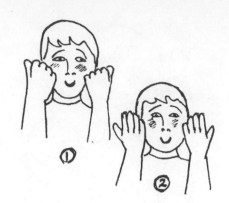

BASHFUL

Palm-in A's on cheeks open to palm-in bent hands on cheeks

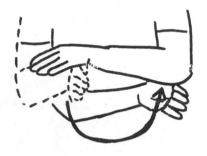

BASKET

Flat hand draws basket under left arm

BASKETBALL

Claw-hands flip ball upward

BATCH

Heel of palm-out B hops from palm to fingers

(See "AMOUNT")

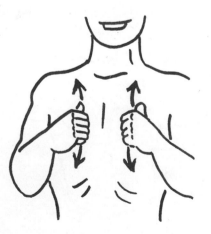

BATH

Rub knuckles up and down on chest

BATHE = BATH + E

BATTER

Fingers pointing down, circle right hand above left horizontal C

BATTERY

Right X-finger bumps side of B; repeat

(See "ELECTRIC")

BATTLE

Palm-in B's point at each other; move together from side to side

(See "WAR")

BAWL ★

S's by eyes drop and open, palms down

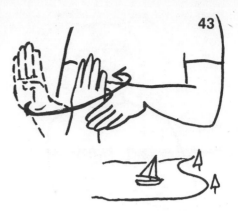

BAY ♛ ★

Palm-out B-hand outlines curve of palm-down left hand, index to thumb ending palm-in

BE

B below lips; move forward

BEEN - BE + P. P.

BEING = BE + -ING

(See "AM")

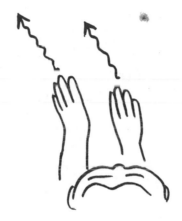

BEACH

Palm-down B's ripple forward left

BEAD ★

Tap side of F across palm, like beads

(See "SEQUIN")

BEAK

G-hand on nose and chin moves forward to close

(See "WOLF")

BEAN ★

(ALT. 1)

Slide thumb of A along thumb-side of B-hand; repeat

BEAN ★

(ALT. 2)

Right X taps down left index

(See "PEA")

BEAR ★

Swing crossed wrists of claw-hands to the right, still crossed

BEARD

Thumb and fingers on chin drop and close to flat-O

BEAST

Thumb-sides of B-s alternately beat on chest

BEAT ♔★

Back of right B hits left index finger

BEAUTY

Circle face with 5-hand closing to O

BEAUIFUL = BEAUTY + -FUL

(See "FACE")

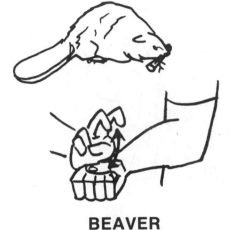

BEAVER

Tap right bent-2 on palm-up left S heels together

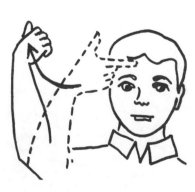

BECAUSE

Index on forehead, left up and right, closing to extended A

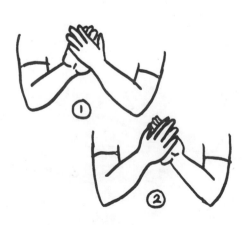

BECOME

Palm-to-palm hands twist to reverse position

BECAME = BECOME + P. T.

BED ♔

Rest cheek on back of palms-together hands

BEE

9 to cheek, then brush off bee
(See "WASP")

BEEF

Right thumb and forefinger grasp side of left B and shake
(See "MEAT")

BEEN

Be + P. P.

BEEP

Palm-out B taps ear

BEER

Vertical palm-out circles on right cheek
(See "WINE")

BEET

Index finger slices side of palm-out B; repeat
(See "TOMATO")

BEETLE

B rides forward on back of wiggling fingers on left hand
(See "ANT")

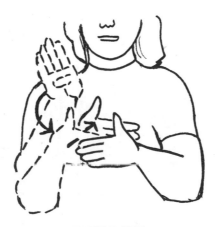

BEFORE

Make palm-out B, then right palm-in hand behind left palm-in hand, right hand moves inward

BEG

Palm-up right hand on back of left; flex fingers
(See "COAX")

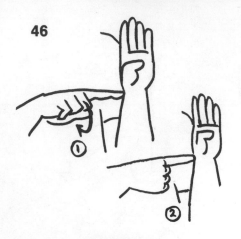

BEGIN

Index twists on wrist of left B

BEGAN = BEGIN + P. T.

BEGUN = BEGIN + P. P.

(See "START")

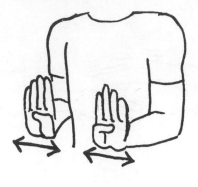

BEHAVE

Palm-out B's move from side to side

BEHAVIOR = BEHAVE + -ER

(See "DO")

BEHIND

B behind A-hand turns to A and arcs to rest against left A-wrist

(See "HIND")

BELIEVE

Right index finger on forehead; drop to clasped hands

BELIEF = BELIEVE + F

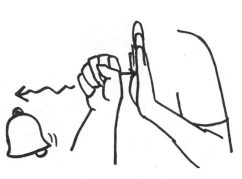

BELL

Right S hits left palm, then shakes to the right

BELLY

Open hands outline big belly

BELONG

Right thumb and finger hold thumb of left B while moving to left shoulder

(See "ATTRACT")

BELOW

B drops to L, which falls slightly

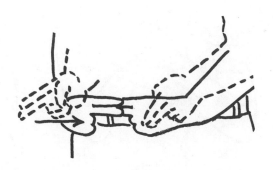

BELT ★

H-hands overlap fingertips across belt-line, snapping at wrists

(See "BUCKLE")

BENCH

Two fingers sit on side of left B-hand

(See "SIT")

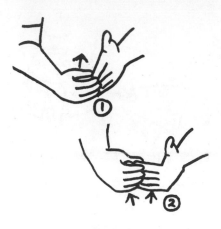

BEND

Grasp left fingertips and bend them inward

BENEATH

B drops; changes to N, circles below left palm

BENEFIT

"Pin" with 9-hand down shoulder

BERRY

Twist C around I-fingertip; shake first letter of name of berry by little finger before signing "berry" e.g., "Raspberry" = shake R, sign "berry."

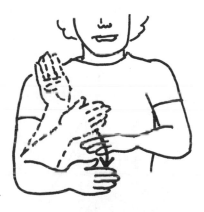

BESIDE

B drops to palm-in flat hand that brushes past side of left palm-down flat-hand

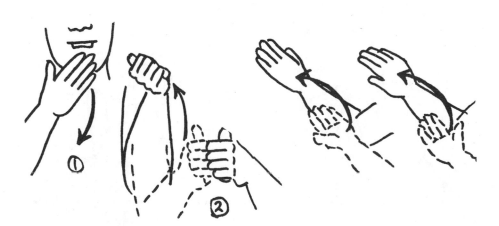

BEST

Hand on chin; add-est: A-hand brushing up from left A

BET

Palm-up hands, right behind left, move forward-left and turn palm-down

(See "COMPROMISE")

BETHLEHEM

Palm-out B circles and then taps fingertips of B's

BETRAY

Index finger flicks around left B, near mouth

BETTER

Flat palm-in hand slides off chin into palm-in

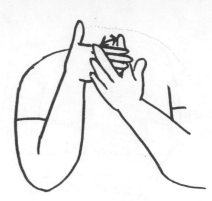

BETWEEN

Right flat hand flutters between 1st and 2nd fingers of left hand

BEYOND

Right B changes to Y against the left Y; right Y moves forward

BIB

Both index fingers outline bib

BIBLE

Praying-hands drop open like book

BIBLIOGRAPHY

Palms-together "book" moves down, opening repeatedly
(See "BOOK")

BICYCLE

Palm-out B-hands pedal

BIG

Palm-out B's arc sideways
(See "MUCH")

BIKE

Palm-down S-hands pedal

(See "BICYCLE")

BILLION

Heel of right B on heel of left
hand; Arc B to fingertips as
both hand move forward

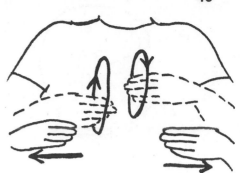

BIND

B's point toward each other,
circle each other, and separate

(See "TIE")

BINOCULARS

O-hands twist around eyes, in
place

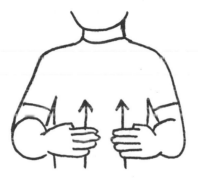

BIOGRAPHY

Palm-in B's move up trunk
(See "ADDRESS")

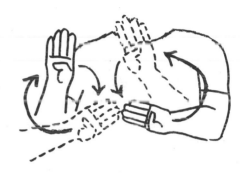

BIOLOGY

Palm-out B's circle alternately
(See "SCIENCE")

BIRD

Close finger on thumb twice,
hand at chin

BIRTH

Palm-up hands move from
sides forward, to rest right on
left   **BORN = BIRTH + P. P.**
BIRTHDAY = BIRTH + DAY

BISCUIT

Thumb and curved index on
left palm lift slightly, rotate and
touch again

(See "COOKIE")

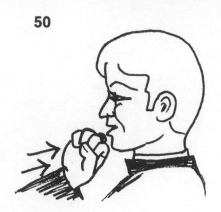

BISHOP

Kiss ring on right fist

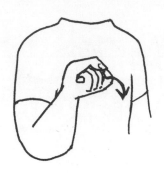

BIT ★

(ALT. 1)
Little finger flips forward from
index finger

BIT ★

(ALT. 2)
Palm-up hand; thumb flips up
from under index

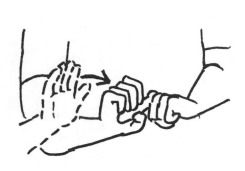

BITE

Right hand bites left index
finger

BIT = **BITE** + **P. T.**

BITTER

Index finger of B on chin, palm-
left, twist to palm-in
(See "SOUR")

BLACK ♔

Palm-down, index moves
across forehead right
BLACKBOARD = **BLACK** + **BOARD**

BLADE

Shake heel of B upward from
left index fingertip
(See "SHARP")

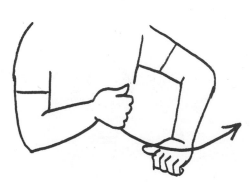

BLAME

A arcs forward, little-finger side
hitting back of left hand

BLANK

Bent middle finger of 5-hand
draws a line in the air
(See "DASH")

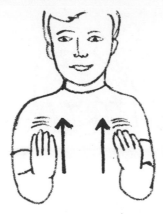

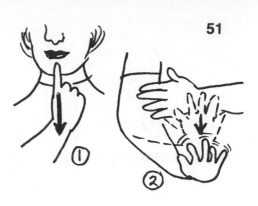

BLANKET

From in front, right arm sweeps across left arm to shoulder near neck (drawing up blanket)

(See "SHEET")

BLAZE ★

Palm-in B's flutter upwards

(See "FIRE")

BLEED

Index at chin drops, changing to palm-in 5 on back of left hand, moving downwards with fluttering fingers

BLED = BLEED + P. T.

(See "BLOOD")

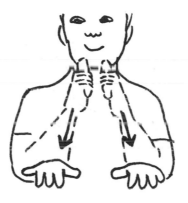

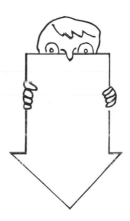

BLEND

Flat hands draw up to A's with knuckles together

BLESS

Thumbs of extended A's on chin; move down, opening slowly to palm-down 5's

BLEW

Blow + P. T.

BLIND

Bent-V, palm-in, jerks toward eyes

BLINK

Hands stationary at eyes, shut and open thumbs and fingers of L's

BLISTER

Right flat-O on palm-down left B pops to claw

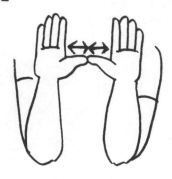

BLOCK ★

Thumb-tips, palms out, tap

BLOND

B makes a wavy motion down side of hair

BLONDE = BLOND + -E

BLOOD

Palm-in 5 touches back of hand, then drops down with fluttering fingers (blood dripping)

(See "BLEED")

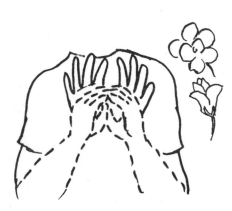

BLOOM

Flat-O's together change to 5's with thumbs touching

BLOSSOM

Flat-O's together, change to 5's, thumbs touching, move slightly to right and repeat

BLOUSE

Palm-out B's on chest move down to waist

(See "COAT")

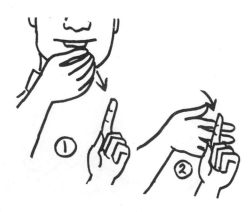

BLOW ★

Palm-in flat-O at mouth moves out and opens to palm-in 5; hits side of index finger

BLEW = BLOW + P. T.

BLUE ♔

Palm-left B shakes from wrist

BLUSH

Flat-O at cheek rises and opens to a 5

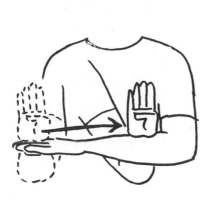

BOARD

Palm-out B moves along left arm

BOAST

Extended A-thumbs strike waist alternately

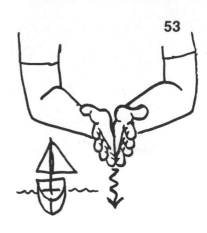

BOAT

Flat hands joined at little finger side, move forward in wavy up-and-down motion

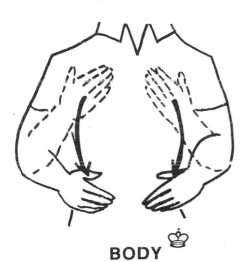

BODY

Touch chest and then ribs

BOIL

Palm-in hands "juggle" alternately while fluttering fingers

BOLD

Little-finger side of fist strikes right chest circularly

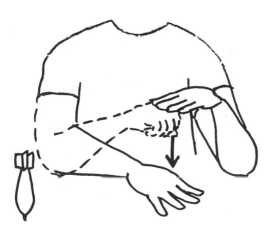

BOMB

Drop bomb from under left hand, right hand opening from S to 5

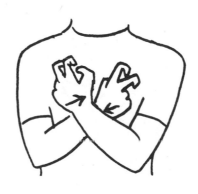

BONE

Bent 3's palm in, wrists tap against each other

BONFIRE

Palm-in 5's flutter fingers as they separate and rise

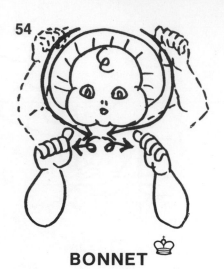

BONNET ♛

Outline and tie on bonnet with A-hands

BOOK ♛

Palm-to-palm hand open, palms up

BOOST

Palm-in S boosts left B

(See "SUPPORT")

BOOT ★

Tap sides of B-hands together twice, palm-out

(See "SHOE")

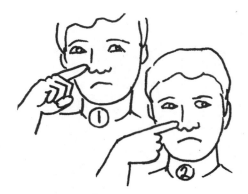

BORE

Tip of index finger on side of nose; twist in place

BORN

Birth + P. P.

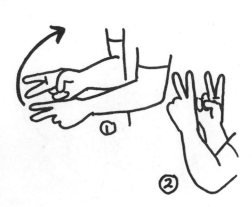

BORROW ♛

Right V on top of left V, both arc up together toward body

BOSS

Tap side of right B on right shoulder

(See "OFFICE")

BOTH

V slides through left C, closing to a U-hand

BOTHER

Side of right hand chops into thumb-base of left hand, several times

BOTTLE

C on palm closes into S, outlining a bottle

BOTTOM

Right fingertips tap heel of palm-out left B

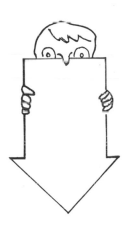

BOUGHT

Buy + P. T.

BOULEVARD

2 B's, palm-out and parallel, move away from body and zag right

(See "AVENUE")

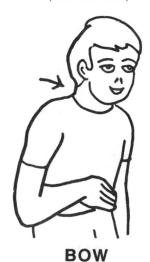

BOUNCE

5-hand bounces

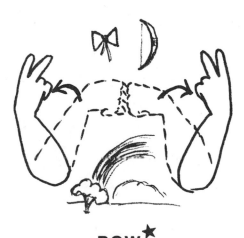

BOW ★

Palm-in S-hands arc out to V's

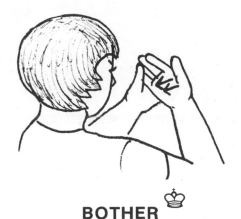

BOW

Arm at waist, bow forward slightly

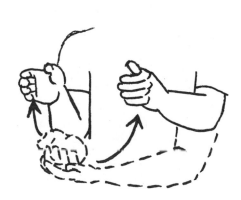

BOWL ★

Palm-up cupped hands, right over left, rise to sides

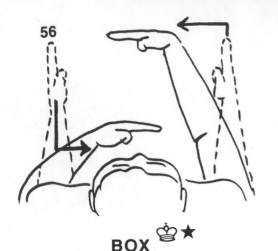

BOX ♕★

B-hands make a box

BOY

4-fingers touch thumb several times near temple, grasping cap-brim

BRA

L-hands, pointing down, move from mid-chest to sides

BRACELET

Middle finger and thumb circle left wrist and twist this "bracelet" slightly

BRAG

Extended A-thumb strikes waist several times

BRAILLE

Flutter fingers slightly across "page" of palm

BRAIN

Thumb of C taps on forehead twice

BRAKE

A-hand presses down abruptly, as if braking

BRANCH ★

Palm-out B, at thumb of left palm-out 5, arcs sideways

(See "LIMB")

BRAND ★

Draw fingers of B across open palm-out palm

(See "LABEL")

BRASS

Heel of right B arcs down and to side hitting side of palm-in left hand

(See "METAL")

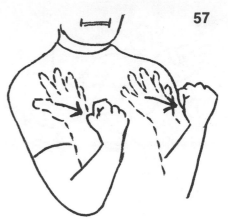

BRAVE

5's on chest; pull out to S-hands

(See "HERO")

BREAD

Side of right hand slices back of hand three times

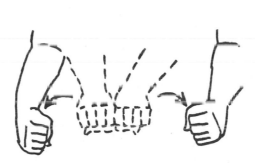

BREAK

Sides of S-hands touch, then separate sharply. twisting to face each other

BROKEN = BREAK + P. P.
BROKE = BREAK + P. T.

BREAKFAST

B-hand rotates at wrist up to mouth

(See "EAT")

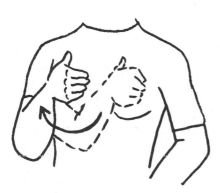

BREAST

Touch fingertips on each side of chest

BREATH

Flat hands move together from and to chest

BREATHE = BREATH + -E

(See "SIGH")

BREED

B on B, palms in, then circle each other vertically

(See "KIND")

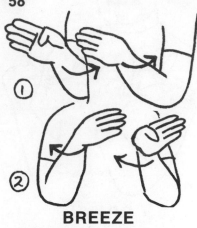

BREEZE

B-hands swing back and forth twisting at wrists (as breeze "blows") (See "WIND")

BRIBE

Palm-up flat-O passes under left palm toward left
(See "UNDER")

BRICK

Back of B taps on back of left S
(See "STONE")

BRIDE

Extended-A thumb strokes down cheek, opens, and goes into clasp of other hand, palms-in

BRIDEGROOM

Fingers and thumb touch near temple, then hand swings down to enter clasp of other hand

BRIDGE

Fingertips of V touch left palm, arc to touch arm near elbow

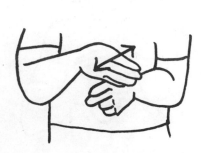

BRIEF

Side of right B slides back and forth on side of left H-index
(See "SHORT")

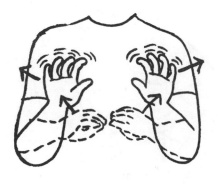

BRIGHT

Flat-O's together change to 5-hands, palm-out; separate upwards with fluttering fingers
(See "CLEAR")

BRILLIANT

Bent middle finger shakes up from forehead

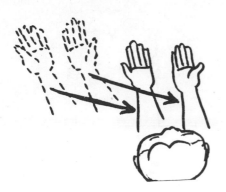

BRING

Palm-up hands at left; move back toward body

BROUGHT = **BRING** + **P. T.**

(See "TRANSPORT")

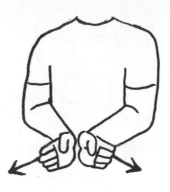

BROAD ♔

Heels of B's together, separate forward

BROCCOLI

Flat-O grows up through C-hand, twisting to palm-out B

(See "GROW")

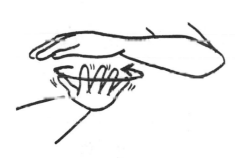

BROIL

Flutter fingers while circling hand under palm

(See "OVEN")

BROKE

Break + P. T.

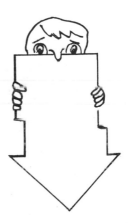

BROKEN

Break + P. P.

BROOCH

Index finger draws a small circle on left shoulder

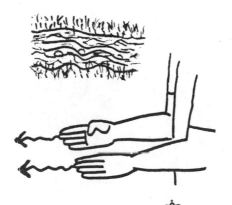

BROOK ♔

Parallel B-hands shake forward slightly to the side (like brook-water)

BROOM

Right S on left, sweep to left; repeat

BROTH

Ladle B-hand up to mouth twice

(See "SOUP")

BROTHER

A-hand at temple drops, index fingers together

(See "SISTER")

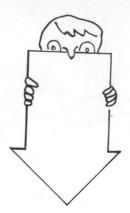

BROUGHT

Bring + P. T.

BROW

Fingertips of palm-out B brush across forehead

BROWN

Palm-left B moves down at side of mouth

(See "TAN")

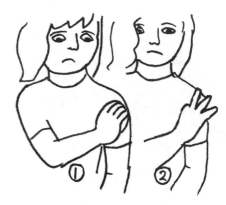

BRUISE

Thumb-side of O on upper arm, open to F

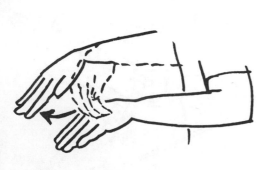

BRUSH ★

Brush top of left hand with back of right fingers several times

BUBBLE

O-hands rise, alternately opening several times with a flicking motion

BUCKET

B-hand points down at side, rises, still pointing down

(See "PAIL")

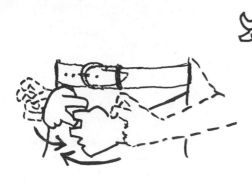

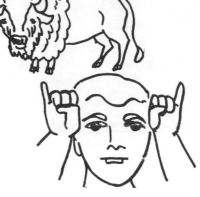

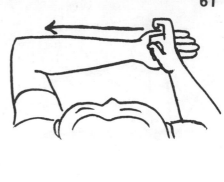

BUCKLE ★

Bent V's curve toward each
other at waist and mesh

(See "BELT")

BUFFALO

I's palm-out at temples

BUFFET

Palm-left X moves from back of
left hand, along arm

(See "CAFETERIA")

BUG

First two fingers wiggle,
thumb on nose

BUGGY

Palm-out B-hands move
straight forward to Y-hands

(See "PUSH")

BUILD

Build palm-down hands
alternately on top of each other

BUILDING = BUILD + -ING

BUILT = BUILD + -P. T.

BULB ♛★

Heels of B-thumbs together,
circle out and together again

BULL

Palm-out Y on center of
forehead

BULLDOZER

Index in the palm of left hand,
push hand forward with index

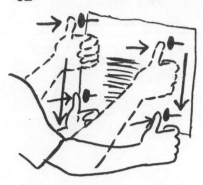

BULLETIN

Extended-A hands tack up bulletin, top and bottom

BUMP ♛ ★

S hits palm from behind and bounces back

BUNCH ★

Palm-out B's circle out to touch again, palm-in

(See "CLASS")

BUNDLE

Right vertical hand quickly rotates around left vertical hand

BUNNY

Fingers of B's at temples flop forward and back

BURDEN

Slightly bent hands push shoulder down

(See "RESPONSIBLE")

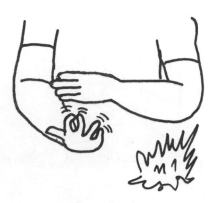

BURN ★

Right fingers flutter under palm-in horizontal B

(See "HEAT")

BURP

Index points at and touches chest, arcs up slightly

BURY ♛

Palm-down hands arc back toward body

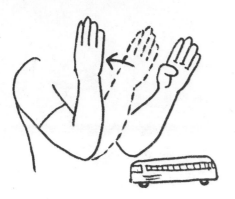

BUS

Left B, palm-right, in from of right B, palm-left; right moves back

(See "CAR")

BUSH ★

Wrist of palm-out B against side of palm-down hand; shake top of B slightly

BUSHY = BUSH + -Y

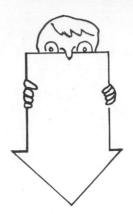

BUSINESS

Busy + -ness

BUSY ♔

Palm-out B arcs from side to side, hitting back of hand

BUSINESS = BUSY + -NESS

BUT

Palm-out crossed fingers separate(wrist action)

BUTCHER

Thumb of extended-A slices side of neck backwards

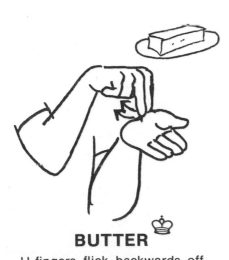

BUTTER ♔

U-fingers flick backwards off left heel to N, twice

BUTTERFLY

Hook thumbs, palms-in, and flutter hands

BUTTON

9-hand taps its side against chest, high, then lower

(May be made wherever button is)

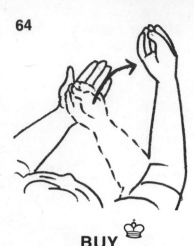

BUY ♛

Palm-up flat-O on palm, lifts off, arcs forward

BOUGHT = **BUY** + **P. T.**

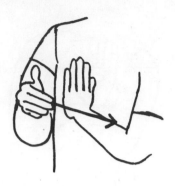

BY

Palm of right hand brushes by side of vertical, palm-right left hand

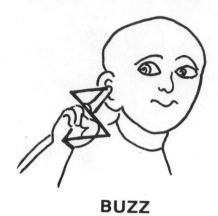

BUZZ

Starting with index finger on ear, draw A

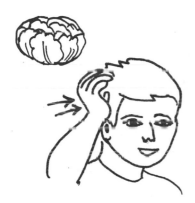

CABBAGE

C-heel taps head

CABIN

Palm-out C's draw roof and sides of cabin

(See "HOUSE")

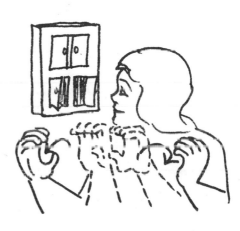

CABINET

Palm-out C's open doors; repeat, lower down

(See "CUPBOARD")

CABLE

Right C moves away from thumb of left C in wavy motion

(See "CORD")

CABOOSE

C thumb rubs back and forth on palm-down left U

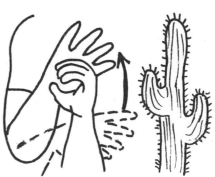

CACTUS

Right 4-hand behind left C, raise 4 from angled-left to vertical

CAFE

C-taps at corner of mouth

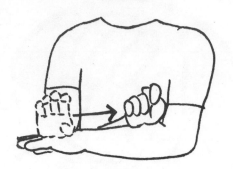

CAFETERIA

(ALT. 1)

C on back of hand slides up left arm into T

(See "BUFFET")

CAFETERIA

(ALT. 2)

C touches at one side of mouth, then at the other

(See "RESTAURANT")

CAGE

Palm-in right 4 hits side of left C

(See "JAIL")

CAKE

Fingertips of right claw-hand bounce on back of left hand

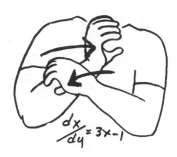

CALCULUS

C's brush past each other at wrists, sideways; repeat

(See "ARITHMETIC")

CALENDAR

Right C slides up palm-in left hand, over, and down back

CALF

Extended A's at corners of head, palm in

(For calf of leg, just point)

CALIFORNIA

L-Y hand wiggles down from ear to Y

CALL

Thumb of right C (palm-left) touches corner of mouth; hand moves short distance forward

CALM

C-hands crossed at chin, separate downwards

(See "QUIET")

CAME

Come + P. T.

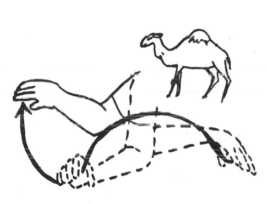

CAMEL

C-hand draws a camel's back

CAMERA

Index finger "clicks the shutter"

CAMP

Tap little and index fingers twice

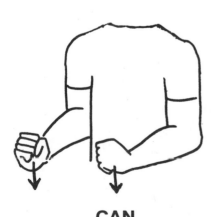

CAN

(ALT. 1)

S-hands face each other, drop sharply downwards a short way   **CANNED = CAN + P. T.**

(See "COULD")

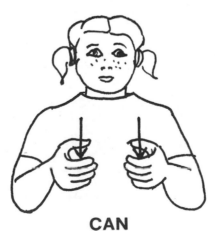

CAN

(ALT.2)

C's face each other and drop

CANNED = CAN + P. T.

(See "COULD")

CANADA

A grasps clothes on right side and taps chest

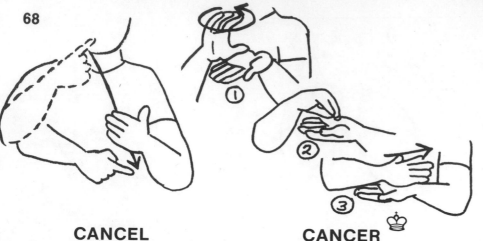

CANCEL

Right index finger slashes diagonally across palm of left hand

CANCER

C circles on palm; changes to flat-O; opens and spreads up arm

CANDLE

Palm of left 5 on tip of right index finger; flutter fingers

CANDY

Index finger on cheek, twist hand

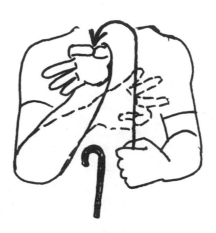

CANE

Drag right-hand 9 from left hand up into shape of cane

CANNON

Indexes pointing forward, upper hand shoots forward and recoils

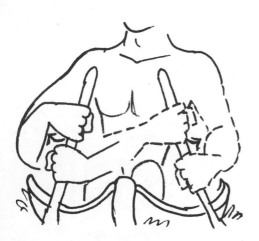

CANOE

Paddle canoe to left and right

CAN'T

Right index strikes down past tip of left index

(May also be signed "Can" + "n't")

CANTALOUPE

Middle finger thumps top of left C

(See "MELON")

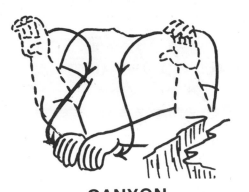

CANYON

C's outline canyon

(See "VALLEY")

CAP ♛★

Flat hand pats top of C

CAPITAL

Thumb of C taps shoulder

(See "OFFICE")

CAPITOL

C circles near temple pivoting at wrist, then thumb touches temple

(See "GOVERN")

CAPTAIN

Claw-hand taps right shoulder twice

(See "OFFICE")

CAPTION

Right 9 arcs downward and to right several times, from left 9-hand

CAPTURE

Claw-hand "attacks" left index; closes, and pulls it back to shoulder

CAR ♛

Right C behind left C; right moves backwards

CARAMEL

C on back of flat hand circles and changes to an L

(See "CHOCOLATE")

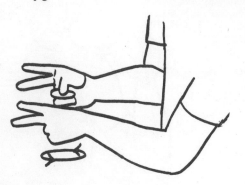

CARE

Right V-hand on left V-hand, circle horizontally

CAREFUL = CARE + -FUL

(See "SUPERVISE")

CARD

Right C grasps left hand, slides back and forth

CAREER

Thumb of C slides forward along side of left B-hand

(See "STRAIGHT")

CARELESS

V fans back and forth at forehead several times

CARGO

Palm-up C arcs over to palm-out on top of palm-down hand

CARNIVAL

Palm-out C arcs down to palm-out L, and moves right

(See "FESTIVAL")

CAROL

C swings to L behind left arm

(See "MUSIC")

CARPENTER

S on open left palm moves forward several times like planing

CARPENTRY = CARPENTER + -Y

CARPET

C-hand drags across back of left hand

CARROT

Scrape top of left C with thumb
of extended A

(See "BEAN")

CARRY

Palms-up, move to side In
small vertical arcs

CART

Palm-out C-hands move
straight forward to T-hands

(See "PUSH")

CARTOON

Index of C brushes downward
twice off nose

(See "DOLL")

CARVE

Flat hand carves side of left C;
repeat

(See "SLICE")

CASE ★

C's outline box

(See "BOX")

CASH

C on palm, arc slightly, moving
forward

(See "BUY")

CASSEROLE

Slide C under flat left hand as if
casserole slides into oven

(See "BAKE")

CASTLE

Bent-V's build a castle shape

(See "PALACE")

CAT 👑

9-hand draws out whiskers; repeat

CATALOGUE

Palm-up C slides forward and off side of palm-right left hand

(See "MAGAZINE")

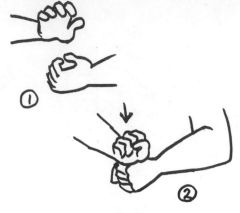

CATCH

Palm-out claw above side of left claw; right drops onto left; both close to S's

CAUGHT = CATCH + P. T.

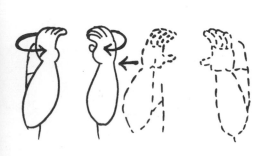

CATEGORY

C's quickly twist from palm-out to palm-in, and repeat

CATEGORIZE = ADD + -IZE

CATERPILLAR 👑

One alternating with X-finger pulls right hand along left arm several times

CATHOLIC

Palm-in H-fingers make a cross near forehead, vertical, then horizontal

CATSUP

(See "KETCHUP")

CATTLE

Y-hands, palm-out at temples, twist slightly

(See "COW")

CAULIFLOWER

Heel of 9 taps on head

(See "CABBAGE")

CAUSE

Palm-up A's, left ahead of right,
drop and open

CAVE

Little-finger side of right hand
hollows out left C, pivoting

CAVITY = CAVE + -ITY

(See "HOLLOW")

CEASE

Right C falls onto left palm

(See "STOP")

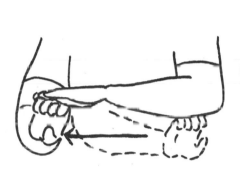

CEILING

C-hand slides along underside
of left arm

CELEBRATE

A-hands spiral upward toward
head

**CELEBRATION =
CELEBRATE + -TION**

CELERY

Flat-O grows up through C,
twisting to palm-out C

(See "GROW")

CELL

With index curved, right thumb
circles on little finger of left
hand   (See "ALGAE")

CELLAR

C circles under flat left hand

(See "BASE")

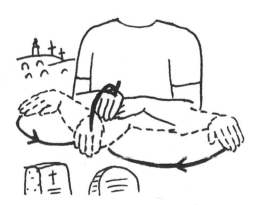

CEMETERY

Palm-down hands arc
horizontally toward each
other, right rests on left, both
arc back toward body

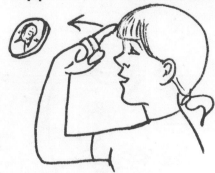

CENT

Touch index finger to forehead, then move hand out with small jerk

CENTER

C circles over, drops on left palm

CENTRAL = CENTER + -AL

(See "MIDDLE")

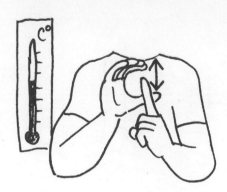

CENTIGRADE

Right C moves up and down behind left index finger

(See "THERMOMETER")

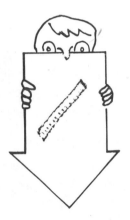

CENTIMETER

SPELL C + M

CENTURY

Side of C on left palm circles once vertically, then touches again

(See "HOUR")

CEREAL

(ALT. 1)

C-hand ladles up to mouth from left hand

(See "SOUP")

CEREAL

(ALT. 2)

Index to X; repeat, moving sideways under lips

CERTAIN

C jerks from chin forward and slightly down

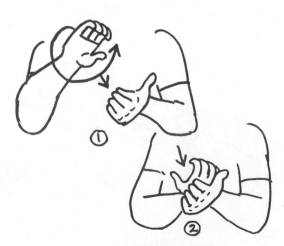

CERTIFY

C-hand inverts and hits flat left palm

CERTIFICATE = ADD - ATE

CHAIN

Link 9-hands, release, reverse, and link again, moving slightly right with each reversal

CHAIR

2 fingers "sit" on thumb of left C

(See "SIT")

CHALK

Thumb of C writes on left palm

(See "WRITE")

CHALKBOARD

CHALK + BOARD

CHALLENGE

Palm-in extended-A's' arc inward, but do not meet

CHAMP

Palm-out bent-3 twists inward to top of forehead

CHAMPION

Palm of claw taps left index

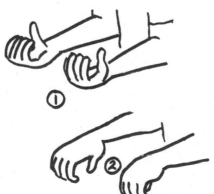

CHANCE

Palm-up C's twist to palm-down C's

(See "HAPPEN")

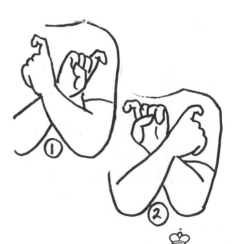

CHANGE

X's touch heels, stay together, twist to reverse hands

CHANNEL

Palm-in C's twist to palm-out, moving forward

CHAPTER

Thumb and fingertips of C slide down left palm

CHARACTER ♔

C circles clockwise, then touches on left chest

CHARGE

Fingers of palm-in C strike downward across left palm
(See "COST")

CHARM ★

Thumb of C slides down outside of left wrist, wriggling fingers

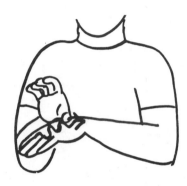

CHART

Thumb of C draws wavy line backwards on back of hand
(See "MAP")

CHASE

Right extended-A behind left extended A; both move forward and left; right hand circles slightly   (See "PURSUE")

CHAT

Hands face each other, open and close, simultaneously and repeatedly

CHATTER

Heels together, right claw fingertips rise and fall quickly on left several times

CHEAP

Right hand slaps down off left palm

CHEAT

(ALT. 1)

Horizontal V-hand chops side of left hand; repeat

CHEAT

(ALT. 2)

Index and little finger out, move right hand from wrist to left elbow (Putting card in sleeve)

CHECK ★

Index finger makes check mark near left palm

(See "EDIT")

CHEEK

Thumb and finger grasp skin of cheek

CHEER

Side of C brushes up side of chest; repeat

(See "HAPPY")

CHEESE

Right heel on left heel mashes and twists slightly

CHEMISTRY

Palm-out C's circle (pour) alternately

(See "SCIENCE")

CHERRY

Twist C first around left hand's upper V-finger, then around lower finger

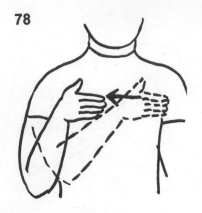

CHEST

Draw hand palm-in across chest

CHEW

Right A circles knuckles on palm-up knuckles of left A

(See "DIGEST")

CHICAGO 👑

C-hand arcs sharply down to right

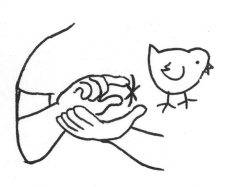

CHICK

G-hand rests on cupped palm, opens and closes

(See "DUCKLING")

CHICKEN

G drops from mouth to close on left palm

(See "BIRD")

CHIEF

C-hand taps top of left index twice

CHILD 👑

Waist-high flat hand pats child's head

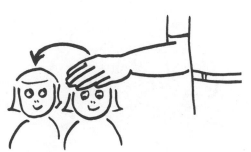

CHILDREN

Palm-down hand bounces to side, waist high

CHILL

C-hands face each other; hands shiver slightly

(See "COLD")

CHIMNEY

Outline chimney upward with C's

(See "TOWER")

CHIN

Index finger circles slightly on chin

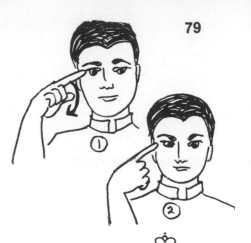

CHINA

Index finger at corner of eye twists slightly forward

CHINESE – **CHINA** + **-ESE**

CHIP

Right C arcs down and up, hitting side of left index with thumb

CHIPMUNK

Paws under chin flap up and down

CHIROPRACTOR

Thumb of C taps left wrist

(See "DOCTOR")

CHOCOLATE

C-thumb circles on back of left hand

CHOICE

Right palm-out C touches index of V, moves back

(See "CHOOSE")

CHOIR

Palm-in C's circle horizontally to shoulders

CHOKE

Chokes self, right hand

CHOOSE ♛

Thumb and finger of 9 pick index and then middle finger of left

CHOP ★

Side of palm-up hand chops at wrist of vertical left hand

(See "AXE")

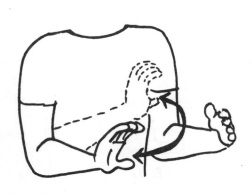

CHORUS

C swings back and forth inside left flat hand and left arm

(See "MUSIC")

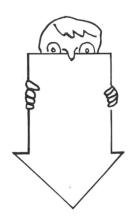

CHOSE

Choose + P. T.

CHOSEN

Choose + P. P.

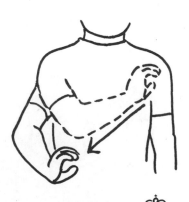

CHRIST ♛

C at left shoulder moves to right side of waist

CHRISTIAN = CHRIST + -AN

CHRISTMAS

Twist C inward

(See "DECEMBER")

CHUBBY

Claw-hands tap on cheeks

(See "FAT")

CHURCH

Palm-out C thumb taps back of left S twice

CIDER

C-thumb cuts down back of left S

(See "JUICE")

CIGAR

Wiggle R; back of hand resting against chin

CIGARETTE

Index and little fingers tap on left index finger

CINNAMON

First 2 fingers tap alternately on top of left C-hand

(See "SALT")

CIRCLE

Palm-out index finger draws circle

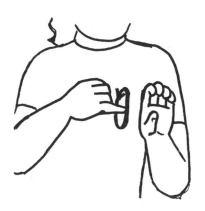

CIRCUIT

Little finger of right hand circles near thumb and index of palm-out C

CIRCUMSTANCE

C on back of left hand, both move in horizontal circle

(See "STANDARD")

CIRCUS

V-fingertips touch, separate in 2 sideways arcs

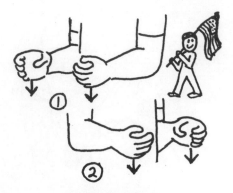

CITIZEN

2 C's, palms-facing, drop downward first at left then at right

(See "INDIVIDUAL")

CITY

Tip of palm-out right C taps fingertips of flat left hand while circling

(See "TOWN")

CIVIL

Top C circles left C vertically
(See "WORLD")

CLAM

Palms together, slightly cupped, right flat hand opens and closes at little-finger side

CLAP

Vertical hands clap

CLASH

A-hands face each other; arc toward each other, opening and meeting sharply

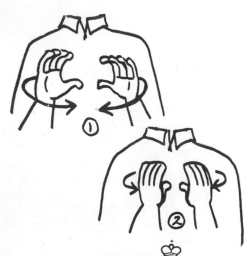

CLASS

Palm-out C-hands circle horizontally out, to palm-in

CLASSIFY = CLASS + -IFY

CLAUSE

Palm-out C's separate to L's

CLAW

Right hand claws forward

CLAY

Cupped hands squeeze clay

CLEAN

Right palm wipes off left palm

(See "NEAT")

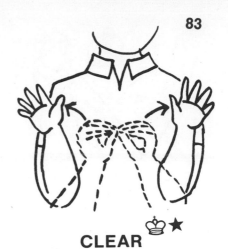

CLEAR ♕★

Flat-O's touching open to 5-hands

CLEVER

Middle finger bent, palm-in hand flicks to palm-out

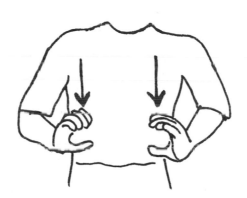

CLIENT

C's move down each side of chest

CLIMAX

Slanted flat hands move upward to touch in a peak

(See "PEAK")

CLIMB

Palm-out bent V's climb, alternately

CLINIC

C draws cross on upper arm

(See "HOSPITAL")

CLIP

Right L clips left index

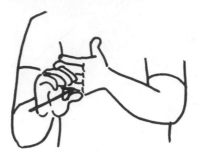

CLOCK

Index circles clockwise in left C

CLOSE

(ADJ.)

Side of C approaches back of bent left hand to the right, but does not touch it

(See "NEAR")

CLOSE

(VERB)

Palms down, flat hands close, sides meeting

CLOSET

Palm-out C-hand beside palm-out left B opens toward you, then returns

(See "DOOR")

CLOTH

Fingertips rub side of chest

CLOTHE = **CLOTH** + **-E**

CLOTHING = **CLOTH** + **-ING**

CLOTHES = **CLOTH** + **-E** + **-S**

CLOUD

C-hands face each other above eyes; move right

CLOVER

Indexes together, right one outlines 3-leaf clover and returns to left fingertip

CLOWN

Claw-hand shakes slightly in front of nose

CLUB ★

C's, palms facing, arc forward and touch as palm-in B's

(See "BAND")

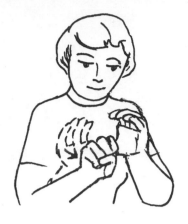

CLUTCH

Grasp thumb of left C

(See "HOLD")

COACH

Right C-hand on left index
finger brushes back and forth

(See "PRACTICE")

COAL

Slide thumb of C across
forehead

(See "BLACK")

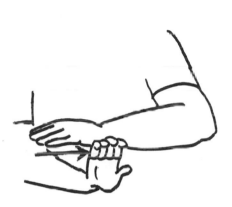

COAST ★

Back of palm-out C moves left
along outside of left hand

COAT ♔

A-hand thumbs slide down
lapels

COAX

Index on back of S beckons

(See "BEG")

COCOA

Index bent, thumb traces circle
on back of hand twice

(See "CHOCOLATE")

COCONUT

Beside ear shake coconut

COCOON

Palms in, hook thumbs
together, close hands on chest

COFFEE

Right-S on left S, circles in a grinding motion

(See "GRIND")

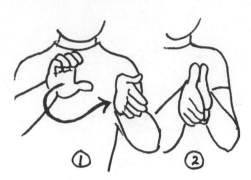

COHESIVE

Palm-out C flattens against left flat hand

(See "ADHESIVE")

COIN

Thumb and index of F lie flat on left palm

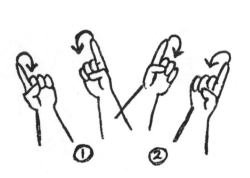

COINCIDE

1-hands turn over from palm-up to palm-down, first toward left, and then toward right

COKE

Index of L sticks left arm

COLD

S's shake as if shivering

COLE SLAW

Palm-up C's toss salad

(See "SALAD")

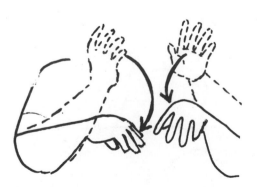

COLLAPSE

5-hands fall toward each other, briefly meshing palm-down, en route

(See "CRUMBLE")

COLLAR

G-fingers draw across neck to front

COLLECT

Right hand fingers together and flapping, circles left palm, gathering in

COLLEGE

Right hand on left, palm to palm; right rises, circling

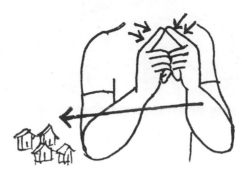

COLONY

With knuckles together, indexes tap moving right

(See "TOWN")

COLOR

Fingers flutter in front of chin

COLORADO

C above left arm outlines big and small mountains

COLT

C at temple nods twice from wrist

(See "HORSE")

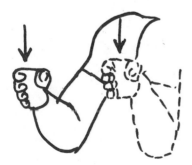

COLUMN

Palm-out C moves downward, shifts to right, and repeats

COMB ★

Palm-left claw near side of hair makes a combing motion

COMBINE

5-hands, palms-in, move together, meshing fingers to point in

COME

Palm-up index points out; beckons once

CAME = COME + P. T.

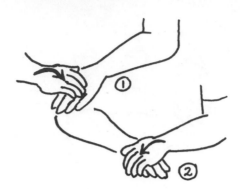

COMFORT

Stroke back of left hand down, then back, then stroke back of right hand

COMFORTABLE =
COMFORT + -ABLE

COMIC

C-hands near face pull up a smile

(See "SMILE")

COMMA

Right hand with bent index fingers twists to make comma near left palm

COMMAND

Index at chin twists to palm-out C, and moves sharply to palm-down

(See "ORDER")

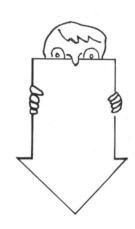

COMMANDMENT

Command + -ment

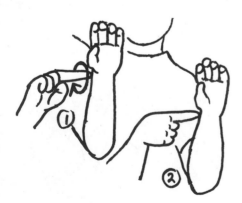

COMMENCE

Index fingertip on wrist of palm-out left C twists to palm-in

COMMENCEMENT =
COMMENCE + -MENT

(See "START")

COMMERCE

C on left S bounces back and forth

(See "BUSY")

COMMERCIAL

Right C in front of palm-right left S, C moves out and back several times

(See "ADVERTISE")

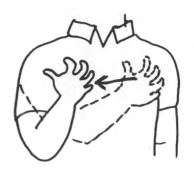

COMMITTEE

Claw-hand on left, then right, shoulder

(See "MEMBER")

COMMON

Both palm-out C's move in a horizontal circle

(See "STANDARD")

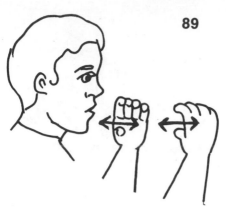

COMMUNICATE

C-hands move alternately to and from chin

COMMUNICATION =
COMMUNICATE + -TION

(See "TALK")

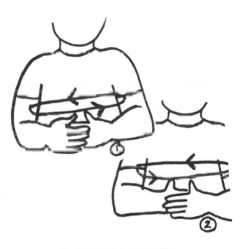

COMMUNITY

Alternate hands in sign for "near", circling in front of you

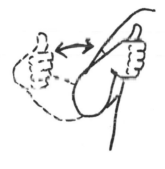

COMMUTE

Palm-in extended-A moves forward and back

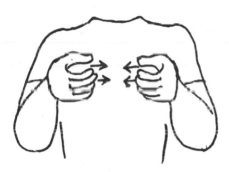

COMPACT ★

C's jerk slightly toward each other; repeat

(See "SMALL")

COMPANY

C-thumbs interlock and circle horizontally

(See "STANDARD")

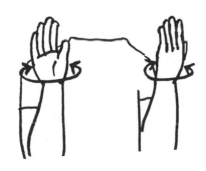

COMPARE

Flat hands alternately pivot in and out several times

COMPARISON = COMPARE + -TION

COMPETE

A's, palms facing, move alternately back and forth, not touching

(See "RACE")

COMPETENT

Right hand grasps side of left C and slides off to A

(See "EXPERT")

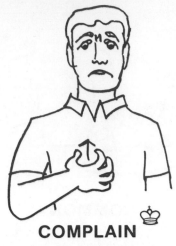

COMPLAIN

Fingertips of claw tap on chest

COMPLAINT = COMPLAIN + -T

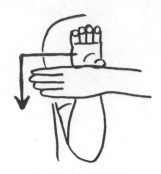

COMPLETE

Palm-out C slides along side of left hand and down at fingertips

(See "FINISH")

COMPLEX

Hands rise alternating X and 1, and cross in front of chest

(See "COMPLICATE")

COMPLICATE

C's shaking slightly, rise from sides, to cross in front of chest

(See "COMPLEX")

COMPLIMENT

Index at chin drops to clap hands

(See "PRAISE")

COMPONENT

Palm-up C arcs slightly up and down to right

(See "THING")

COMPOSE

C-hands face each other at sides; shake C's together to link, right above left

COMPOSITION = COMPOSE + -TION

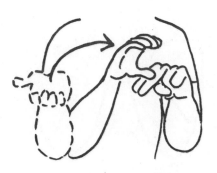

COMPOUND

Palm-up C arcs over to rest on top of palm-down left U-fingers

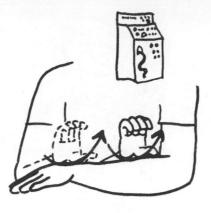

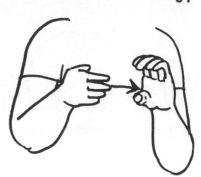

COMPROMISE

Index on forehead, then palm-up C's turn to palm-down, left head of right

(See "BET")

COMPUTE

Right C bounces up left arm

COMPUTER = COMPUTE + -R

CON

Flat right hand approaches left C til fingertips hit side

(See "AGAINST")

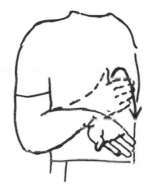

CONCEAL

Right C moves from chin to under left hand

(See "HIDE")

CONCEDE

Flat hand on chest swings to palm-up

CONCEIT

Thumb and bent indexes near head jerk forward and out

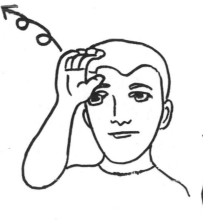

CONCENTRATE

C's at temples move forward a short distance

(See "ATTEND")

CONCEPT

Thumb of C on forehead; spiral up and out

CONCEPTUAL = CONCEPT + -L

(See "IDEA")

CONCERN

Middle fingers alternately touch chest

CONCRETE

Back of C strikes back of left S

(See "STONE")

CONDENSE

Right above left, open hands come together as palm-together S's

CONDITION

Right C-thumb into palm, pull left hand toward body

(See "REQUIRE")

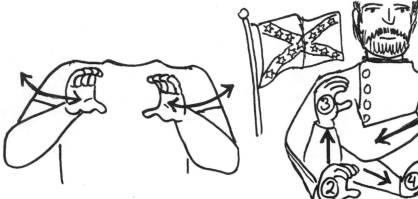

CONDUCT ★

Palm-out C's swing apart and together

(See "ORCHESTRA")

CONFEDERATE

C's make confederate flag on chest

CONFESS

C-hands on chest turn over and out to palm-up open hands

(See "ADMIT")

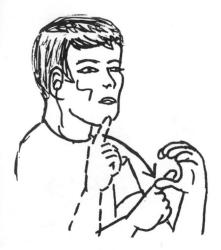

CONFIRM

Index on chin drops to cross thumbs of left C

(See "POSITIVE")

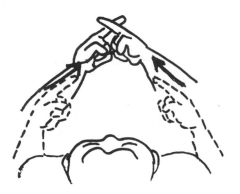

CONFLICT

Index fingers move forward to hit

(See "PARADOX")

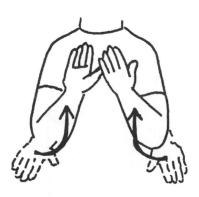

CONFRONT

Flat palms swing to face each other, not touching

(See "PRESENCE")

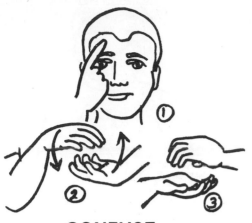

CONFUSE

Index on temple, then claws, right above left, reverse

CONGRATULATE

Clasped hands shake near head

CONGRESS

Right C touches left side of chest, then right side

(See "MEMBER")

CONQUER

Right S behind palm-down left S, jerks down at wrist to palm-down, wrist on wrist

(See "DEFEAT")

CONSCIENCE

Index finger taps heart twice

(See "GUILT")

CONSCIOUS

Thumb of C taps head behind ear

(See "SENSE")

CONSERVE

Palm-in V taps wrist of palm-out left C

CONSERVATION –

CONSERVE + -TION

(See "SAVE")

CONSIDER

Palm-in index fingers circle alternately in front of face

CONSONANT

Palm-out C moves over fingers of palm-in left 5

(See "ALPHABET")

CONSTANT

C-hands, thumbs touching move forward

(See "CONTINUE")

CONSTELLATION

Side of right C strikes upwards off 1-hand, then 1-hand off C, moving upwards

(See "STAR")

CONSTIPATE

Extended A-thumb moves up into left A

CONSTITUTE

Side of right C touches on left fingertips, then on heel

CONSTITUTION =

CONSTITUTE + -TION

(See "LAW")

CONSTRUCT

C's alternately build on top of each other

(See "BUILD")

CONSUME

Bent hand arcs up past cheek

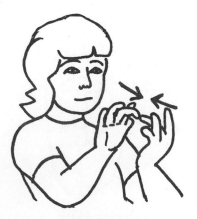

CONTACT

Bent middle fingers, left palm-in and right palm-out, make contact

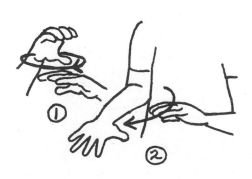

CONTAGIOUS

C circles slightly over left palm-down hand and opens to spread outward

(See "INFLUENCE")

CONTENT

Sides of C on chest, one above the other, move down slightly

(See "SATISFY")

CONTINENT

Palm-out C on back of left hand circles out and back along arm

(See "GROUND")

CONTINUE

Thumb of right extended A on thumb of left, both move forward

(See "MOMENTUM")

CONTOUR

Palm-out C's outline form

(See "SHAPE")

CONTRAST

Right index points at left palm-out C; jerk hands apart

(See "OPPOSE")

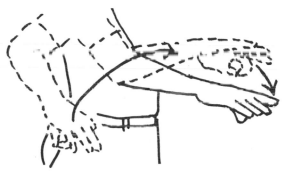

CONTRIBUTE

F pulls out of pocket, moves forward and opens to palm down 5

(See "PROVIDE")

CONTROL

X-hands alternately move forward and back

(See "MANAGE")

CONTROVERSY

Indexes point at each other; swing sharply up and out

**CONTROVERSIAL =
CONTROVERSY + L**

CONVENIENT

Thumb of C brushes up back of bent fingers; repeat

(See "EASE")

CONVERSE

Slightly bent 4-hands face each other, move back and forth from wrists

**CONVERSATION =
CONVERSE + -TION**

(See "TALK")

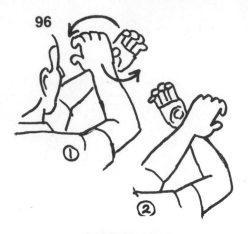

CONVERT

C-heels together; reverse position

(See "CHANGE")

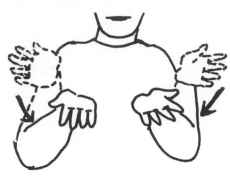

CONVINCE

Palm-up hands jerk sharply toward each other

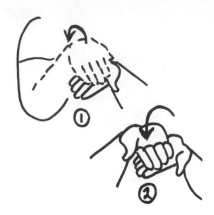

COOK

Flip right hand from palm-down to palm-up on left palm

(See "FRY")

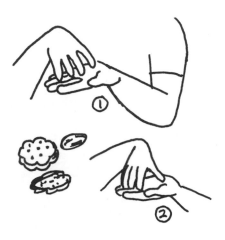

COOKIE

Fingertips touch palm, twist and touch again (Cookie-cutter)

(See "BISCUIT")

COOL

Palm-in, fingers flap by sides of head

COOPERATE

9's interlock; both circle horizontally

COPPER

Thumb of C arcs right, twisting, hitting side of left index (See "METAL")

COPY ♔

Palm-down 5 arcs back to make a flat-o on left palm

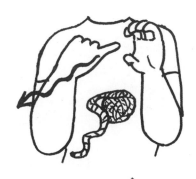

CORD ♔

Right I-hand wiggles down and to side from C

CORK

Right extended-A thumb pushes cork into side of left S

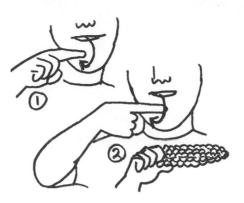

CORN

1-hand twists inward and out near chin

CORNER★

Flat hands tap fingertips in corner shape

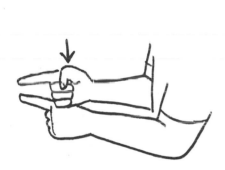

CORRECT

Right 1-hand drops on top of left 1; index fingers at slight angles

CORRELATE

Interlocked 9's move side to side

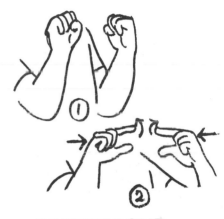

CORRESPOND

Right hand slightly behind left, index fingers flick from S to G-hands toward each other several times

COSMETIC

Flat O's decorate cheeks

COST

Palm-in X; knuckle strikes downward on left palm

COSTUME

Thumbs of C's brush down chest near shoulders; repeat
(See "DRESS")

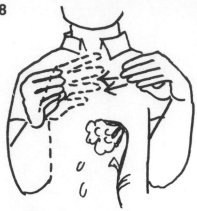

COTTON

Pull cotton off left flat-O to right flat-O; repeat

COUCH

Two fingers sit on thumb of left C; slide off to right

(See "SIT")

COUGH

Fingertips of claw remain stationary on chest; hand swings up and down

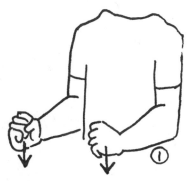

COULD

(Alt. 1)

S-hands palms-facing, drop slightly; then flat hands, palms facing, drop to palms-down

COULD

(Alt. 2)

Palm-out right C, near head, arcs forward to D

COUNSEL

C on back of left hand brushes forward; repeat

COUNSELOR = COUNSEL + -R

(See ("ADVICE")

COUNT

Thumb and index finger of 9 slide up left palm

COUNTER

Right C above left elbow, C and elbow bounce on left arm

(See "TABLE")

COUNTRY

Palm-in Y rubs in circle near elbow

COUNTY

C circles on left elbow

(See "COUNTRY")

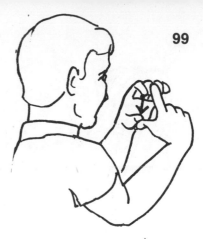

COUPLE ★

Thumb and finger of right hand close fingers of C to left thumb

(See "PAIR")

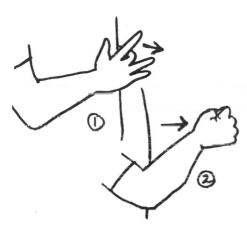

COURAGE

Bent middle finger on heart, then 5-hand moves out to palm-in S

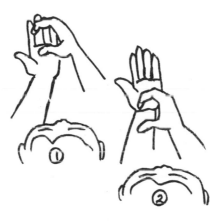

COURSE ★

Side of C touches left fingertips, then heel of left hand

(See "LESSON")

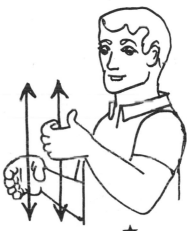

COURT ★

C-hands palms-facing, move alternately up and down

(See "BALANCE")

COURTESY

Side of C taps upward twice in middle of chest

COURTEOUS = COURTESY + -OUS

(See "FINE")

COUSIN

Shake C near ear

(See "AUNT")

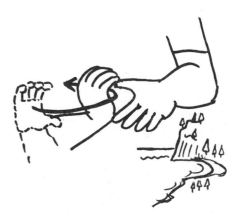

COVE

Right C outlines curve of palm-down left thumb and index

(See "BAY")

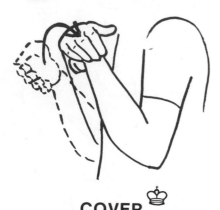

COVER 👑

Curved palm-up covers left S-hand

COW

Y-hand, twist slightly at temple
(See "CATTLE")

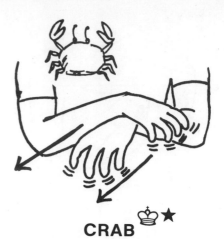

CRAB 👑★

Crossed hands move forward to right, wiggling fingers

CRACK ★

Flat hand outlines crack in wall

CRACKER 👑

Palm-in A taps arm near elbow

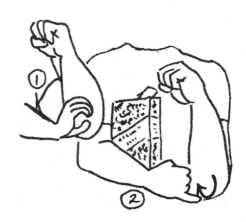

CRACKERJACK

Make C and J at left elbow
(See "CRACKER")

CRADLE

Both palms-up, right U in left C, rock both

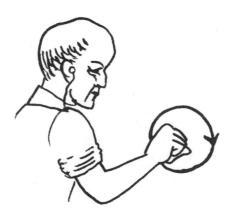

CRANK ★

Right fist cranks

CRASH

Right S hits side of left C
(See "BUMP")

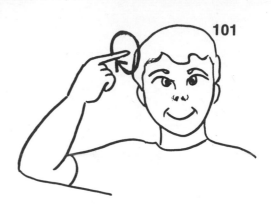

CRAWL

Bent-V's twist from "knee to knee" across left palm

CRAYON

Index circles on left palm

CRAZE

Index rotates near temple

CRAZY = CRAZE + -Y

CREAM ★

C-hand to S-hand moves across back of left hand

CREATE

Right C on left, twist to palm-in; rest right on left again

CREATIVE = CREATE + -IVE

CREATURE = CREATE + -URE

(See "MAKE")

CREDENTIAL

Tips of C-thumbs tap

(See "LICENSE")

CREDIT

Right C resting on left, both moving toward body

(See "BORROW")

CREEK

Palm-out C's ripple up and down forward

(See "BROOK")

CREEP

Fingers creep up left arm

CREPT = CREEP + P. T.

(See "CATERPILLAR")

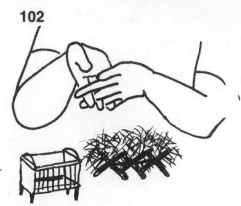

CRIB

Mesh fingers downward

CRICKET

C rides forward on wiggling fingers of left hand

(See "ANT")

CRIED

Cry + P.T.

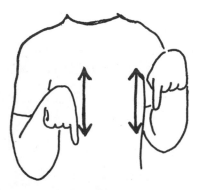

CRIPPLE

1-hands point down; alternately move up and down

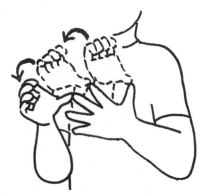

CRITERIA

Palm-in left 5, pointing right; thumb of palm-out right C bounces off left thumb, index and middle fingers

(See "PRIORITY")

CRITIC

Index makes large X on left palm

CRITICAL = CRITIC + -AL
CRITICIZE = CRITIC + -IZE
(See "DISCRIMINATE")

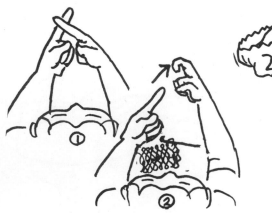

CROCHET

Cross horizontal index fingers; right slides off end of left into X; repeat several times

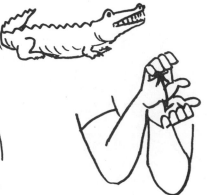

CROCODILE

Top "jaw" of C snaps open and closed, C-heels touching

CROP

C brushes up through left C twice

(See "GRAIN")

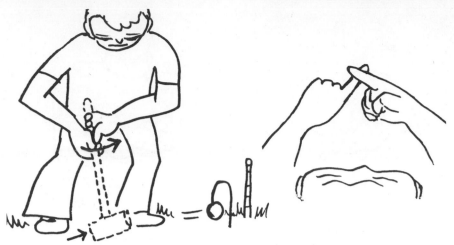

CROQUET

Bend over with mallet and strike ball to left

CROSS⭐

Palm-in right index on palm-down left index

(See "HYBRID")

CROW⭐

At chin flat-O opens and closes beak

(See "BIRD")

CROWD

S's approach each other, then press outward, lifting shoulders (elbowing through a crowd)

CROWN⭐

C's hold crown above head, put it on

CRUCIFY

Side of S strikes left palm at side; reverse hands, strike palm on the other side

CRUEL

Thumb of C strikes of back of left S

CRUMB⭐

Flat-O opens to scatter crumbs in circling motion, fingers fluttering, on left palm

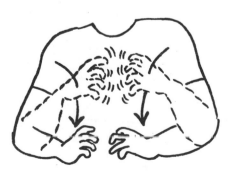

CRUMBLE

Palm-down 5's point at each other, converge downward, fingers fluttering

(See "COLLAPSE")

CRUSADE

C's face each other and move
from side to side
(See "WAR")

CRUSH

5-hands heels twist forcefully
on each other
(See 'SQUASH")

CRUST

C moves around edge of left
hand
(See "EDGE")

CRY ♔ ★

Drag index fingers alternately
move down cheeks, marking
tear-tracks

CRIED = CRY + P. T.

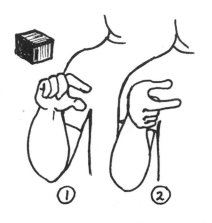

CUBE ★

Thumb and index outline 2
sides of cube

CUBIC = CUBE + -IC

CUCUMBER

Right index slices past thumb
of C several times
(See "TOMATO")

CUFF ★

Thumb and index finger
outline cuff on left wrist

CULTURE

Right C curves around vertical
left index (See "ATMOSPHERE")

CUP ★

X is set on palm, as if holding a
cup handle

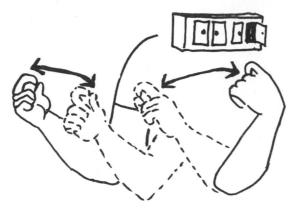

CUPBOARD

Open and close cupboard doors

(See "CABINET")

CUPID

Right fist pulls back to a horizontal V from left palm-out C

(See "ARROW")

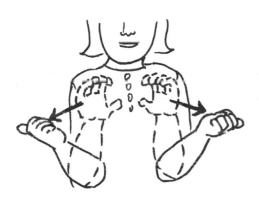

CURE

Palm-out C's turn over and slide closed to palm-up A's

(See "MELT")

CURIOUS

Right F on adam's apple twists

CURL ★

Index outlines curl from ear down

CURRENT ★

Palm-down flat hand flows through left C

CURRICULUM

Side of C on fingers of vertical left palm, then side of M on heel

(See "LAW")

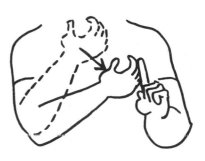

CURSE

(Alt. 1)

Right C from front of mouth strikes side of vertical left index

(See "BEAT")

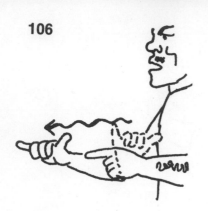

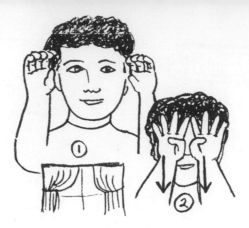

CURSE

(Alt. 2)

Palm-down Y above left horizontal index shakes along index and off

CURTAIN

C-hands meet, change to 4, and slide down

(See "DRAPE")

CURVE

Palm-out C curves downward

CUSTOM

Wrist of right C on wrist of left, both drop slightly

(See "HABIT")

CUT ♔

V-fingers snip off end of middle fingertip of flat left hand

CUTE

Palm-in U- to N-fingers brush chin down

(See "SUGAR")

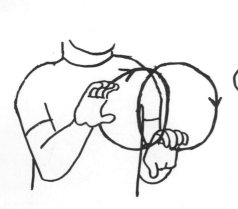

CYCLE

C's alternately pedal forward

(See "BICYCLE")

CYCLONE

Right above left, flat O's rotate around each other, rising to the right

(See "STORM")

CYMBAL

"Holding cymbals" with A's strike cymbals together

DAD

D touches temple
(See "FATHER")

DAFFODIL

D touches on each side of nose
(See "FLOWER")

DAISY

G-hand plucks petals from left index

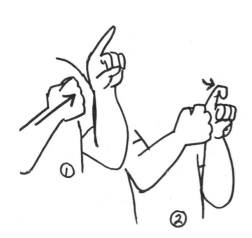

DAMAGE

S strikes side of left D-hand;
left index bends to X
(See "BUMP")

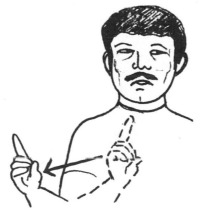

DAMN

D moves sharply to the right
(See "HELL")

DANCE

Palm-in V-fingertips arc from side to side, brushing left palm

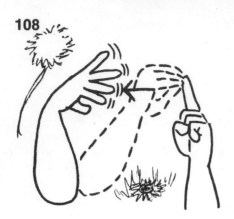

DANDELION

Flat O on left index-tip, pull fluff off to side, fingers fluttering

DANDY

Palm-out, near shoulders, D's jerk out slightly; repeat

DANGER ♛

Thumb-side of A arcs up, hitting back of left S; repeat

DANGEROUS = DANGER + -OUS

DARE

D on heart moves sharply forward slightly

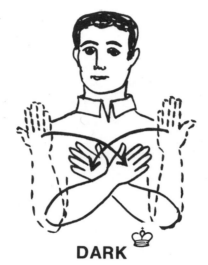

DARK ♛

Palm-in hands cross in front of body

DARLING

Right D-hand circles on back of left hand over heart

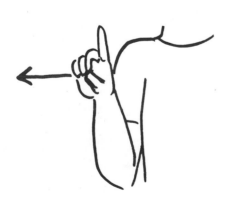

DASH ★

Palm-out D moves toward the right a short distance
(See "BLANK")

DATE ★

D taps on palm

DAUGHTER

Extended A-hand drops in an arc to palm-up and opens on left arm

DAWN

D rises past outside of palm-down left hand

DAY

Right 1-hand drops down on left arm

DAILY = DAY + -LY
TODAY = TO + DAY

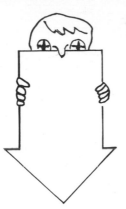

DEAD

Die + D

DEAF

Touch ear then sides of palm-down B's touch

DEAL

Deal several cards

DEAR

D-hands cross on heart
(See "LOVE")

DEATH

Die + -th

DEBATE

Pointing at each other, 1-hands move together back and forth

DEBT

Index finger taps heel of palm-up left hand
(See "OWE")

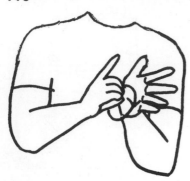

DECADE

Side of D on left palm, circles
once then touches palm again

(See "HOUR")

DECEMBER

(Alt. 1)

D twists inward

(See "CHRISTMAS")

DECEMBER

(Alt. 2)

D arcs over side of vertical flat
left hand

(See "CALENDAR")

DECIDE

Index on forehead, then both
9's jerk slightly down

DECISION = DECIDE + -SION

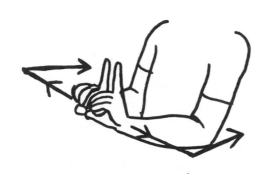

DECK ♛ ★

Palm-out D's touching; move
to sides and then toward body

DECLARE

Palm-in D's touch at corners of
mouth, swing out and twist to
palm-out

(See "ANNOUNCE")

DECORATE

Palm-out flat-O's twist while
putting up decorations

DECREASE

Right H on left H, right H twists
off to palm-up

(See "REDUCE")

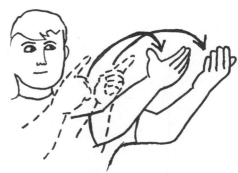

DEDICATE

D's, palms facing, arc forward
to left and upward to palm-up

(See "GIFT")

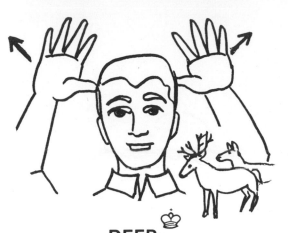

DEEP

Side of index pointing down, slides down vertical palm-right palm

DEPTH = DEEP + -TH

DEER

5-hands move up from temples to sides

DEFEAT

Right D behind palm-down left S jerks down at wrist to palm-down, wrist on wrist

(See "CONQUER")

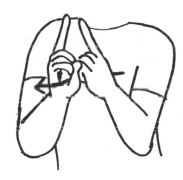

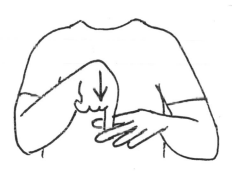

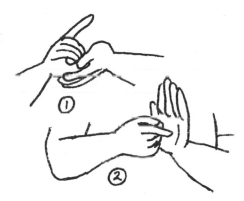

DEFEND

Left D behind right D; both move forward slightly

(See "GUARD")

DEFICIT

Index slides down between index and middle fingers of left palm-down hand

DEFINE

Palm-down D touches left palm twice, turning between contacts

(See "MEAN")

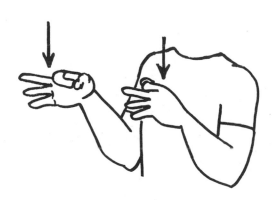

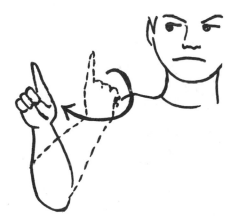

DEFINITE

Facing each other, horizontal 9's jerk down

(See "DETERMINE")

DEFLATE

C-thumb, on palm-up left fingertips; close C-fingers to thumb

DEFY

Palm-in D near shoulder swings sharply to palm-out

(See "REBEL")

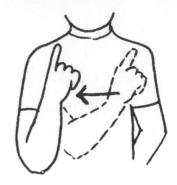

DEGREE

Thumb and finger of right D move up and down left index finger

(See "THERMOMETER")

DELAY

Palms-facing D's touch; right D arcs forward

(See "POSTPONE")

DELEGATE

D-fingers touch one shoulder, then the other

(See "MEMBER")

DELICATE

Index of D-hand does pushups on left palm

(See "WEAK")

DELICIOUS

Bent middle finger on mouth twists out and slightly up

DELIGHT

D's brush up shoulders; repeat

(See "GAY")

DELIVER

Fingers of palm-down D on back of left hand flip forward to palm-out

(See "SEND")

DEMAND

Thumb and fingers of D on left palm; both arc toward body

(See "REQUIRE")

DEMON

D at temple, crook index sharply to X

(See "DEVIL")

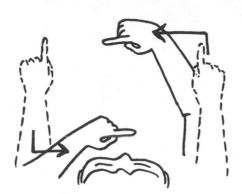

DEMONSTRATE

D on left vertical palm; both move forward

(See "SHOW")

DEN

Palm-down D-hands shape box

(See "BOX")

DENMARK

(American Sign)
D circles near forehead

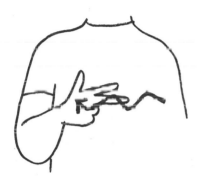

DENMARK

(Danish Sign)
Palm-in 3 moves in wavy motion across chest to right

DENOMINATOR

D circles below left index

(See "FRACTION")

DENTIST

D taps at corner of mouth twice, palm-in

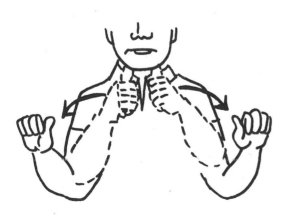

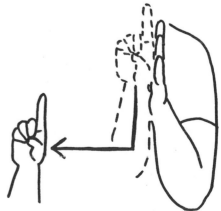

DENY

Thumbs of both A-hands under chin , brush forward to palm-out

DEODORANT

Spray deodorant can under palm of left hand

DEPART

Side of D moves down left palm, then away to the side

(See "APART")

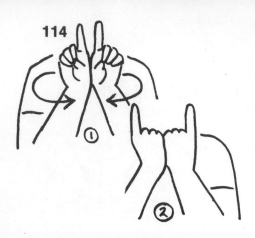

DEPARTMENT

D-hands, palm-out, circle horizontally out to palm-in

(See "CLASS ")

DEPEND

Right X hangs on horizontal left index, drop slightly

DEPENDENT = DEPEND + -ENT

(See "PARASITE")

DEPRESS

Middle finger slides down middle of chest

(See "ILL")

DESCRIBE

D-hands, right behind left; move hands alternately forward and back

(See "EXPLAIN")

DESERT

D moves across forehead to right

(See "SUMMER")

DESERVE

Side of D on left palm moves toward body, closing

(See "EARN")

DESIGN

Palm-down D draws "S" on back of left S

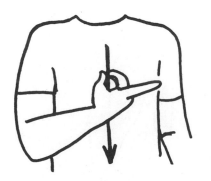

DESIRE

Palm-in D moves down chest

(See "HUNGER")

DESK

Right D and elbow bounce on left arm

(See "TABLE")

DESPERATE

Palm-up D's pull back toward
body as index fingers crook

(See "WANT")

DESSERT

(Alt. 1)

D-hand ladles up to mouth
twice from left palm

(See "SOUP")

DESSERT

(Alt. 2)

Palms facing tap horizontal D's
together

DESTINE

D near head arcs forward

DESTINY = DESTINE + Y

(See "WILL")

DESTROY

Palm-down right hand sweeps
back over palm-up left; close
left; right closes, then brushes
forward, striking left in passing

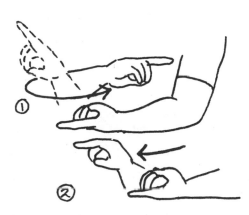

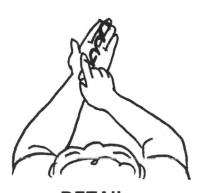

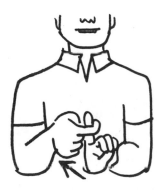

DESTRUCT

Right palm-down D sweeps
back, brushing palm-up D;
then forward again, striking
palm-up D fingertips sharply

DESTRUCTION = DESTRUCT + -ION

(See "DESTROY")

DETAIL

D taps down left palm

(See "LIST")

DETAIN

Right X pulls index of left D
backwards

DETENTION = DETAIN + -TION

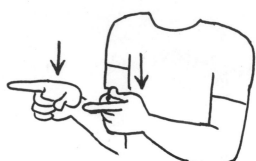

DETERIORATE

Side of right hand on back of left arm, hops down arm

(See "REGRESS")

DETECT

D near eye drops to left palm

(See "NOTE")

DETERMINE

Horizontal D's jerk downward

(See "DEFINITE")

DETROIT

With D-hand, arc sharply down to right, palm-out

(See "CHICAGO")

DEVELOP

Thumb and finger of D slide up palm

(See "TALL")

DEVIATE

Palm-down indexes touch; one curves off to side

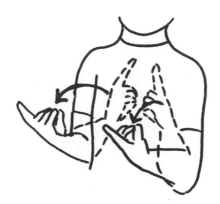

DEVIL

Thumb on temple, bend 2 fingers at the same time; repeat

DEVOTE

Palm-in D's touch heart, then arc outward to palm-up

DEVOTION = DEVOTE + -TION

DIAGONAL

Right D moves up to right diagonally

DIAGNOSE

Thumb and fingertips of D's together, separate in small downward twists; repeat

(See "ANALYZE")

DIALECT

(Alt. 1)

D shakes from lips outwards

DIALECT

(Alt. 2)

Horizontal D's touch fingertips, separate to sides, shaking slightly

DIALOGUE

Alternately, D's move from near corners of mouth and back

(See "TALK")

DIAMOND ♔

D rises shaking from left ring-finger

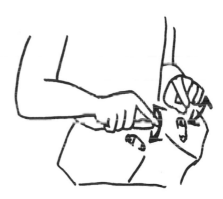

DIAPER

G-hands open and close at hips (like 2 pins)

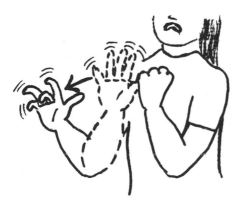

DIARRHEA

Left hand grasps right 5-thumb, which pulls out, fingers fluttering

DICE ★

D-hand shakes dice, then throws to side, opening hand

DICTIONARY

Palm-down D arcs down and left brushing left palm; repeat

(See "ENCYCLOPEDIA")

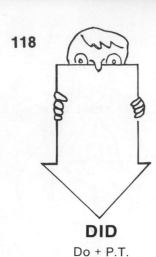

DID
Do + P.T.

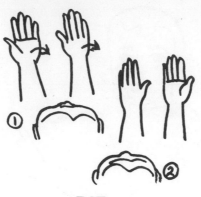

DIE
Right hand palm-down, left palm-up, turn hands over to the right

DEAD = **DIE** + **D**
DIED = **DIE** + **P. T.**
DEATH = **DIE** + **-TH**

DIET
D's twist inward and down body

(See "SLIM")

DIFFER
Palm-out crossed index fingers separate

DIFFERENT = **DIFFER** + **-ENT**
DIFFERENCE = **DIFFER** + **-ENCE**

DIFFICULT
Fingers of bent V's brush up and down

(See "HARD")

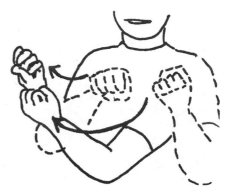

DIG ★
S's, one palm-up and one palm-down, (like holding handle of a shovel) make digging motion

DIGEST ★
Palm-down D on palm-up left D grind on each other alternately

(See "CHEW")

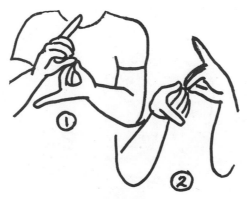

DIGIT
Fingers and thumbs of D's touch, one palm-up, one palm-down; reverse position and repeat

(See "NUMBER")

DIM
Palm-out D's cross in front of face, moving down

(See "DARK")

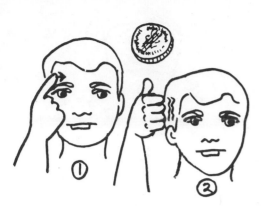

DIME

Index finger touches temples; moves out to extended-A hand; shake

(See "CENT")

DIMPLE

Index pokes dimple in cheek

DINE

Palm-in D's circle alternately up toward mouth

DINING = DINE + -ING

(See "BANQUET")

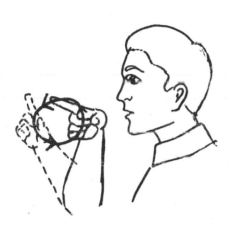

DINNER

D circles in and up near mouth
(See "EAT")

DINOSAUR

Arm of flat-D moves along behind left arm

DIP ♔ ★

Palm-down flat-O's dip down

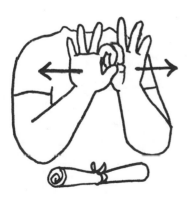

DIPLOMA

Palm-out F's touching, move outward

DIRECT ★

Right D on left index, D slides forward

DIRECTOR = DIRECT + -OR
DIRECTION = DIRECT + -TION

(See "STRAIGHT")

DIRT

Fingers wiggle under chin
DIRTY = DIRT + -Y

DISAGREE

Index at temple moves to touch end of left index tip to tip, then hands pull sharply apart

(See "OPPOSE")

DISAPPEAR

Index between fingers of palm-down left hand, then drops down

(See "DROWN")

DISAPPOINT

Index finger rises sharply to chin

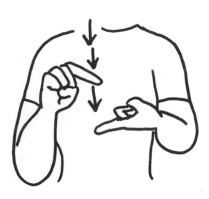

DISCOUNT

Palm-down index finger lowers in stages toward palm-up index, not touching

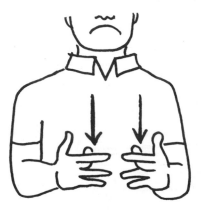

DISCOURAGE

Both middle fingers slide down chest

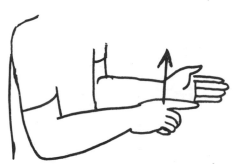

DISCOVER

Palm-down D moves up across palm

(See "FIND")

DISCRIMINATE

Thumb and fingertips of D make large X on palm

(See "CRITIC")

DISCUSS

Palm-in index taps heel of left palm

DISEASE

Palm-in D's rest on forehead and stomach

(See "SICK")

DISGUISE

D-hand, palm-in, passes across face

DISGUST

Palm-in claw-hand circles on chest

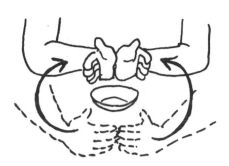

DISH ★

With palms outline dish

(See "PLATE")

DISPLAY ♛

Thumb and fingers of D on palm-left hand; circle both hands horizontally

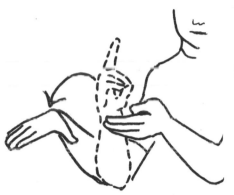

DISPOSE

Palm-left D on left palm slides out and off to palm-down 5-hand

DISSOLVE

Palm-up D's separate, closing to A's

(See "MELT")

DISTANT

D's touch, one D moves forward, arcing slightly up

DISTANCE = DISTANT + -ANCE

(See "FAR")

DISTORT

Heels of D's touch, crossing, stay together as hands reverse

(See "CHANGE")

DISTRACT

Thumb and fingers of D touch palm; D moves forward and slightly to the side

DISTRIBUTE

Right D curves forward past 5-fingers

(See "POPULATE")

DISTRICT

Palm-out D's circle back towards body

(See "PLACE")

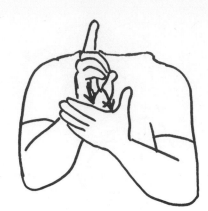

DISTURB

Thumb-side of D chops into thumb-base of open hand several times

(See "BOTHER")

DITTO

Palm-left D circles by left palm rapidly several times

(See "MIMEOGRAPH")

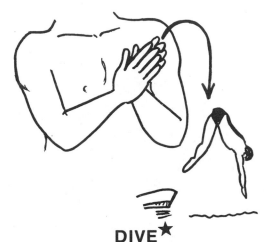

DIVE★

Hands together dive

DIVED/DOVE = DIVE + P. T.

DIVERGE

Index points at vertical index and veers off to side

DIVIDE

Palm-out D moves down thumb and out finger

DIVISION = DIVIDE + -TION

DIVISIBLE = DIVIDE + -IBLE

(See "ADD")

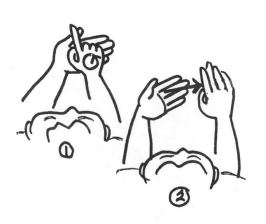

DIVINE

D circles above palm, then open hand slides straight off end of palm

(See "HOLY")

DIVORCE

D-hands touch fingers and twist to sides

DIZZY

Palm-in right claw circles counter-clockwise in front of eyes

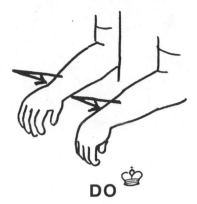

DO ♛

Palm-down C-hands move side-to-side

DOES = DO + -S
DONE = DO + P. P.
DID = DO + P. T.

DOCK ♛★

D outlines left palm-down arm, starting on outside

DOCTOR ♛

Thumb and finger of D tap pulse of left wrist

DOCTRINE

Index side of D touches fingers and then heel of left vertical hand

(See "LAW")

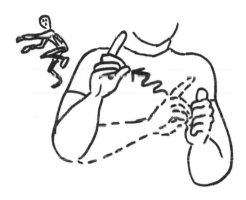

DODGE

D wiggles back toward body from A

(See "AVOID")

DOG

Fingers of D-hand snap several times (to call a dog)

(See "PUPPY")

DOLL ♛

Right X-finger brushes off tip of nose

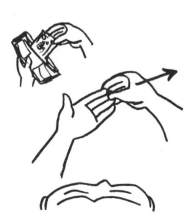

DOLLAR

Flat-O grasps end of horizontal hand, then slips off; repeat

DOLPHIN

D makes 2 curves to the left, outside arm

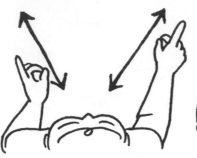

DOMINATE

D's point forward at each side of body, move forward and back alternately in large motions tending slightly outward

(See "MANAGE")

DOMINO

Two G-hands make the shape of a domino

DONKEY

Thumbs on temples, fingers together flap forward

(See "STUBBORN")

DOOR

Swing right hand open backwards and return

DOOR KNOB

Door + Knob

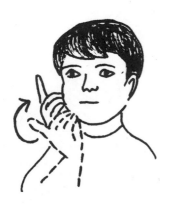

DORMITORY

D on chin, then on cheek

(See "HOME")

DOT

D moves forward to make dot

DOUBLE

D on left palm arcs up to palm-up

(See "ONCE")

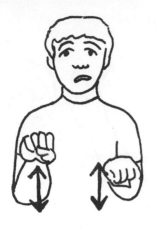

DOUBT

Palm-down S-hands move alternately up and down

(See "BALANCE")

DOUGH ♔

Palms-in, circle D on back of S

DOUGHNUT

R's touching, circle downward to palm-up and touching

DOWN ♔★

Palm-in hand moves down

DRAG

S's near shoulder, left in front of the right, both move forward

DRAGON

Palm-out S's at chin move forward to palm-down 5's; fingers fluttering, move forward

DRAIN

D rotates as it falls through left C-hand

(See "SINK")

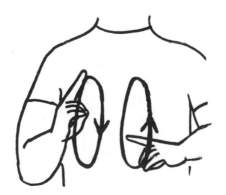

DRAMA

Thumbs and fingers of D's brush down chest alternately

DRAMATIC = DRAMA + -IC

(See "ACT")

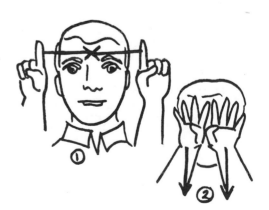

DRAPE

Palm-out D-hands meet, change to 4's, and slide down

(See "CURTAIN")

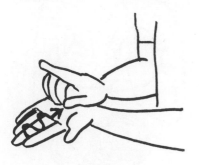

DRAW ★

With D-hand draw backwards
on palm in wavy line

DREW = DRAW + P. T.

DRAWN = DRAW + P. P.

(See "ART")

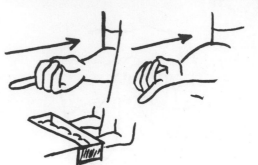

DRAWER

D-hands draw toward body,
palm-up

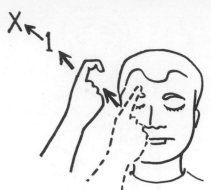

DREAM

Palm-in 1 on forehead, move
up to right, alternating X and 1

(See "SCHEME")

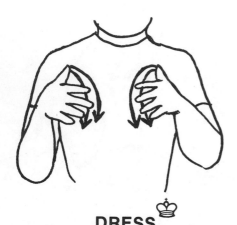

DRESS ♛

Thumbs of palm-in 5-hands
brush down chest twice

DRIFT ♛

D drifts forward on back of left
hand

DRILL ★

D moves back and forth on side
of left index

(See "PRACTICE")

DRINK

Thumb on chin, drink from C

DRANK = DRINK + P. T.

DRUNK (VERB) = DRINK + P. P.

DRIP

Left index on base of right
thumb; right one "drips"
repeatedly by flicking down

DRIVE ★

S-hands grasp invisible wheel,
then steer

DROVE = DRIVE + P. T.

(See "TRACTOR")

DROOL

Index of 4 at corner of mouth, pointing left; hand moves downward with fluttering fingers

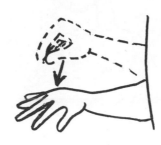

DROP★

Flat-O drops and opens (can be done with 2 hands)

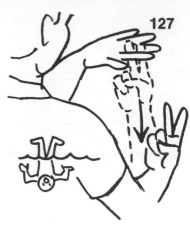

DROWN

Palm-in right V-fingers between left fingers, right hand drops, twisting slightly

(See "DISAPPEAR")

DRUG

D circles on palm

(See "MEDICINE")

DRUM

Both A-hands drum alternately

DRUNK

(Noun, Adj.)
A-hand with thumb extended swings past mouth, palm-out

DRUNK

Drink +P. P.

DRY

X-drags along chin as if wiping it

(See "PRUNE")

DUCK★

Two fingers close on thumb twice

(See "BIRD")

DUCKLING

Right hand resting in left palm, two fingers open and close on thumb (See "CHICK")

DUKE

D at shoulder arcs down to waist

(See "CHRIST")

DULL

Side of X pulls back across fingertips of left D

(See "STALE")

DUMB

Palm-in A hits forehead

DUMP

Left palm-up to palm-down hand dumps D off palm

DUPLICATE

Palm-out D closes down to flat-O on left palm

(See "COPY")

DURING

Indexes near right shoulder, D's arc down and out

DURABLE = DURING + -ABLE

(See "WHILE")

DUST

Back of palm-up D circles on back of palm-down left S

(See "WAX")

DUTY

Right D taps back of left hand twice

(See "WORK")

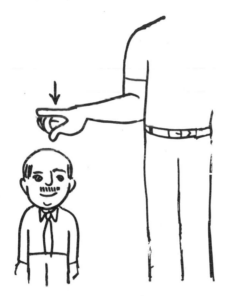

DWARF

Palm-down D shows height of dwarf

(See "CHILD")

DYE

Parallel palm-down 9-hands move down and up several times

(See "DIP")

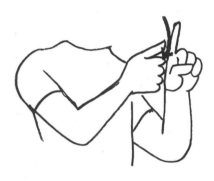

EACH

Thumb of right A rubs once down side of left index

EAGER

Palm-to-palm E-hands rub back and forth on each other

(See "ENTHUSE")

EAGLE

X pointing forward on nose

EAR

Point to ear

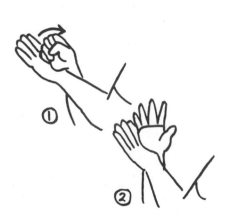

EARLY

(Alt. 1)

S on back of left hand slides inward, opening to 5

EARLY

(Alt. 2)

Right middle finger on back of left hand stays put as right hand moves forward

EARMOLD

Index and thumb of open hand put mold in ear

EARN

C, moving across left palm toward you, closes to S

(See "DESERVE")

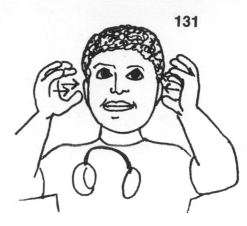

EARPHONES

Claw-hands tap over ears

EARRING

With thumb and index clip earring on ear

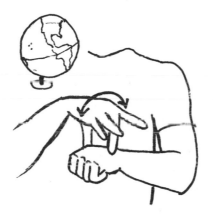

EARTH

Thumb and middle finger hold sides of left S; right hand rocks back and forth as on axis

EARTHQUAKE

Earth + quake

EASE ♔

Right fingertips stroke upwards on back of bent left fingers, circling up and out 2 or more times

EASY = EASE + -Y

EASEL

Palm-left V angles down from flat palm like an easel's legs

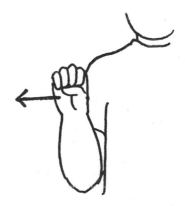

EAST

Palm-out E moves right

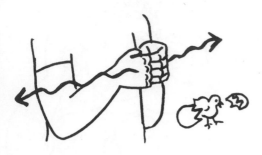

EASTER

Palm-to-palm E-hands separate, shaking

EAT ♔

Extended-A circles in and up near mouth spooning food in

ATE = EAT + PAST

ECHO

Side of E hits left palm, shakes to right, "Bouncing off"

(See "BELL")

ECOLOGY

Palm-up E on back of left hand circles slightly out and back

(See "GROUND")

ECONOMY

Palm-up E taps left palm twice

ECONOMIC = ECONOMY + -IC

(See "MONEY")

EDGE ♔

E moves around fingertips of palm-down left hand

EDIT

Palm-out E makes check mark over left palm

EDITOR = EDIT + -OR

(See "CHECK")

EDUCATE

Palm-out E's near temples move forward slightly; repeat

(See "TEACH")

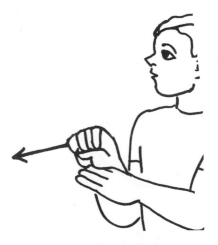

EFFECT

E on back of left hand moves forward

(See "ADVICE")

EFFORT

Palm-out E's move forward
with slight arc

(See "ATTEMPT")

EGG ★

Right H breaks on the left H

(See "OMELET")

EGYPT

Palm-out X on forehead

EITHER

Palm-out E moves off left
thumb, then off fingertip of
index

(See "THEN")

EJECT

Palm-out E rockets up side of
vertical palm and away

(See "ASTRONAUT")

ELABORATE

Palm-out claws in front of body
circle vertically in opposite
directions

(See "FABULOUS")

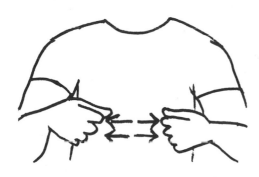

ELASTIC

Palm-in A's mime pulling
elastic twice

ELBOW ★

Index finger taps left elbow

ELDER

E waves downward from chin

(See "OLD")

ELECT

Right 5-hand moves to touch as 9 at left index, then moves back.

ELECTION = ELECT + -ION

(See "CHOOSE")

ELECTRIC

Palm-in X-fingers bump twice

ELECTRICITY = ELECTRIC + -ITY

ELEGANT

5's facing, alternately circle upward, thumbs brushing chest

(See "FANCY")

ELEMENT

E circles under palm

(See "BASE")

ELEPHANT

From nose, trace elephant's trunk

ELEVATE

Palm-left E rises

ELEVATOR = ELEVATE + -ER

(See "UP")

ELF

E-hands inward on shoulders turn outwards

(See "ANGEL")

ELIMINATE

From index of left 5-hand flick right thumb out and away

ELK

Palm-out E's move up and out
from temples

(See "DEER")

ELSE

Palm-down E twists over to
palm-up

EMBARRASS

As hands move up past cheeks
flutter fingers

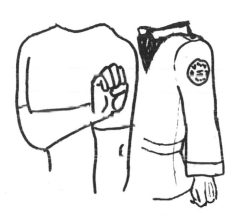

EMBLEM

Index side of E touches left
upper arm

EMBROIDER

9 sews up and down between
fingers of palm-down left hand

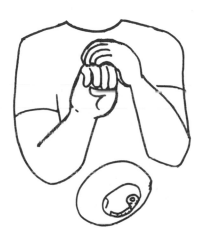

EMBRYO

Left C covers right E

EMERGE

Palm-out E grows up through
left C

(See "GROW")

EMIT

Upside-down E pulls out of left
C to palm-out

(See "OUT")

EMOTION

E brushes up chest

(See "FEEL")

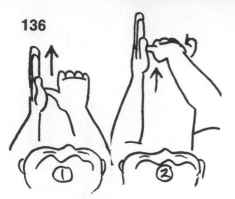

EMPHASIS

Tip of extended-A thumb on left palm twists to palm-in

EMPHASIZE = EMPHASIS + -IZE

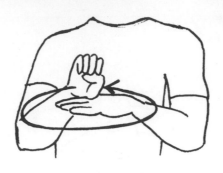

EMPIRE

Palm-out E on back of left hand circles out, around, and back along arm

(See "GROUND")

EMPLOY

Palm-out E arcs side-to-side, hitting back of left S

EMPLOYEE = EMPLOY + -EE
EMPLOYER = EMPLOY + -ER
EMPLOYMENT = EMPLOY + -MENT

(See "BUSY")

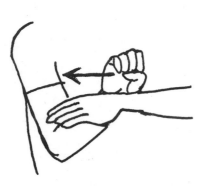

EMPTY

E brushes along back of left hand and off

(See "BARE")

ENCHILADA

E-hands, palm-up; right "folds" over, then the left "folds" on top

(See "TORTILLA")

ENCOURAGE

Flat hands push (someone) forward; repeat

(See "MOTIVE")

ENCYCLOPEDIA

Palm-down E arcs down and toward signer, brushing left palm; repeat

(See "DICTIONARY")

END

Palm-out E slides along side of left hand and down fingertips

(See "FINISH")

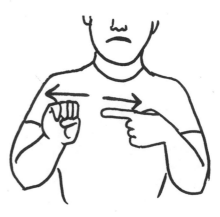

ENEMY

Palm-out E and left index pull away from each other

(See "OPPOSE")

ENERGY

E-hand draws muscle on left upper arm

(See STRONG")

ENGAGE

Palm-out E circles once horizontally over left S and drops on back of S

(See "APPOINT")

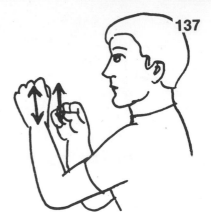

ENGINE

Right S behind left, hands move piston-like alternately up and down

ENGINEER = ENGINE + -EE + -ER

(See "MOTOR")

ENGLAND

(U. S. Sign)
Palms-down, right hand, pulls left toward body

ENGLAND

(United Kingdom Sign)
Thumb and bent index grasp chin and waggle it slightly

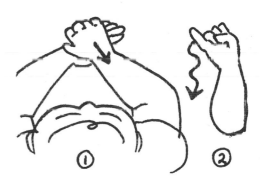

ENGLISH

Palms-down right pulls left hand toward body and add -ish

ENJOY

Palm-in hands, on body, right above left, circle in opposite directions

(See "HAPPY")

ENOUGH

Flat palm brushes forward across left S; may repeat

ENTER

Right palm-down flat hand arcs down under horizontal left palm

ENTRANCE = ENTER + -ANCE

(See "INVADE")

138

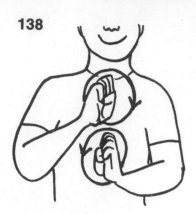

ENTERTAIN

In opposite directions circle
E's on chest
(See "ENJOY")

ENTHUSE

Palms rub together
ENTHUSIASTIC = ENTHUSE + -IC
ENTHUSIASM = ENTHUSE + -ISM
(See "EAGER")

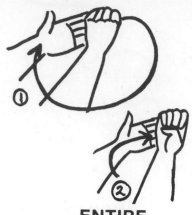

ENTIRE

E circles horizontally from
palm-down to end palm-up on
left palm
(See "WHOLE")

ENTRANCE

Enter + -ance

ENVELOPE

Hand passes under lip and
inserts in left hand

ENVIRONMENT

Right E curves around vertical
left index

(See "ATMOSPHERE")

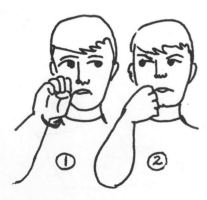

ENVY

Palm-out E at side of mouth
twists to palm-in
(See "JEALOUS")

EPIDEMIC

E on back of hand moves
forward to palm-down 5 over
left hand and circles
(See "PLAGUE")

EPISCOPAL

With right index, outline full
sleeve under left horizontal
arm

EQUAL

Fingertips of bent hands tap; repeat

EQUATOR ♔

Right E circles left palm-in S, from palm-out to palm-in position

EQUIP

Palm-up E skips to the right

EQUIPMENT = EQUIP + -MENT

(See "THING")

ERA

Side of E on left palm, circles forward once, then touches palm again

(See "HOUR")

ERASE

E rubs back and forth on left palm

ERASER = ERASE + -ER

ERECT

Palm-out E slides up left palm

(See "TALL")

ERROR

With side of E, hit chin lightly; repeat

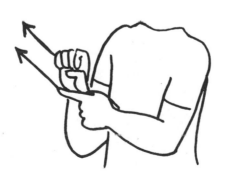

ESCALATE

E on side of left index; both move forward and up together

ESCALATOR = ESCALATE + -ER

ESCAPE ♔

Index finger between fingers of left hand; "escapes" sharply to side

ESCORT

Vertical 1-hands come together and move forward

(See "WITH")

ESKIMO

E-hands outline parka hood

ESPECIALLY

Palm-out E on tip of middle finger of palm-in left 5, both move up

(See "EXCEPT")

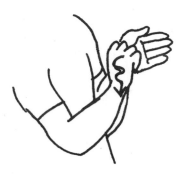

ESSAY

Right E moves down across left palm in wavy motion

(See "READ")

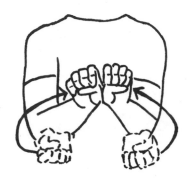

ESSENCE

E's, palm-up to palm-down in vertical circle

ESSENTIAL = ESSENCE + -AL

(See "IMPORTANT")

ESTABLISH

A-hand twists to palm-left and comes down on back of left hand

(See "FOUND")

ESTEEM

E arcs down in front of face

(See "GOD")

ESTIMATE

Palm-left E arcs sideways in front of forehead

(See "GUESS")

ETCH

With palm-down E "draw" on palm

(See "ART")

ETERNAL

Palm-out E circles and then moves forward

EUROPE

E faces temple, circles vertically

EVACUATE

E-hand from between fingers of palm-down left hand moves sharply away

(See "ESCAPE")

EVADE

Right E wiggles back from left A

(See "AVOID")

EVALUATE

Palm-to-palm E's move alternately up and down

(See "BALANCE")

EVAPORATE

E shakes up out of left C

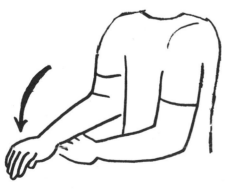

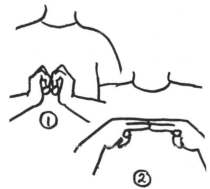

EVE

Flat right hand "sets" over left to a level position

EVENING = EVE + -ING

EVEN

E-fingertips touch, and then N-fingertips

EVENT

Palm-up E's twist to palm-down

(See "HAPPEN")

EVER

Palm-out E circles

(See "CIRCLE")

EVERY

Thumbtip of right A slides twice down thumb of left A

(Can be EVER + -Y)

EVIDENT

Palm-up E fall on left palm

EVIDENCE = EVIDENT + -ENCE

(See "PROVE")

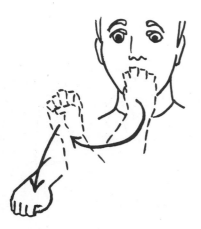

EVIL

Palm-in E at mouth twists to palm-out, moves sharply to palm-down

(See "BAD")

EVOLVE

Heels of E's touch, crossing, and stay together as hands reverse

(See "CHANGE")

EXACT

Right X circles and drops on palm-up left X

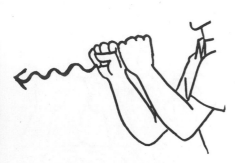

EXAGGERATE

Right S in front of left; right S shakes forward

(See "PROPAGANDA")

EXAM

Index faces left palm, moves downward, alternating index and X

EXAMINE = EXAM + -INE

EXAMPLE

Palm-out E on left palm; both move forward

(See "SHOW")

EXCAVATE

Palm-up E digs upward from left palm

EXCEED

Bent right on bent left hand; right swings upward in an arc

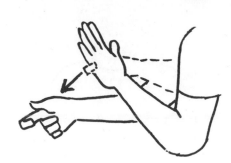

EXCEL

X holds side of left hand, jerks away forward

EXCELLENT = EXCEL + -ENT
EXCELLENCE = EXCEL + -ENCE
(See "EXPERT")

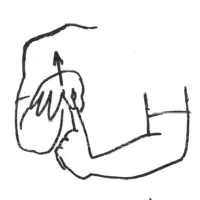

EXCEPT ♕

9 grasps finger of palm-in left hand and pulls hand up

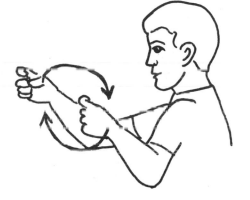

EXCHANGE ♕

Horizontal X-hands, right in front of left, circle each other once

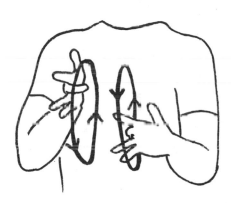

EXCITE

Middle fingers alternately brush upward on chest

EXCUSE ♕

Right fingertips brush off left fingertips several times

EXERCISE

S's move up and down above shoulders

EXHIBIT

E against palm-out left palm; both circle

(See "DISPLAY")

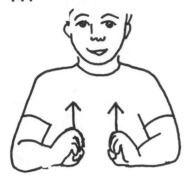

EXIST

Palms-facing E's move upwards on body

(See "ADDRESS")

EXIT

Right E rises toward body from under left palm

EXPAND

S-palms together, separate vertically, opening

EXPECT

Index at temple, then slightly to side, hands face each other, right behind left, and bend quickly

EXPENSE

Palm-up flat-O on palm rises, throws (money) down and opens to 5

EXPENSIVE = EXPENSE + -IVE

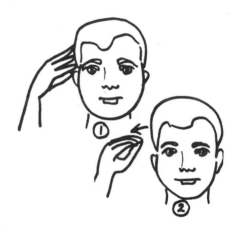

EXPERIENCE

Palm facing head, 5 on temple closes into flat-O; repeat

(See "VETERAN")

EXPERIMENT

Palm-out E's circle alternately

(See "SCIENCE")

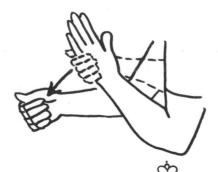

EXPERT

Grasp side of left hand, slide off forward into A

EXPIRE

Palm-out X slides along index of palm-in left hand and down fingers

(See "FINISH")

EXPLAIN

9-hands, palms facing, alternately move forward and back   (See "DESCRIBE")

EXPLODE

S's face each other, cross at wrists, jerk apart

EXPLORE

Palm-out E at eye moves down and out across left palm
(See "INSPECT")

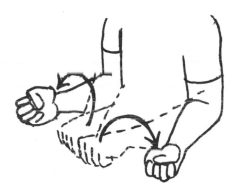

EXPORT

Palm-down E on back of hand flips forward to palm-out
(See "SEND")

EXPOSE

E's, palms-down and touching, twist apart sideways to palms-up

(See "OPEN")

EXPRESS

E's facing each other near chin, left ahead and right, move forward together in slight arc

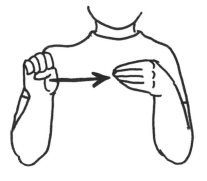

EXTEND

F's touch, palms facing; one arcs forward
(See "POSTPONE")

EXTRA

Palm-out right E moves toward and touches left flat-O
(See "MORE")

EXTRACT

Upside-down E pulls sharply upward through palm-in C, tilting forward   (See "OUT")

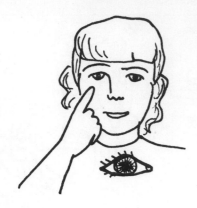

EYE

Point to eye

EYEBROW

Outline eyebrow with index

FABLE

Palm-out, right F-hand shakes away fron stationary left F

(See "SENTENCE")

FABRIC

Three last fingers of F rub shoulder

(See "CLOTH")

FABULOUS ♛

Palm-out F's near temples make small outward circles, then palm-out, flat hands push forward

FACE ♛

Index finger circles face

FACT

Fingers of F at chin; move forward

(See "CERTAIN")

FACTOR

Side of F arcs across left palm

(See "SOME")

FACTORY

Palm-out F-hands touch, and
outline roof and sides
(See "HOUSE")

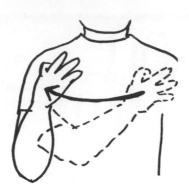

FACULTY

F-hand at left, then right
shoulder
(See "MEMBER")

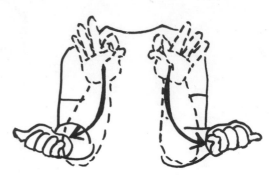

FADE

Palm-out F's fall; gradually
close to palm-up A's
(See "MELT")

FAHRENHEIT

Middle fingertip of F moves up
and down left index
(See "THERMOMETER")

FAIL

Back of V slides forward across
left palm

FAILURE = **FAIL** + **-URE**

FAINT

Palm-down, A's drop from near
temples to 5's

FAIR

With middle finger of F, tap
chin

FAIRY

Fingers of F's on shoulders,
twist to point out (wings)
(See "ANGEL")

FAITH

Touch forehead with index;
drop to S on S at shoulder level

FAKE

Fingers of F brush past mouth

(See "FALSE")

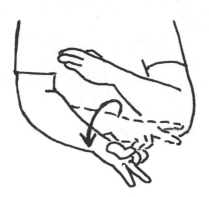

FALL ★

Palm-down V on elbow twists
over and out to palm-up

FELL = FALL + P. T.

FALLEN = FALL + P. P.

FALSE

Index brushes past mouth

FAME

Index fingers at corners of
mouth spiral up and out

FAMOUS = FAME + -OUS

FAMILIAR

Fingertips of palm-in F tap side
of forehead

(See "THINK")

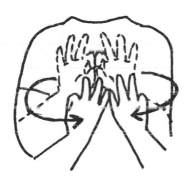

FAMILY

F-hands first touch index, and
then circle to touch little
fingers

(See "CLASS")

FAMOUS

Fame + -ous

FAN

4-hand fans face

FANCY ♛★

Thumb of palm-left 5 brushes
upward on chest several times

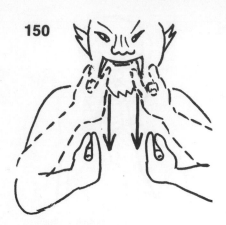

FANG

Closing G-hands pull fangs downward from mouth

FANTASY

Palm-out 4 off temple loops forward

FANTASTIC = FANTASY + -IC

(See "IDEA")

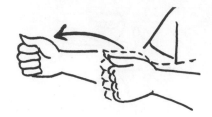

FAR ♛

A-hands together, right arcs forward

FARTHER = FAR + -ER

FARTHEST = FAR + -EST

(See "YONDER")

FARM

Right thumb of open hand is drawn across the chin left to right

FARMER = FARM + -ER

(See "RANCH")

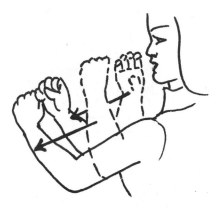

FASCINATE

C-hands, right behind left in front of face, draw forward, closing to S's

FASHION

Index and little finger out, hand nods down, arcs, and nods to right

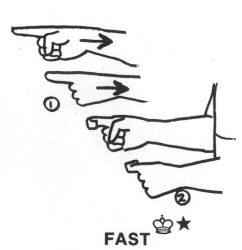

FAST ♛★

Indexes point forward, one ahead of the other, jerk back to X's

FASTEN

Right index drops to hook X into hole of horizontal F

FAT

Claw-hands face the neck, move out to sides

(See "CHUBBY")

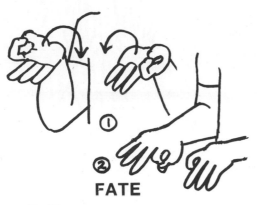

FATE

F's flip over

FATAL = FATE + -AL

(See "HAPPEN")

FATHER

Thumb of 5 on forehead

(See "DAD")

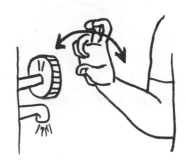

FAUCET

Thumb and bent-fingers turn faucet twice to the right

FAULT

Palm-in fingertips of F on right shoulder

FAVOR

Fingertips of right B-hand move up and down toward left index finger several times

FAVORITE

Tap middle finger on chin; repeat   May be signed FAVOR + -ITE

FEAR

Slightly at left, palm-out F's shake downward

(See "AFRAID")

FEAST

F's circle alternately to and from mouth

(See "BANQUET")

FEATHER

F-hand arcs up from back of head

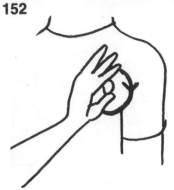

FEATURE

F-hand circles heart clockwise
on chest

(See "CHARACTER")

FEBRUARY

(Alt. 1)
Draw heart over own heart

(See "HEART")

FEBRUARY

(Alt. 2)
F arcs over at side of vertical
left hand

(See "CALENDAR")

FEDERAL

F circles once near temple,
then touches temple with
middle fingertips

(See "GOVERN")

FEE

Middle fingertip of F brushes
down across left palm

(See "COST")

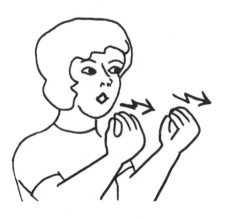

FEED ★

Flat O's hand some food from
near mouth, left hand ahead of
right in 2 small jerks

FED = FEED + P. T.

FEEDBACK

Palm-out F moves back toward
body, changing to B

FEEL

Bent middle finger brushes
middle of chest upwards

FELT = FEEL + P. T.

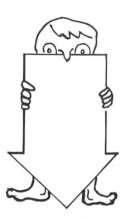

FEET

See "FOOT"

FELLOW

F moves diagonally forward from temple

(See "HE")

FEMALE

Middle fingertip of palm-out F brushes down jawline

FEMININE = FEMALE + -INE

(See "GIRL")

FENCE★

Fingers of hands mesh; separate sideways

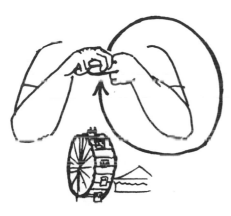

FERRIS WHEEL

Two fingers sit on side of left H; make large circle forward with both hands

FESTIVAL

Palm-out F curves right and down, changes to L and continues right

(See "CARNIVAL")

FEVER

Back of flat hand on right forehead

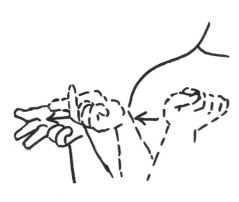

FEW

Palm-up A, while moving to right opens slowly to 3-hand

FIB

Palm-down index passes left, under lip; may repeat

(See "LIE")

FICTION

Middle finger of F on temple circles up to right

(See "IDEA")

FIELD ★

F on back of hand, circle out, back to elbow, along arm to hand

(See "GROUND")

FIG

Finger and thumb of F on palm-in left S goes around S

(See "APRICOT")

FIGHT

S-hands face each other, jerk to cross at wrists; repeat

FOUGHT = FIGHT + P. T.

FIGURE ★

Palms of F's brush sideways twice

(See "ARITHMETIC")

FILE ★

Side of F-hand pushes toward left wrist along each finger

FILL

Palm-down flat hand rises inside palm-right left C

FILM ★

Heel of F-hand stays on side of left, fingers of F move side-to-side slightly

(See "MOVIE")

FILTH

Right hand opens sharply under chin from S to 5

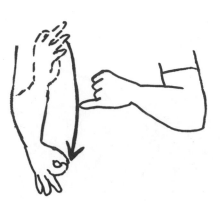

FINAL

Right F-hand moves down past the little finger of the left I-hand

FINALLY = FINAL + -LY

(See "LAST")

FINANCE

Palm-up right F taps left palm twice

FINANCIAL = FINANCE + -AL

(See "MONEY")

FIND

F-hand pulls up past palm of left hand

FOUND = FIND + P. T.

(See "DISCOVER")

FINE ♔

Thumb of palm-left 5-hand on chest, move hand forward.

(May be done sharply with F-hand)

FINGER

Fingertip rubs back of index finger

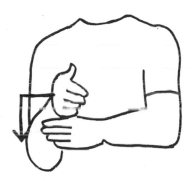

FINISH ♔

Side of right hand on side of left moves to end and drops down

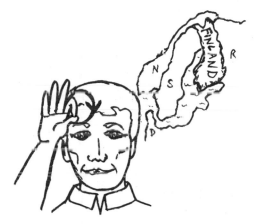

FINLAND

(U.S. Sign)
F circles near forehead

(See "DENMARK")

FINLAND

(Finnish Sign)
Bent index taps teeth

FIRE ★

Palm-up bent 5's move upward fluttering fingers

(See "BLAZE")

FIRST ♔

Index hits tip of extended left thumb

FISH ♛
Hand flutters forward like swimming

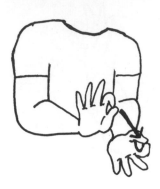

FIT
Palm-out right F moves down to touch thumbtips with palm-up left F

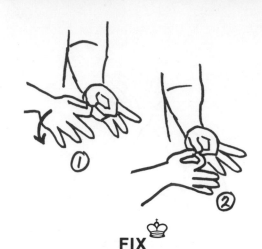

FIX ♛
Thumbs of F's together; left is stationary, right twists down from wrist; repeat

(See "REPAIR")

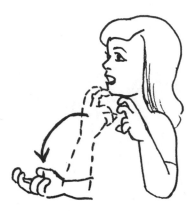

FLABBERGASTED
Palm-in bent-V's face each other; one falls from chin to palm-up (dropping jaw)

FLAG ♛
Flat hand waves in breeze, left index on arm

FLAKE
Palm-up F arcs downward, striking side of left index in passing

(See "CHIP")

FLAME
Palm-in F moves up, fluttering fingers

FLANNEL
Palm-down right F-thumb and index, flat, circle on palm-up left hand

FLAP
Right hand hangs over left index and flaps up and down

FLAPJACK

Palm-up F slides forward and flips

(See "PANCAKE")

FLARE

Wrist of right O rests against left index finger, then opens to 5 and rises, fingers fluttering

(See "TORCH")

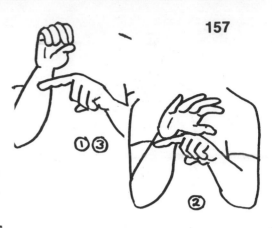

FLASH

Flat-O and 5-hand open and close supported on index; can repeat

FLASHLIGHT

Left index on wrist of right 5, both pointing forward, move around like flashlight

FLAT

Open hand swings right, on a level

(See "LEVEL")

FLATTER

Right hand "paints" left index finger

FLAVOR

Palm-in, middle finger of F taps chin

(See "TASTE")

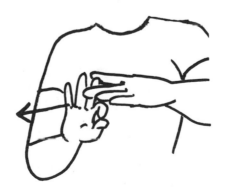

FLEE

F between fingers of palm-down left hand moves sharply away

(See "ESCAPE")

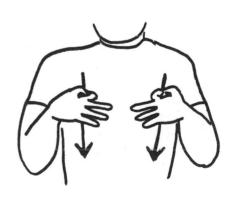

FLESH

Palm-in sideways F-hands move down body from chest

(See "BODY")

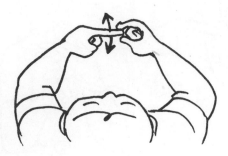

FLEX

Right hand seizes left index finger and flexes forward and back

FLEXIBLE = FLEX + -ABLE
(See "PLASTIC")

FLING

Palm-up F throws forward
(See "THROW")

FLIRT

Palm-down 5-hands, thumbs together, wiggle fingers (Like a pair of eyelashes)

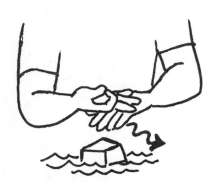

FLOAT

Right F, palm-up on back of left flat hand; float forward together
(See "DRIFT")

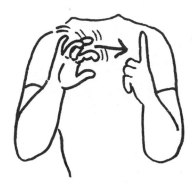

FLOCK ★

Palm-out 5 moves toward vertical index while fluttering fingers

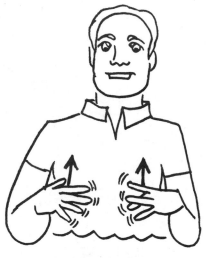

FLOOD

Palm-down 5-hands point to each other; rise, fluttering fingers

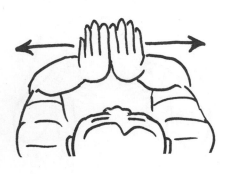

FLOOR

Palm-down flat hands separate

FLOUR

Palm-in F circles on back of palm-in S-hand
(See "DOUGH")

FLOW

Right behind left, fingers flutter; hands flow forward left

FLOWER ♔

Flat-O at right of nose, then at left

FLU

Palm-in F's, right on forehead, left on stomach

(See "SICK")

FLUID

Right F moves downward from lips with wavy motion

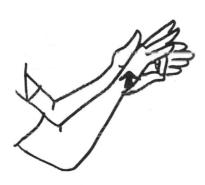

FLUNK

Thumb-and-finger side of F hits left palm sharply

(See "FORBID")

FLUSH ★

Palm-out F, move down and back up again

FLUTE

Palm-in F's play flute, fluttering fingers

FLUTTER

Fingers of Palm-out F's flutter downward

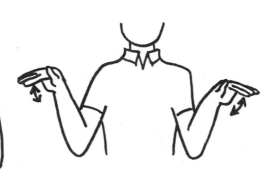

FLY ★

Bent hands at shoulders flap fingers like wings

FLEW = FLY + P. T.
FLOWN = FLY + P. P.
FLIGHT = FLY + T

FOAM

F-hand spirals up from palm

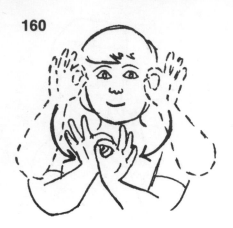

FOCUS

F's at side of eyes drop and come together to a focus

FOE

F-hand and left index move sharply apart

(See "OPPOSE")

FOG

From sides, arc up and cross palm-in F's at wrists, near face

(See "DARK")

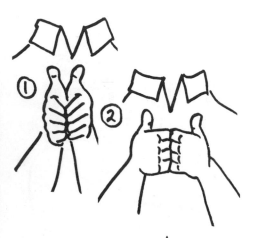

FOLD ★

Palm-to-palm, keep fingertips together and roll hands back-to-back

FOLDER = FOLD + -ER

FOLK

F-palms face each other; circle alternately up and down forwards

(See "PEOPLE")

FOLLOW

Right A follows left A; both move forward left

FOND

F's cross over heart

(See "LOVE")

FOOD

Palm-in flat-O nods toward mouth (Putting food in)

FOOL

Palm-left F arcs in front of eyes

FOOLISH = FOOL + -ISH

(See "STRANGE")

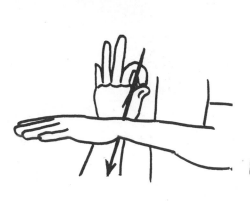

FOOT

F-hand moves down past flat
left wrist

FEET = **Make the sign twice**

(See "PAW")

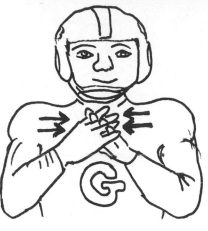

FOOTBALL

Mesh fingers of almost-
horizontal 5-hands several
times

(Can be "FOOT" + "BALL")

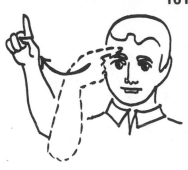

FOR

Index on forehead twists to
palm-out

(See "PRO")

FORBID

Side of vertical 1-hand strikes
left palm

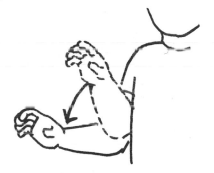

FORCE

Thumb of palm-left C at
shoulder; move sharply
forward

FORE

Bent right hand behind bent
left; right moves back

(See "PRE")

FOREIGN

Fingers of F rub left arm in
circles near elbow

(See "COUNTRY")

FOREST

Elbow of F on back of left hand,
shake F slightly to right

(See "TREE")

FOREWORD

Fore + word

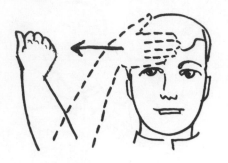

FORGET

Palm-in hand on forehead; wipe off to right, to palm-in A

FORGOT = FORGET + P. T.

FORGOTTEN = FORGET + P. P.

FORGIVE

Fingertips brush off palms, right off left; turn over, then left off right

FORK ★

"Tines" of W stab palm

FORM

Palm-out F-thumbs outline form

FORMAL = FORM + -AL

(See "SHAPE")

FORMER

Open hand brushes backward on front of shoulder several times

FORMERLY = FORMER + -LY

FORMULA

Side of right F on left fingers, then on heel

(See "LAW")

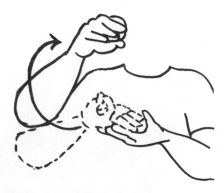

FORTUNE

Palm-up F on left palm, swing up over palm, inverting

(See "RICH")

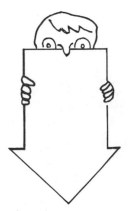

FORWARD

Fore + ward

FOSSIL

Fingertips and thumb of right F make elongated circle in palm-up left hand

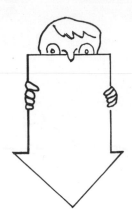

FOUND

Palm-down F twists, and side of F falls on back of left hand

FOUNDATION = FOUND + -TION

(See "ESTABLISH")

FOUND

Find + P. T.

FOUNTAIN

F rises behind left S, fingers fluttering, and "flows" down other side

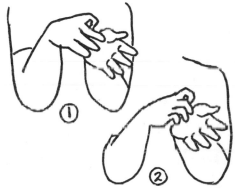

FOX

Nose in center of F, twist F around nose, wrist stationary

FRACTION

Place F above and then below left index

FRAGILE

Three fingers of F do pushups on left palm

(See "WEAK")

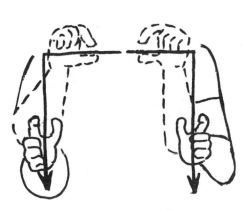

FRAGRANT

Palm-in F circles vertically near nose

FRAGRANCE = FRAGRANT + -ANCE

(See "SMELL")

FRAME ★

Palm-out G's outline frame

FRANCE

(U. S. Sign)

Palm-in F twists to palm-outward

FRENCH = FRANCE + -H

FRANCE

(French Sign)
F twists outward from heart
FRENCH = FRANCE + -H

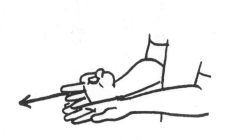

FRANK

Side of F on palm; slide F
straight forward
(See "HONEST")

FRANKFURTER

C to S hand pulls alternately
out of left F
(See "BALONEY")

FREAK

F-fingers flutter past forehead
(See "WEIRD")

FRECKLE

Spot face with thumb and
fingertip of F
(See "MEASLES")

FREE

Palm-in F's, crossed at wrists,
separate and twist to palm-out

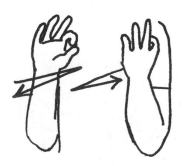

FREEWAY

F's brush past each other,
moving rapidly back and forth
(Can be Free + Way)
(See "TRAFFIC")

FREEZE

Open, palm-down hands draw
back to claws
FROZE = FREEZE + P. T.
FROZEN = FREEZE + P. P.

FREIGHT

Palm-up F arcs over to palm-
down on top of left palm-down
hand
(See "CARGO")

FREQUENT

Fingertips of palm-down F
strike left palm several times

(See "OFTEN")

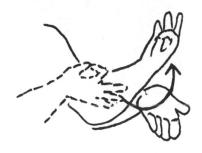

FRESH

Back of F-hand slides left
across left palm, arcing up

(See "NEW")

FRESHMAN

Right index taps left 5's ring
finger

FRIDAY

Palm-out F-hand circles
slightly

(See "MONDAY")

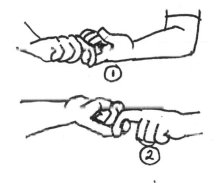

FRIEND

Index fingers hook, first right
over left, then left over right

FRIGHT

Palm-in F's jerk toward each
other and cross

FRIGHTEN = FRIGHT + P. P.

(See "SCARE")

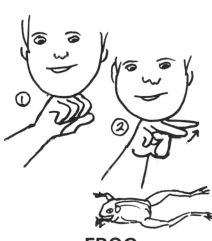

FROG

S under chin; two fingers flick
out twice

FROM

Back of palm-in X touches
palm-out left index, then
moves toward body

FRONT

Palm-in flat hand moves
downward in front of face

FROST ★

3-fingers of F smooth up and over back of S-hand

(See "COVER")

FROWN

Indexes above eyes drop to point downwards over eyes

FRUIT

Finger and thumbtip of F on cheek; twist wrist

(See "APPLE")

FRUSTRATE

Flat hand flips up in front of mouth

FRY

Palm-down F flips palm-up

(See "COOK")

FUDGE

F circles on back of left hand

(See "CHOCOLATE")

FULL

Palm-down flat hand brushes inward across top side of left S

(See "MATURE")

FUN

Palm-in U on nose strokes downward to palm-in N

FUNNY = **FUN** + **-Y**

(See "DOLL")

FUNCTION

Palm-out F arcs, side-to-side, hitting back of left S

(See "BUSY")

FUNDAMENTAL

Circle palm-out F below left palm

(See "BASE")

FUNERAL

Palm-out right V behind left; move both forward in slightly down and up motion twice

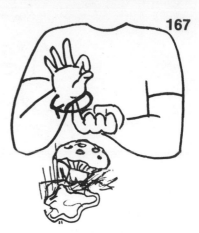

FUNGUS

Heel of F-thumb circles on little fingertip of palm-up left I

(See "ALGAE")

FUNNEL

Open C's approach each other and close to S's, moving down to one on the other

FUR

F-hand slides up arm and over shoulder

(See "WOOL")

FURNISH

F-hand, palm-up, arcs to the right

(See "THING")

FURNITURE

Furnish + -ure

FURY

F jerks up chest

(See "ANGER")

FUSS

Palm-in F taps on chest sharply

(See "COMPLAIN")

FUTURE

Palm-left F near side of head
arcs forward

(See "WILL")

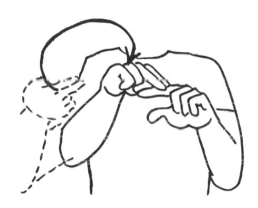

GAIN

Right palm-up H swings over to hit top of left G; may be repeated

(See "INCREASE")

GALLAUDET

G closes and moves backwards from side of eye

GALLON ♔

Right G passes down to N through left C

GALLOP

Bent V's leap forward to open V's; repeat

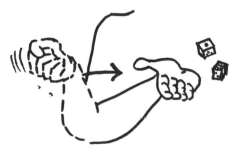

GAMBLE

Mime shaking dice and throwing them

GALOSHES

Sides of palm-out G's hit each other twice

(See "SHOE")

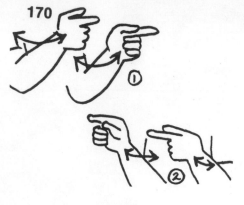

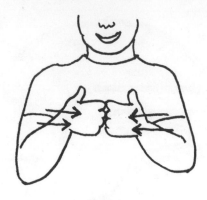

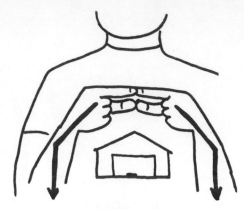

GAME
(Alt. 1)
G-hands, one palm-out, one palm-in, swing back and forth, pivoting at wrists
(See "PLAY")

GAME
(Alt. 2)
Palm-in A's, thumbs up, bump knuckles; repeat

GARAGE
Thumb and fingertips of G's touch, outline garage
(See "HOUSE")

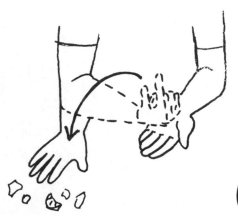

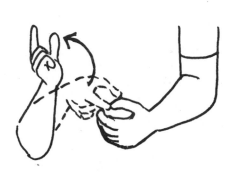

GARBAGE
Back of G on palm, slide forward and off, throwing down as 5
(See "DISPOSE")

GARDEN
Box in a garden with G-hands
(See "BOX")

GAS
G rises out of and up from top of C
(See "EVAPORATE")

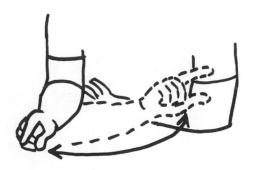

GATE
(Alt. 1)
G swings out from elbow and back

GATE
(Alt. 2)
Fingers of palm-in hands mesh; right opens outward and closes again

GATHER ★

Starting at sides, flat hands flap forward several times to meet, palm-in

(See "COLLECT")

GAY

Sides of G-hands brush upwards on sides of chest; repeat

(See "DELIGHT")

GEESE

Sign for goose works down to left wrist, opening and closing

GEM

G shakes away from left ring finger

(See "DIAMOND")

GENDER

G at temple, then at jaw

(See "PARENT")

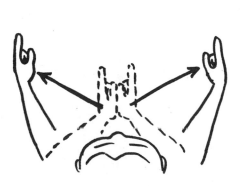

GENERAL

Palms of G-hands touch; then separate forward

(See "BROAD")

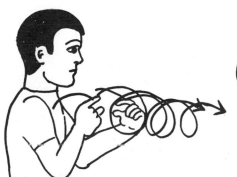

GENERATE ♔

Palms facing each other; G's circle each other forward from right shoulder

GENERATION = GENERATE + -TION

GENEROUS

Bent-hands circle each other vertically near heart

(See "KIND")

GENIUS

Thumb of horizontal C on forehead; thumb of other C on fingertips of first one

GENTLE

G-hands, crossed at chin; separate downward

(See "QUIET")

GENTLEMAN

A-thumb on forehead drops to 5 on chest

(Can be signed GENTLE + MAN)

GENTLEMEN

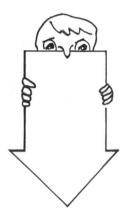

Make the sign for "Gentleman" twice

(Or sign GENTLE + MEN)

GENUINE

Side of palm-out G hand on palm, slide off forward

(See "HONEST")

GEOGRAPHY

Right G on left; then circle each other vertically once

(See "WORLD")

GEOMETRY

Little-finger side of G hits thumb and finger of left G twice

(See "ARITHMETIC")

GERBIL

G brushes off nose-tip; repeat

(See "MOUSE")

GERM

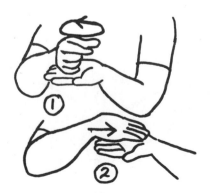

Side of G circles on left palm, flat-O opens over palm and spreads up arm

(See "CANCER")

GERMAN
(U. S. Sign)
S-hands cross at wrists, open to 5's

GERMANY = GERMAN + -Y

GERMANY
(German Sign)
Back of hand with vertical index touches forehead

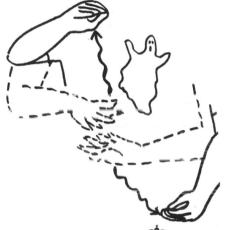

GET
Right open hand above left, draw toward body, closing to S-hands

GOT = GET + P. T.

GOTTEN = GET + P. P.

(See "RECEIVE")

GHOST
Palms face each other, right rises and left drops in wavy motions, closing to flat O's

GIANT
G's move in big arcs out from shoulders

(See "GIGANTIC")

GIFT
G's point up, left ahead of right, drop to left to level position

GIGANTIC
G's at shoulders move in large arcs to sides, change to palm-out C's

(See "GIANT")

GIGGLE
Wiggle indexes of palm-in L's at corners of mouth

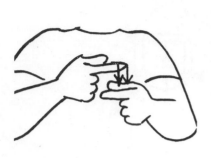

GINGER

Right G above left, tap twice

GIRAFFE

C-hand traces up neck

GIRL ♔

Thumb of extended-A hand
moves down jawline

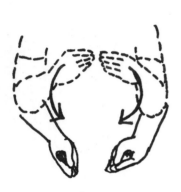

GIVE

Palm-in flat-O's near body turn
outwards to palm-up
GAVE = GIVE + P. T.
(See "ISSUE")

GLAD

G-hand brushes chest upward;
repeat

(See "HAPPY")

GLASS

Drop G from temple to palm
GLASSES = GLASS + -S

GLAZE

Fingers of palm-down G arc to
cover back of left S
(See "COVER")

GLIDE

G glides forward on back of left
hand

(See "DRIFT")

GLIMPSE

Palm-in flat hand covers eye;
index opens and closes once

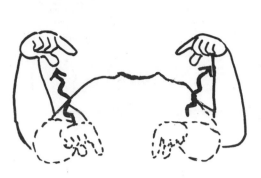

GLISTEN

G's move up and out with wavy motion

(See "CLEAR")

GLOBE

2 G's separate, outline globe and touch again

(See "BULB")

GLORY

Palm of 5 on palm, right lifts off, fingers fluttering

GLOVE

Draw on invisible gloves

GLOVES = GLOVE + -S

GLOW

G-thumb and finger on back of left hand; raise hand up and off, shaking

(See "SHINE")

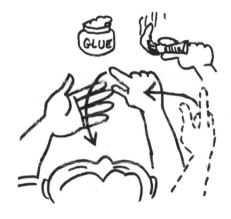

GLUE

G-hand twists to palm-down; sweeps across left palm

(See "PASTE")

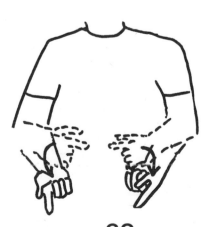

GO

G-hands face each other, roll out to point forward

WENT = GO + P. T.

GOAL

Left G at head height, slightly to left; right index, behind left G, turns down to point at G

(See "AIM")

GOAT

Palm-in fist on chin moves to forehead; two fingers flick out on both chin and forehead

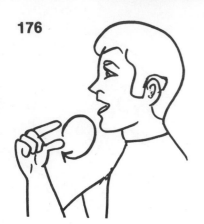

GOBBLE

Palm-in G circles in and up near mouth; repeat

(See "EAT")

GOBLIN

G's pull away from each other vertically with wavy motion

(See "GHOST")

GOD

Palm-left B arcs down from above to near forehead

GOLD

G at ear shakes downward to right

GOLDEN = GOLD + -EN

(See "CALIFORNIA")

GOLF

Hold and swing invisible golf club

GOOD

Palm-in fingers on chin drop to palm of left hand

GOOSE

Arm on back of left wrist, first two fingers open and close on thumb; repeat

GOPHER

Tips of G's tap under chin

GORGEOUS

G circles face

(See "FACE")

GORILLA

G-hands thumbs scratch sides

(See "MONKEY")

GOSPEL

Little-finger side of G-hand brushes up left palm; repeat

(See "NEW")

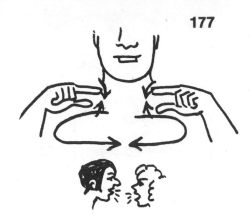

GOSSIP

G-hands face each other near chin, circle outwards, horizontally, with indexes and thumbs opening and closing

(See "RUMOR")

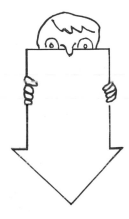

GOT

Get + P. T.

GOVERN

Index circles near temple, then touch temple

GOVERNOR = GOVERN + -ER
GOVERNMENT = GOVERN + -MENT

GOWN

Thumbtips brush down off chest twice

(See "DRESS")

GRAB

Palm-down hand closes to S, grabbing something

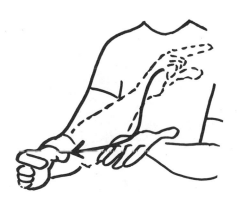

GRACE

G from heart glides off left palm and forward

GRADE ★

G circles over and drops on left palm

178

GRADUATE

G on left palm circles up
(See "COLLEGE")

GRAHAM

G circles on back of palm-in
left S-hand
(See "DOUGH")

GRAIN

G brushes up twice through
left C-hand

GRAMMAR

G-hands touch, then separate,
shaking slightly
(See "SENTENCE")

GRAND

G-hands face each other, twist
apart to palm-out D's

GRANDDAUGHTER

G from chin falls to inside of
left elbow

GRANDFATHER

From temple, palm-left 5
makes two arcs diagonally
right

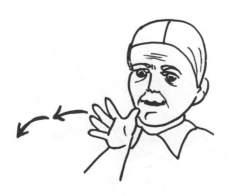

GRANDMOTHER

From chin, palm-left 5 makes
two arcs diagonally to right

GRANDSON

G at temple falls to inside of left
elbow

GRANT

G-hands point downward, then swing upward

(See "ALLOW")

GRAPE

Fingers of claw–hand hop across back of left hand

(See "RAISIN")

GRAPEFRUIT

G fingertips twist on cheek

(See "APPLE")

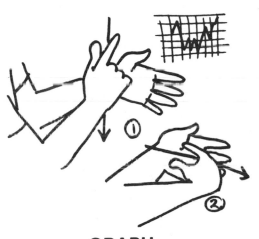

GRAPH

G draws a cross on left palm

GRASP

Right hand grabs thumb of palm-out G

GRASS

Fingers of palm-up claw move up through fingers of left claw several times

GRASSHOPPER

G rides forward on hopping bent-V hand

(See "LOCUST")

GRATE

Mime holding grater; grate downwards

GRAVE ★

Palm-down G-hands arc back toward body, ending palm-out

GRAVITY = GRAVE + -ITY

(See "BURY")

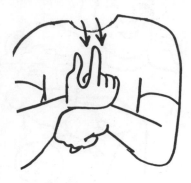

GRAVEL

Back of G taps on back of left S
(See "STONE")

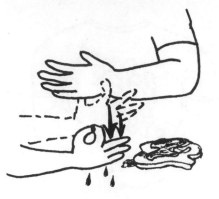

GRAVY ♔

Right 9-hand slides off lower
edge of left hand and closes;
repeat

GRAY (GREY)

Side of G moves right across
forehead
(See "BLACK")

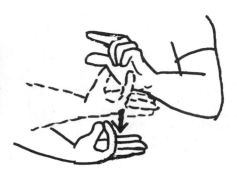

GREASE

Thumb and index grasp
thumb-base of left G and pull
off downward, closing
(See "GRAVY")

GREAT

G-hands face each other, arc
apart
(See "MUCH")

GREECE

G arcs down inward near nose
GREEK = GREECE + -K

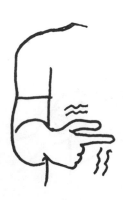

GREEN

Palm-left G shakes
(See "BLUE")

GREMLIN

G's on shoulders swing off
(See "ANGEL")

GRIEF

Middle right finger touches
heart; A-hands knuckles
pressed together and twist
slightly

GRILL ★

Palm-up G circles under left palm

(See "OVEN")

GRIM

G-hands at sides of mouth curve slightly downward

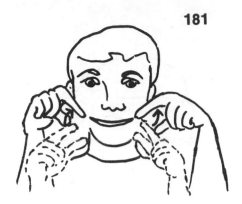

GRIN

G-hands twist upwards near corners of mouth

(See "SMILE")

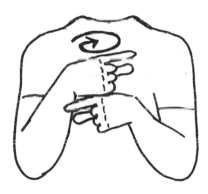

GRIND

G circles on G in grinding motion

GROUND = GRIND + P. T.

GRIP

G grips vertical left index finger

(See "HOLD")

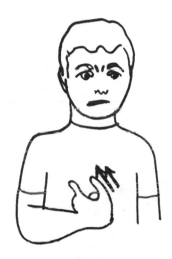

GRIPE

Two fingertips of G hit chest sharply; repeat

(See "COMPLAIN")

GROAN ♔

G-hand at throat shakes up and out under chin

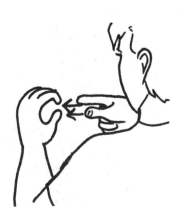

GROCER

Right G nods toward side of left C

GROCERY = GROCER + -Y

(See "STORE")

GROUCH

G outlines half of sour mouth

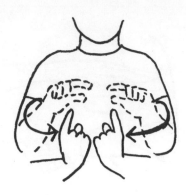

GROUND
(Noun)
G on back of left hand circles
out and back

GROUND
(Verb)
Grind + P. T.

GROUP
G-hands circle horizontally
from palm-out to palm-in
(See "CLASS")

GROVE
Right elbow on back of left
hand, shake right G slightly to
right

(See "TREE")

GROW
Palm-in flat-O "grows"
through left C, to a palm-in 5
GREW = GROW + P. T.
GROWN = GROW + P. P.
GROWTH = GROW + -H

GROWL
Palm-in claw-hand at throat
shakes slightly

(See "GROAN")

GRUMBLE
Claw-hand on chest circles,
fingers fluttering and tapping

GUARANTEE
Index from chin moves to rest
as a G against top of left hand
(See "PROMISE")

GUARD
Left G behind right G, both jerk
forward, not touching

GUESS

Open hand palm left arcs past eyes, closing to S

(See "ESTIMATE")

GUEST

Palm-up G curves horizontally toward body

(See "INVITE")

GUIDE

Right hand grasps G-thumb and pulls left hand toward right

(See "LEAD")

GUILT

G taps on left chest; repeat

GUILTY = GUILT + -Y

(See "CONSCIENCE")

GUINEA PIG

G under chin, and flap fingers together for "pig"

GUITAR

Hold and strum on invisible guitar

GULF

Palm-out to palm-in G outlines curves of left palm from index to thumb (See "BAY")

GULL

Nod G hand, resting elbow on back of left hand

(See "OSTRICH")

GULP

Thumb and index of 9 at throat move forward and back to throat

184

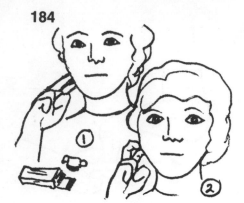
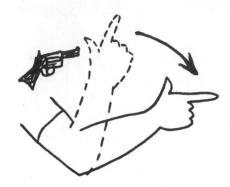

GUM

Fingertips of V-hand touch cheek; bend and straighten fingers (See "TOBACCO")

GUN

L-hand drops down and forward

GUY

G at temple moves forward slightly right (See "HE")

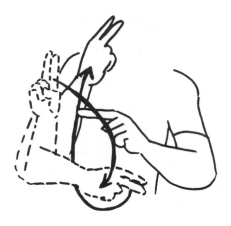

GYM

Thumbs of palm-in extended-A's hit upward and inward on shoulders; repeat

GYMNASTIC

Palm-out U-hand twists around left index finger and moves upward

GYPSY

Index and thumb of L open and close on earlobe

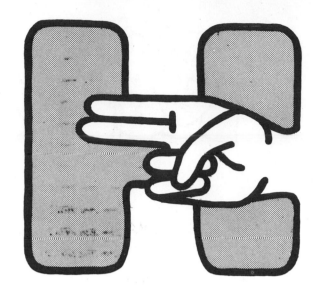

HABIT

Wrist of right S on wrist of left S, drop slightly

(See "CUSTOM")

HAD

See "Have"

HAIL ★

H beats on back of left hand as both move diagonally left down

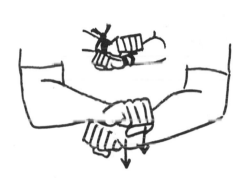

HAIR

Hold hair with 9-hand

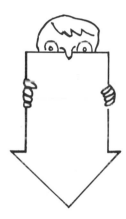

HALF

Palm-in 1 drops to palm-in 2

(½)

HALL ♛

Parallel vertical-H-hands move forward, not touching

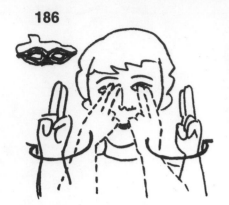

HALLOWEEN

Palm-in U's at eyes move around to sides

(See "MASK")

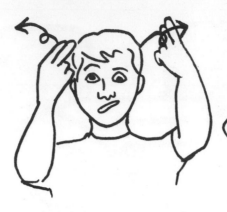

HALLUCINATE

H's circle alternately at sides of head

(See "IMAGINE")

HALO

Index fingers and thumbs outline halo above head

HALT ★

Side of right H falls on left palm

(See "STOP")

HAM

Thumb and finger of 9 pinch side of H-hand and shake hand slightly

(See "MEAT")

HAMBURGER

Clasp hands, right on left, separate, then left on right (make a patty)

HAMMER

A-hand pounds with invisible hammer; repeat

HAMPER ★

H outlines hamper from wrist to elbow of left arm

(See "BASKET")

HAMSTER

Horizontal H-hand brushes off tip of nose; repeat

(See "MOUSE")

HAND

H-finger draws across back of left hand

HANDICAP

H changes to C

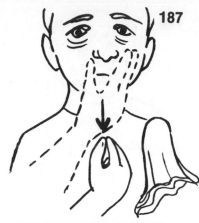

HANDKERCHIEF

H at nose--thumb extended--pulls away, and thumb and 2 fingers meet; repeat

HANDLE

Alternately H's move in and out (Like reins)

(See "MANAGE")

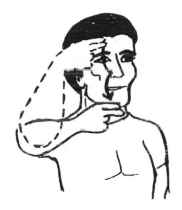

HANDSOME

H moves down at side of face in two arcs

(See "PROFILE")

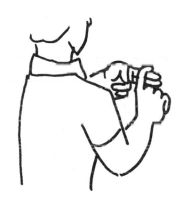

HANG

Hook right X on side of left H

HANGED = HANG + -D
HUNG = HANG + P. T.

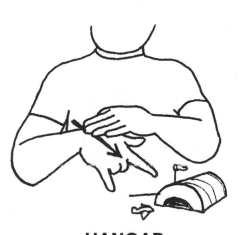

HANGAR

I-L-Y hand slides beneath palm as in sheltering a plane

HANUKAH

Palms in, H's swing up to 4's

(See "MENORAH")

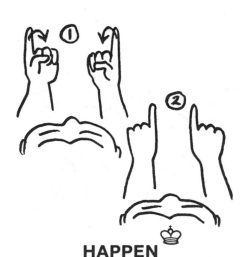

HAPPEN

Palm-up index fingers twist to palm-down

HAPPY

Open hand brushes middle of chest upward; repeat

HARBOR

Palm-out vertical H outlines curves of palm-down left hand's index and thumb, ending palm-in

(See "BAY")

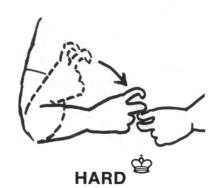

HARD

Palms-in, bent-V hits bent-V

HARDLY = **HARD** + **-LY**

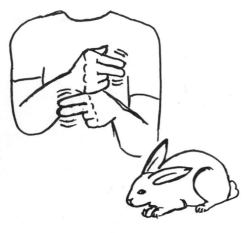

HARE

H-hands wiggle fingers together in and out

HARM

H arcs up, striking back of left S

(See "DANGER")

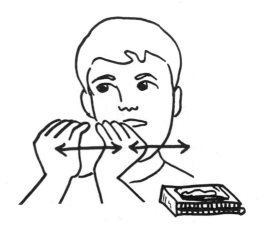

HARMONICA

Palm-in flat-O's move harmonica back and forth in front of mouth

HARP

Fluttering fingers, draw 5-hand toward body past flat left hand

HARVEST

Curved right index slices toward and across left S

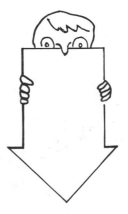

HAS

See "HAVE"

HASSLE

Palm-in H's point at each other, move rapidly up and down from wrist; repeat

(See "ARGUE")

HAT

Pat head

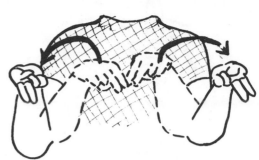

HATCH ★

H's together, turn over and out to palm-up

(See "OPEN")

HATCHET

Side of palm-up H chops at wrist of vertical left hand

(See "AXE")

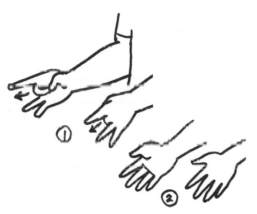

HATE

Parallel 8's snap open to 5's

HAUL

Palm-up H's pull toward body

(See "PULL")

HAUNT

H's pull away from each other vertically in wavy motion

(See "GHOST")

HAVE

Fingertips of slightly bent hands approach and touch chest

HAS = HAVE + -S
HAD = HAVE + PAST
(Or sign HAS = "HAVE" with S-hands
HAD = "HAVE" with D-hands)

HAWAII

H-hand circles face

(See "FACE")

HAY

H brushes up through left C-hand

(See "GRAIN")

HAZE

Palm-in H's arc from sides to cross in front of face

(See "DARK")

HE ♛

E at temple moves forward, slightly right

HEAD

Fingertips of bent hand touch temple, then jaw

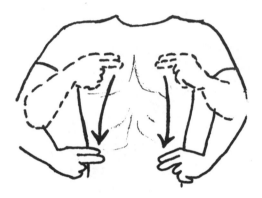

HEALTH

Palm-in H's touch chest, then ribs

(See "BODY")

HEAP

H touches heel of left hand then tips of fingers

(See "AMOUNT")

HEAR

H-hand rises to ear

HEARD = HEAR + P. T.

(See "SOUND")

HEART

(Alt. 1)

Index or bent middle fingers draw heart over heart

HEART

(Alt. 2)

Middle finger taps over heart

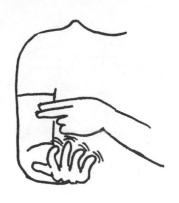

HEAT

Palm-up, right fingers flutter under left H

(See "BURN")

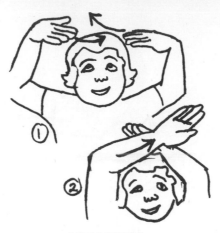

HEAVEN

Right flat hand passes above head under left hand and up (entering heaven)

(See "PARADISE")

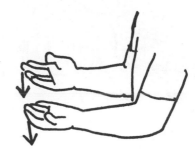

HEAVY

Slight bent palms-up drop slightly

HEBREW

Palm-in M's on chin drop a few inches

HEEL ★

Right L-thumb touches heel of left hand (can tap)

HEIGHT

High + T

HELICOPTER

Palm of bent-5 on left index fingertip; shake 5-hand

HELL

H moves sharply to the side

(See "DAMN")

HELLO

Flat hand, fingertips at forehead, moves forwards slightly right

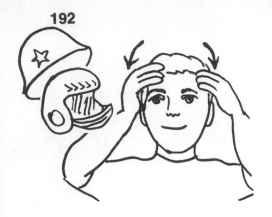

HELMET

Claw-hands put on helmet

HELP

Palm lifts bottom of left S

HEN

S's on chest, flap elbows twice

HER

Palm-out R slides down jawline forward

HERS = HER + -S
(See "GIRL")

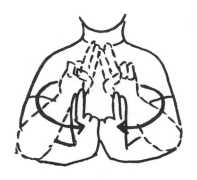

HERD

Palm-out U-hands circle horizontally to palm-in
(See "CLASS")

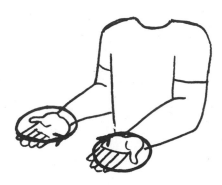

HERE

Palm-up hands circle horizontally in opposite directions
(See "AVAIL")

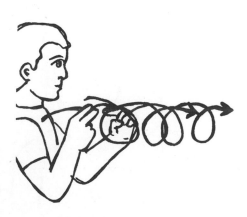

HEREDITY

Palms in, H's circle each other forward from right shoulder
(See "GENERATE")

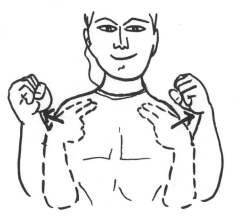

HERO

H's on upper chest move out to S's
(See "BRAVE")

HESITATE

H points to palm-up left hand that flutters fingers
(See "WAIT")

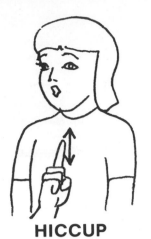

HICCUP

Index finger jumps up and down chest

HIDE ♔ ★

A at chin moves down under bent hand, top of thumb against left palm
HIDDEN = HIDE + P. P.
HID = HIDE + P. T.

HIGH

H hand moves upward
HEIGHT = HIGH + -T
(See "UP")

HIGHWAY

High + way

HIKE

Palm-down H's walk alternately forward
(See "WALK")

HILL

Palm-down hand draws hill

HIM

M at temple moves forward and slightly right
(See "HE")

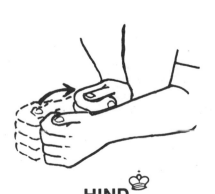

HIND ♔

A-hands together; right arcs sideways behind left

HINGE

Palm-in right H-tips touch side of left palm-in vertical hand; right H hand rocks forward and back on hinge

HIP

Pat hip

HIPPOPOTAMUS

Wrists together, Y's snap open and closed

HIRE

Palm-up, extended H moves in toward body

(See "INVITE")

HIS

S at forehead moves forward and slightly right

(See "HE")

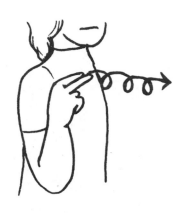

HISTORY

H circles forward from right shoulder

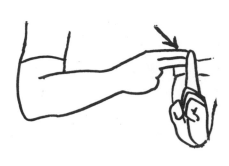

HIT ★

Back of H hits left vertical index

(See "BEAT")

HOCKEY

X scrapes across left palm; repeat

HOE

Bent hand hoes on left palm; repeat

HOG

H under chin; H-fingers flutter

(See "PIG")

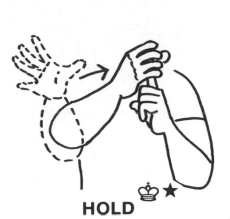

HOLD ♛★

Right claw-hand seizes left index finger

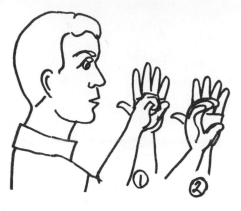

HOLE

Side of S on left palm opens to C-hand

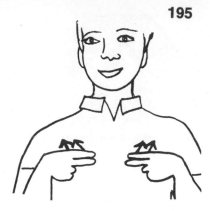

HOLIDAY

Palm-in H's tap on sides of chest

(See "LEISURE")

HOLLAND

Thumb of Y, at mouth arcs out

HOLLER

H from chin shakes upward

(See "SCREAM")

HOLLOW

Palm-up H carves out left C, ending palm-down

(See "CAVE")

HOLLY

Starting on left index-lip, outline holly leaf with thumb and finger

HOLSTER

L index sticks into C on hip

HOLY ♛

Right H circles above left palm, then flat hand wipes off palm

HOME

Flat-O fingertips on chin then flat palm on cheek

(See "DORMITORY")

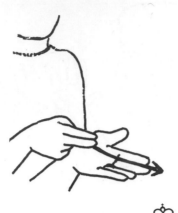

HONEST

Middle fingertip of H slides forward on left palm

HONEY

H rubs chin in circle

(See "SWEET")

HONOR

H arcs down and back to near forehead

(See "GOD")

HOOD ★

Vertical H's, palm to palm, cock forward at wrists

HOOF

Fingers of H move around fingertips of palm-down left hand

(See "EDGE")

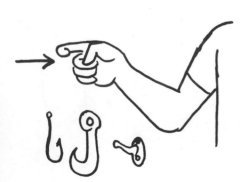

HOOK

Horizontal X-hand hooks toward body

HOOP

H draws circle in midair

(See "CIRCLE")

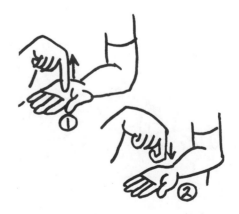

HOP

Index fingertip on left palm hops up to X several times

(See "JUMP")

HOPE

Palms facing, left hand in front of right, cross fingers

HOPSCOTCH

P hops to H on palm of hand

HORIZON

Palm-in H moves along flat arm to right

HORIZONTAL = HORIZON + -AL

HORN ★

Palm-in, right H on left H near lips; right moves forward and then returns
(Sign can be made where horn is, e.g. on head)

HORROR

H-hands shake down toward body

HORRIBLE = HORROR + -IBLE

(See "AFRAID")

HORSE

Thumb on temple, flap H-fingers

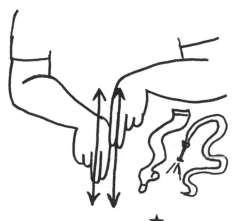

HOSE ★

H-hands slide up and down against each other alternately
(See " STOCKING")

HOSPITAL

H draws cross on upper left arm

HOSTILE

H twists sharply down from chest

(See "RESENT")

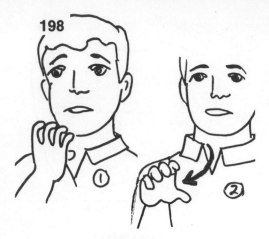

HOT

Palm-in claw at mouth; twist downward and to side

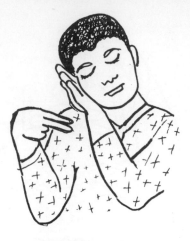

HOTEL

Cheek rests on back of left hand; H under palm

(See "BED")

HOUR ♔

Palm-left H touches left palm, circles forward once, touches again

HOUSE ♔

Flat palms outline roof and sides

HOW

Backs of palm-down bent hands touching, roll hands from inward to outward

HOWL

Palm-in H at throat vibrates slightly outward

(See "GROAN")

HUG

Hug self with H's

(See "LOVE")

HUGE

H-hands face each other; arc sideways

(See "MUCH")

HULA

Do hula on each side

HUMAN

H-hands face each other, move down

(See "PERSON")

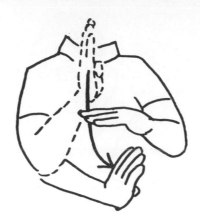

HUMBLE

Right B-hand, palm-left, moves down under left palm-down hand

(See "SUBTLE")

HUMID

Palm-in H-hand moves right across forehead.

(See "SUMMER")

HUNDRED

Fingers pull inward to palm-out C

HUNG

Hang + P. T.

HUNGER

Palm-in C moves once down chest

HUNGRY - HUNGER + -Y

HUNT

H-hands with extended thumbs, left a bit ahead of right, drop to shoot twice

HURRICANE

H's rotate around each other, rising to right

(See "CYCLONE")

HURRY

Parallel H-hands palms facing, shake forward

(See "RUSH")

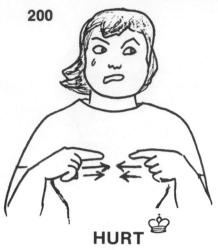

HURT

Palm-in index fingers jerk toward each other; repeat

HUSBAND

A at temple drops to clasped C-hands

(See "WIFE")

HUSH

H fingers palm-left tap closed mouth

HUT

H-hands draw hut

(See "HOUSE")

HYBRID

H-s move toward each other and cross

(See "CROSS")

HYMN

Palm-left H swings from side-to-side behind palm-in left hand

(See "MUSIC")

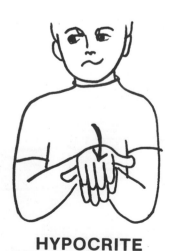

HYPOCRITE

Palm-down flat hands, right on left; eight fingers flap together down once

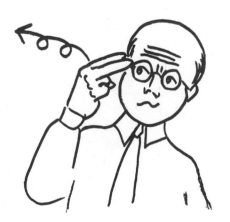

HYPOTHESIS

H circles from forehead up to right

(See "IDEA")

HYSTERIC

H's point at sides of head and circle alternately

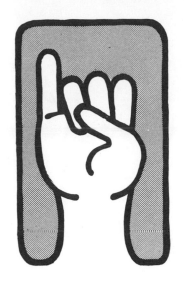

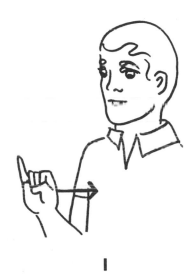

I

Palm-left I-hand touches chest

ICE

W on chin moves forward, fingers bending (contracting)

ICE CREAM

Right S circles inward at mouth

(Can be "Ice" + "Cream")

ICICLE

I's touch fingertips; right wiggles downward from left

IDEA

From side of forehead, palm-in I arcs up and out

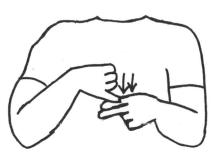

IDENTIFY

Side of little fingers taps index of left H

(See "NAME")

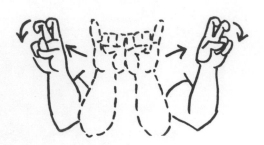

IDIOM

Palm-out I's together, separate to bent-V's that twist slightly down

(See "QUOTE")

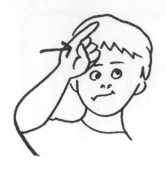

IDIOT

Back of I-hand strikes forehead

(See "DUMB")

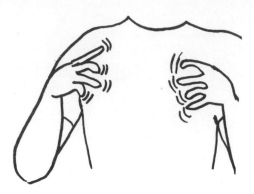

IDLE

Thumbs resting on side of chest, wiggle fingers

(See "LEISURE")

IF

I-hand; two middle fingers move up into a F-hand; may repeat

IGLOO

Palm-out I's outline igloo

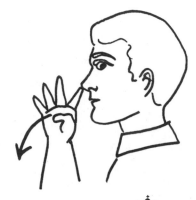

IGNORE

Index of 4 on nose, flip hand down and to left

ILL

(Alt. 1)

Brush little finger of I-hand down chest

(See "DEPRESS")

ILL

(Alt. 2)

Fingertips of palm-in I's touch forehead and stomach

(See "SICK")

ILLUSTRATE

Side of palm-out I-hand moves from right eye to left palm

(See "PICTURE")

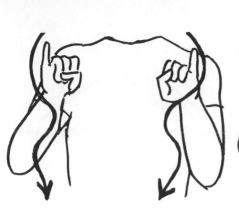

IMAGE

Palms facing each other, I's
outline shape downward

(See "SHAPE")

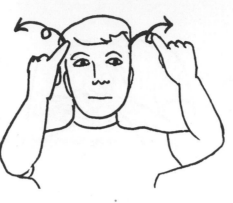

IMAGINE

Palm-in I's on forehead,
alternately circle up and out

IMAGINATION = IMAGINE + -TION

(See "HALLUCINATE")

IMITATE

Palm-out I-hand closes to flat-
O on left palm

(See "COPY")

IMMACULATE

Heel of palm-out I on left palm;
right I slides along left palm

(See "CLEAN")

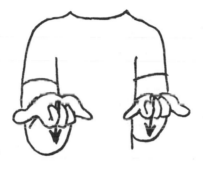

IMMEDIATE

Palm-up   Y-shapes   slightly
drop

(See "NOW")

IMMENSE

I's facing each other   arc to
each side

(See "MUCH")

IMPAIR

Litle finger side of I strikes side
of palm-down left hand

(See "OBSTACLE")

IMPLY

Palm-in I-hand circles out at
mouth

(See "SAY")

IMPORTANT

F's, palm-up to palm-down in
vertical circle

**IMPORTANCE =
IMPORTANT + -ANCE**

IMPRESS

Extended A on left palm, move both back toward body

(See "REQUIRE")

IMPRINT

Heel of I on left heel; little finger taps left palm

(See "PRINT")

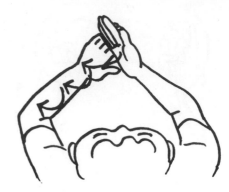

IMPROVE

Side of right hand on back of left hops up arm

IN

Fingertips of right flat-O enter left O   **INTO = IN + TO**

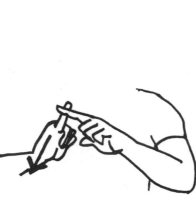

INCH

Palm-left I moves down on first joint of left index finger

INCIDENT

Palm-up I's twist to palm-down

(See "HAPPEN")

INCLUDE

Palm-out I circles to palm-in, goes into grasp of left hand

(See "WHOLE")

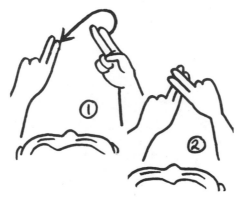

INCREASE

Palm-up H twists up and over onto palm-down H; may be repeated

(See "GAIN")

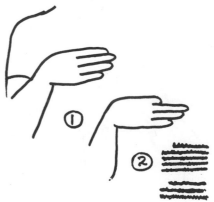

INDENT

Palm-in flat hand bends index

INDEPENDENT

Crossed wrists of palm-in I's turn outward and separate

(See "FREE")

INDIA

Thumb of extended A marks dot in middle of forehead

INDIAN

F from corner of mouth to ear draws on warpaint

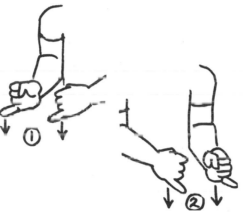

INDICATE

Palm-out I against left palm, both arc forward together

(See "SHOW")

INDIVIDUAL

I-hands face each other, move downwards; first at right, then at left

(See "CITIZEN")

INDUSTRY

Palm-out I arcs side-to-side, hitting back of left S

(See "BUSY")

INFANT

Wrists crossed and hands crooked up, rock tiny infant

(See "BABY")

INFATUATE

Palm-up flat-O opens and closes slowly at heart, moving slightly up and down

INFECT

I-hand circles on left palm, changes to flat-O, opens, and spreads up arm

(See "CANCER")

INFERIOR

I-hand rotates under left palm
(See "BASE")

INFEST

Palm-out I on back of left hand
moves outward to palm-down
5 and circles
(See "INFLUENCE")

INFILTRATE

Left hand curved palm-down in
front of chest, right palm-down
fingers creep beneath and out

INFINITE

Palm-out I circles slightly then
moves forward
(See "ETERNAL")

INFIRMARY

I-finger draws cross on
shoulder
(See "HOSPITAL")

INFLATE

Flat-O on left palm opens
(inflates) to C

INFLUENCE

Flat-O on back of left hand
opens to 5 and then moves in
an outward arc (Spreading
influence)

INFORM

Flat-O at forehead moves
forward and down, opening to
palm-up

INGREDIENT

Side of I taps down left palm
(See "LIST")

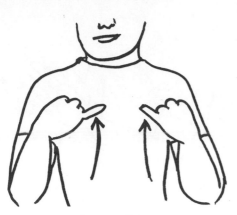

INHABIT

Palm-in I's move up chest
(See "ADDRESS")

INHERIT

Palm-in I-hands roll forward
from right shoulder, little
fingers circling each other
(See "GENERATE")

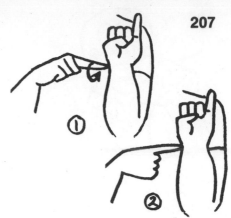

INITIATE

Index on wrist of palm-out left
I; twist index
INITIAL = INITIATE + -AL
(See "START")

INJURE

Palm-in I-hands jerk toward
each other twisting slightly
INJURY = INJURE + -Y
(See "HURT")

INNOCENT

Palm-in I-fingers, near mouth,
swing out, twisting to palm-out
(See "NAIVE")

INSECT

I rides forward on wiggling left
fingers
(See "ANT")

INSERT

Flat palm-down hand slides in
between index and middle
finger of left hand

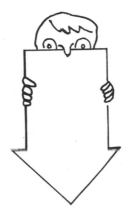

INSIDE

In I side

INSIST

Tip of I on palm, both arc
toward body
(See "REQUIRE")

INSPECT

Index at eye, then brushes forward off left palm two or more times

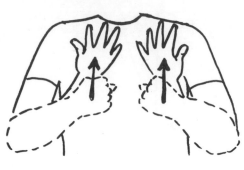

INSPIRE

Palm-in S's on chest slide up, opening to 5's

INSTANT

Palm-out I-hand rests against other palm; twist forward to palm-down

(See "MINUTE")

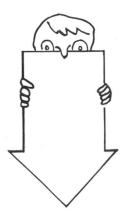

INSTEAD

In + stead

INSTINCT

Back of I-hand on left palm; I twists down and under to palm-down

(See "NATURE")

INSTITUTE

Side of right I taps on index-side of left I

INSTRUCT

I-hands at forehead jerk slightly forward; repeat
(See TEACH")

INSTRUMENT

Back of I on heel of left palm, bounce across palm to fingertips

INSULT

Index finger, pointing forward, moves sharply out and up (jab)

INSURE

Palm-out I shakes

INSURANCE = INSURE + -ANCE

INTEGRATE

Palm-in 5-hands arc toward each other, meshing fingers

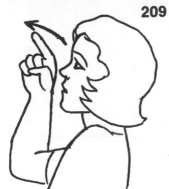

INTELLECT

Side of index on forehead, slide up and forward

INTELLIGENCE = INTELLECT + -ENCE
INTELLIGENT = INTELLECT + -ENT

(See "INVENT")

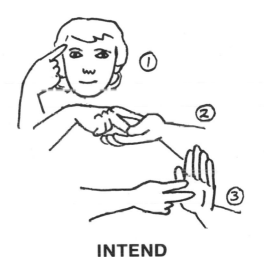

INTEND

Index on temple drops to palm-down V on left palm; hands separate; right twists to palm-in V

(See "MEAN")

INTENSE

Little finger of right I outlines muscle on upper left arm

(See "STRONG")

INTERCOURSE

Spell "I-C"

INTEREST

Palm-in 5's on chest move out to 8's

INTERFERE

Side of I-hand chops into thumb-joint of left hand

(See "BOTHER")

INTERMEDIATE

Circle I over left palm, then touch tip to mid-palm

(See "MIDDLE")

INTERN

I-hand brushes back and forth on left index

(See "PRACTICE")

INTERNATIONAL

I-hands, one on top of other; circle each other vertically and touch again

(See "WORLD")

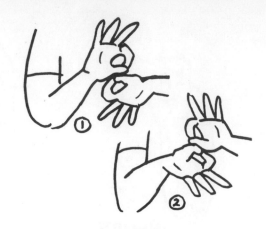

INTERPRET

9's, thumb-on-thumb, one palm-up and one palm-down; reverse; repeat

INTERROGATE

Hands move in small in-and-out circles while changing from 1 to X

INTERRUPT

Little-finger side of I hits left palm

(See "STOP")

INTERVAL

Right flat hand arcs to palm-up over left thumb and jerks toward finger-gaps

INTERVIEW

I's move alternately to and from face

(See "TALK")

INTIMATE

(Adj.)
I moves near back of palm-in left hand

(See "NEAR")

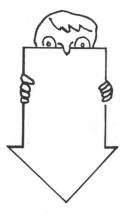

INTO

In + To

211

INTRIGUE

I moves from chin to under left hand

(See "HIDE")

INTRODUCE

Palm-up hands swing to point at each other

INTRODUCTION = INTRODUCE + -TION
(See "PROLOGUE")

INTRUDE

Flat hand swings down between index and middle finger of palm-in left hand

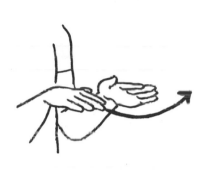

INVADE

Palm-down right hand arcs sharply out under palm-down left hand

(See "ENTER")

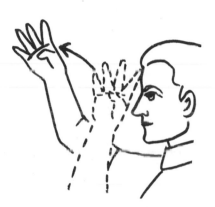

INVENT

Index of 4 on forehead; arc up and out

(See "INTELLECT")

INVERT

Palm-down V swings over to palm-up

INVEST

Extended thumb of palm-out bent-V on left palm; then bent-V arcs forward

(See "BUY")

INVESTIGATE

V at eye; then V brushes forward on palm twice

(See "INSPECT")

INVITE

Palm-up flat hand moves in toward body

INVOLVE

Palm-down right hand circles horizontally, goes into grasp of left C

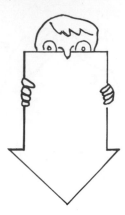

INWARD

In + ward

IRELAND

Bent-V circles over, then drops on back of left hand

IRISH

Ireland + -ish

IRON ★

Palm-in I arcs right, hitting side of left index and ending palm-out

(See "METAL")

IRONY

Fingertip of right I touches side of mouth, then arcs down past outside of palm-down left I, as left I twists

(See "TRICK")

IRRIGATE

I at mouth, side of I then slides across left palm and to right, palm up

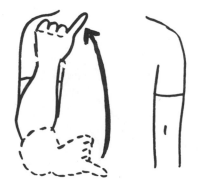

IRRITATE

Palm-in I jerks up body
(See "ANGER")

IS

I on chin moves straight forward

(See "AM")

ISLAND
(Al. 1)
I's face each other, circle horizontally toward body and touch   (See "PLACE")

ISLAND
(Alt. 2)
Side of I circles on back of left S

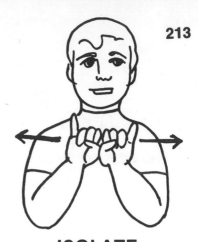

ISOLATE
Palm-out I-hands touch and separate sideways
(See "SEPARATE")

ISRAEL
Palm-in I strokes downward on chin several times

ISSUE
I's, palm-down to palm-up, arc outwards

(See "GIVE")

IT
Tip of I touches palm of left hand
ITS = IT + -S
IT'S = IT + 'S

ITALY
Little finger makes cross near forehead
ITALIAN = ITALY + -AN

ITCH
Scratch left arm

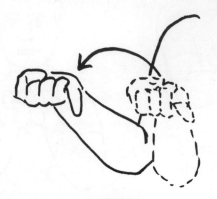

ITEM

Palm-up I-hand arcs to the right

(See "THING")

IVY

I grows up and out of left C and spirals downward

(See "GROW")

JACKET

Palm-in I-fingertips draw lapels down chest

(See "COAT")

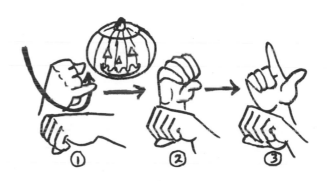

JACK O'LANTERN

Make J + O + L above back of left S

(See "MELON")

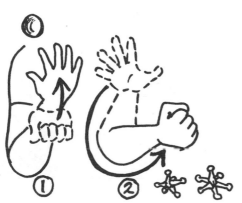

JACKS

Toss up ball and snatch up jacks

JAIL

Palm-in V-hands, right behind left; right hits left

JAM ★

I flicks off palm inwards twice

(See "BUTTER")

JANITOR

Right S on top of left, push broom in front; repeat

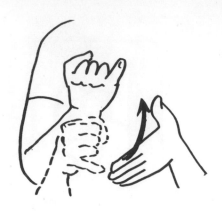

JANUARY
(Alt. 1)

Little I-finger brushes off thumb of left hand

(See "FIRST")

JANUARY
(Alt. 2)

J arcs over at side of vertical hand

(See "CALENDAR")

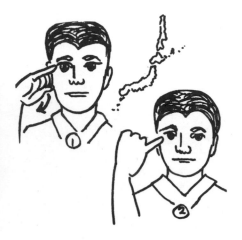

JAPAN
(U. S. Sign)

Little fingertip at corner of eye, hand twists slightly forward

(See "CHINA")

JAPAN
(Japanese Sign)

Index and thumb of horizontal G's touch, separate and close

JAR

I-fingers outline jar-bottom

JAY

G on head rises back and closes

JEALOUS

Draw a J near corner of mouth

JEALOUSY = JEALOUS + -Y

(See "ENVY")

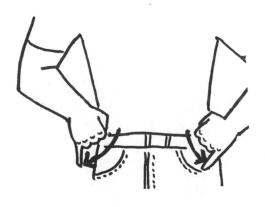

JEANS

Little fingers inwards, make J's at waist

JEEP

Make J's, one in front of the other, and then move apart

(See "CAR")

JELL

Claw jiggles over palm

JELLY = JELL + -Y

JELLO = JELL + -O

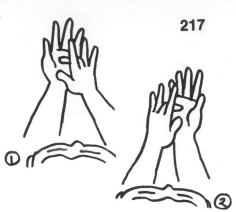

JESUS

Bent right middle finger touches left palm; reverse

(Nails in the hands of Jesus)

JEW

Four fingers and thumb grasp chin, drop slightly to flat-O; repeat

(See "ISRAEL")

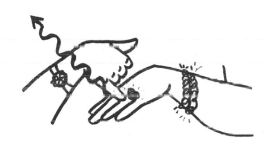

JEWEL

I-finger shakes off left ring-finger

JEWELRY = JEWEL + R + Y

(See "DIAMOND")

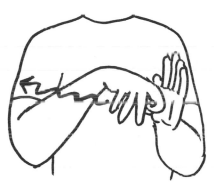

JINGLE

Palm-down F strikes left palm and shakes to side

(See "BELL")

JOB

Side of I-hand arcs once from right to left, hitting back of S

(See "TASK")

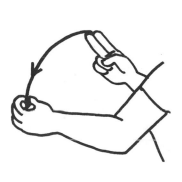

JOIN

H - fingertips arc into side of left O

(See "PARTICIPATE")

JOKE

Palm-in H-hands cross before face; repeat

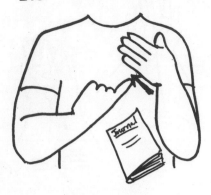

JOURNAL

Little finger of I brushes off
edge of flat hand twice

(See "MAGAZINE")

JOY

Fingertip of palm-in I brushes
up chest; repeat

(See "HAPPY")

JUDGE

Palms-facing parallel 9-hands
move alternately up and down

(See "BALANCE")

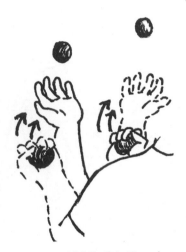

JUGGLE

Palm-up S's throw balls
alternately up to 5-hands;
repeat

JUICE

Thumb-side of Y cuts down
back of S

JULY

(Alt. 1)
Palm-in little finger brushes
straight across forehead

(See "SUMMER")

JULY

(Alt. 2)
J arcs over vertical left hand at
side to Y

(See "CALENDAR")

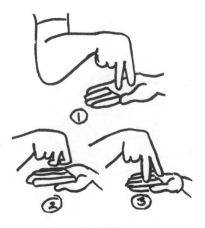

JUMP

V-fingertips on left palm, jump
up with bent fingers and down
again

(See "HOP")

JUNE

(Alt. 1)
I traces J around left fingertips

JUNE

(Alt. 2)
J arcs to E at side over vertical left hand

(See "CALENDAR")

JUMBLE

Left J palm-up, right J palm-down above left; reverse positions

(See "MESS")

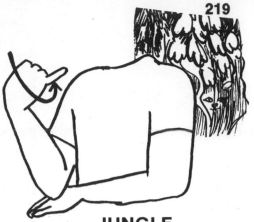

JUNGLE

Elbow resting on back of hand, J swings back and forth; repeat slightly to right

(See "TREE")

JUNIOR

Right index taps left index

(See "FRESHMAN")

JUNK

Back of palm-up I brushes off left palm, twists to palm-out, then throws (junk) down to 5

(See "DISPOSE")

JUST

I-fingertip draws "J" on left palm

JUSTICE = JUST + -ICE

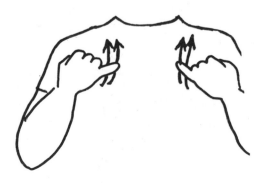

JUVENILE

J-hands brush upward twice off chest; repeat

(See "YOUNG")

KANGAROO
Body stationary, bent hands
hop forward together

KARATE
Mime several karate chops

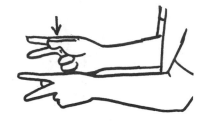

KEEP
Right K drops on left K
KEPT = KEEP + P. T.

KERCHIEF
K's outline and tie kerchief on
(See "BONNET")

KETCHUP/CATSUP
Side of K shakes downward,
like a bottle

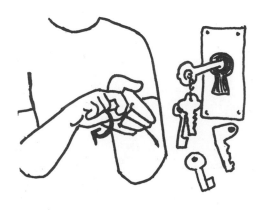

KEY
Thumbtip and finger of X twist
on left palm

KICK

Side of right hand arcs from below to strike side of left hand sharply

(See "SOCCER")

KID

K-hand shakes in front of nose

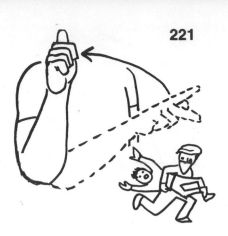

KIDNAP

K pulls back sharply to A-hand near shoulder

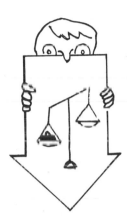

KILOGRAM

(Kg)
Spell K + G

KILOMETER

(Km)
Spell K + M

KILL

Side of index twists under left palm

KIND

K-hands circle vertically around each other, stopping one on top of the other

KINDERGARTEN

K circles under left palm

(See "BASE")

KING

Right K on left shoulder, then right side of body

(See "CHRIST")

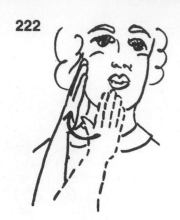

KISS

Fingertips of palm-in hand touch below lips and on cheek

KITCHEN

Palm-down K-hands form box-shape

(See "BOX")

KITE

Palm-out K moves upward in wavy motion

KITTEN

Right K moves to side from mouth; repeat

(See "CAT")

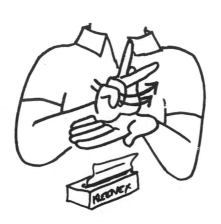

KLEENEX

Heel of right K strikes across left heel several times

(See "PAPER")

KNEE

Tap knee twice

KNEEL

First two fingers kneel on left palm

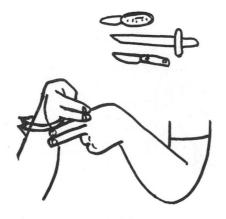

KNIFE

H flicks off H twice

KNIVES = KNIFE + -S

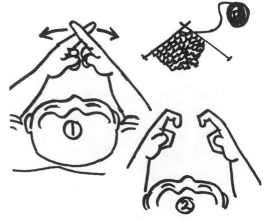

KNIT

Horizontal index fingers cross; separate to X's; repeat several times

KNOB

C-hand twist knob

DOORKNOB = **DOOR** + **KNOB**

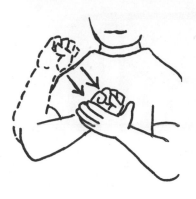

KNOCK ★

Right S-hand knocks several times on left palm

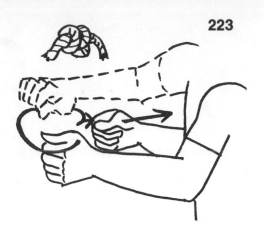

KNOT

Right A circles thumb of left A and jerks back to tie knot

KNOW

Fingers of palm-in hand hit forehead lightly; may repeat

KNEW = **KNOW** + **P. T.**
KNOWN = **KNOW** + **P. P.**
KNOWLEDGE = **KNOW** + **-AGE**

(See "THINK")

KOOL AID

K moves to A at mouth

(See "LEMONADE")

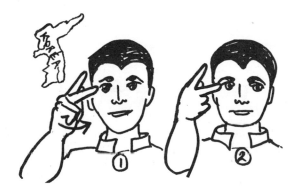

KOREA

Middle fingertip of K at corner of eye; hand twists slightly forward

(See "CHINA")

KOSHER

Side of palm-left flat hand moves from mouth to slide along top of palm-right left hand

LABEL

H-fingers slide across heel of left palm

(See "BRAND")

LABOR

Palm-out L brushes side-to-side hitting back of left S

(See "BUSY")

LADDER

Two fingers walk up inverted V

LADY

A, thumb on chin, moves to 5-hand, thumb on chest

LADIES = LADY + -S

LAKE

Palm-down L-thumbs touch; circle outward, shaking, and touch again

(See "POND")

LAMB

Palm-up L moves twice up left arm

(See "SHEEP")

LAMINATE

Horizontal L-hand covers palm -down left S

(See "COVER")

LAMP

Place thumb on chin and flick middle finger out from thumb several times

LAND ★

L on back of left hand circles out, back to elbow and along arm to hand

(See "GROUND")

LANE

Palms-facing, parallel vertical L's move forward

(See "HALL")

LANGUAGE

Thumbtips of palm-down L's touch, then separate, shaking slightly

(See "SENTENCE")

LANTERN

Palm-down 5 swings side to side under left S

LAP ★

L arcs forward twice, knuckles hitting left palm; repeat

(See "SLIP")

LARD

H-fingers brush toward body off heel of palm-up left L

(See "BUTTER")

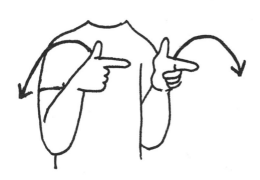

LARGE

L-hands face each other, arc apart

(See "MUCH")

LASH ★

Index of palm-in L moves out to
strike vertical left index
(See "BEAT")

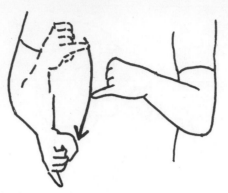

LAST ★

Right little finger chops past
end of left little finger
(See "FINAL")

LATE

Thumbtip of palm-out L on left
palm, twist to palm-down
LATER = LATE + -ER
(See "MINUTE")

LATIN

Palm-in open N-fingertips
touch forehead, then nose
(See "ROME")

LATITUDE

Thumb of right L slides around
palm-in left S
(See "EQUATOR")

LAUGH

Index fingers of L's brush up
and outward at corners of
mouth several times

LAUNCH ★

Side of right L on flat left palm,
pointing forward, arc L forward
and off

LAUNDER

L-knuckles circle on left palm
LAUNDRY = LAUNDER + -Y
(See "WASH")

LAW

L on left fingertips, then on
heel
LAWYER = LAW + -ER

LAWN

L moves from inside left palm-down hand around to the outside

(See "EDGE")

LAY ★

Set back of palm-up 2 on back of left hand

LAID = **LAY** + **P. T.**

(See "SET")

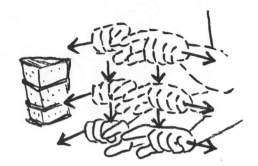

LAYER ★

Palm-out G's outline layers

LAZY

L taps below shoulder

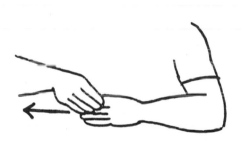

LEAD

Grasp tip of left hand and pull forward at an angle leading hand   (See "GUIDE")

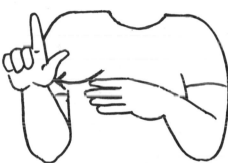

LEAD

(Metal)
Heel of L strikes off left index

(See "METAL")

LEAF

Right wrist of 5 on left index; wave 5 side-to-side

LEAVES = **LEAF** + **-S**

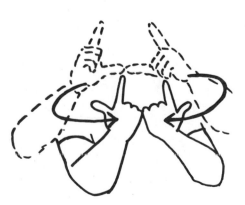

LEAGUE

Thumbtips together, L's circle out and touch little fingers

(See "CLASS")

LEAK

4-hand "leaks" down from left S, fingers fluttering

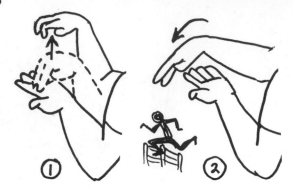

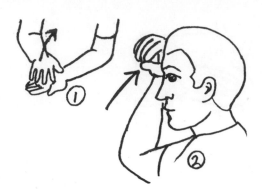

LEAP

Inverted V jumps up and bends, then leaps forward off left palm, straightening

LEARN

Open palm-down fingers on palm-up left hand rise, closing to flat-O at forehead

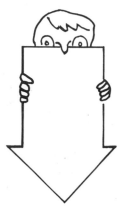

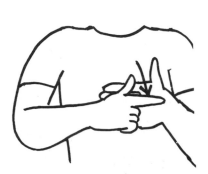

LEAST

Less + -est

LEATHER

L brushes down across back of palm-in left hand

LEAVE

Flat palms face each other at side, pointing slightly up; drop down to point forward, then withdraw back and up, closing to palm-down A's

LEFT = LEAVE + P. T.

LECTURE

Palm facing side of head, shake hand slightly and quickly forward and back from wrist

LEDGE

Right L draws ledge from fingertips of left palm-in hand

LEDGER

Thumb of right palm-down L brushes off bottom edge of palm-in left flat hand

(See MAGAZINE")

LEFT
Palm-out right L moves left

LEFT
(Verb)
Leave + P. T.

LEG
L-hand pats thigh

LEGAL
Right L pointing outward, hand slides across left palm to point slightly upward

(See "ALL RIGHT")

LEGEND
L's circle each other forward from right shoulder

(See "GENERATE")

LEGISLATE
Thumb of L touches left, then right side of chest

LEGISLATURE = LEGISLATE + -URE

(See "MEMBER")

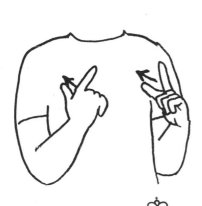

LEISURE
L-thumbs tap into sides of chest

LEMON
L-thumb taps chin

LEMONADE
L on chin closes to A

(See "KOOL AID")

LEND

Right V on left V, arc both forward

LENT = **LEND** + **P**

(See "LOAN")

LEOPARD

From cheeks move L's to sides; repeat

(See "CAT")

LEPRECHAUN

L's at shoulders swing out

(See "ANGEL")

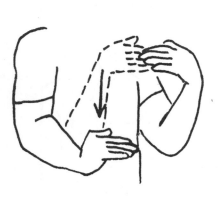

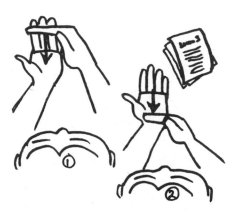

LESS

Bent hand under other bent hand; drop downward

LEAST = **LESS** + **-EST**

LESSON

Side of bent hand on left fingertips, then on heel of palm-up hand

LET

L-hands face each other, pointing down; swing to point forward

(See "ALLOW")

LETTER

Extended A-thumb at mouth moves down to touch palm-up left index

LETTUCE

Heel of L taps upwards on side of head; repeat

(See "CABBAGE")

LEVEL ★

L, palm-down, moves to right

(See "FLAT")

LIBERTY

Palm-in L's, crossed at wrists, separate and twist to palm-out (breaking bonds)

(See "FREE")

LIBRARY

Palm-out L makes a small circle twice

LICENSE

Palms-out L-thumbs tap

(See "CREDENTIAL")

LICK ★

Fingertips of right hand brush upward against left palm; repeat

LID

Palm-down L drops on side of left S

(See "CAP")

LIE

(To tell a ....)
Side of palm-down B moves left across chin

LIED = LIE + P. T.
LIAR = LIE + -ER

(See "FIB")

LIE

(Recline)
Back of V on left palm; slide toward body

LAY = LIE + P. T.
LAIN = LIE + P. P.

LIFE

Palm-in 9-hands move up body

(See "ADDRESS")

LIFT

Palms-up, L's lift

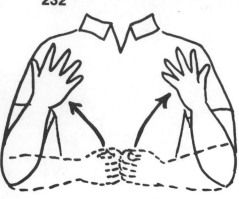

LIGHT ★

Palm-in O-hands touch and open to palm-in 5-hands while moving upward

LIGHTNING

Index finger draws a large Z rapidly

LIKE

Palm-in L on chest moves forward, closing thumb and finger

LIMB ★

Palm-out L at thumb of left palm-out 5 arcs sideways
(See "BRANCH")

LIME

Thumb-edge of L cuts down back of left S
(See "JUICE")

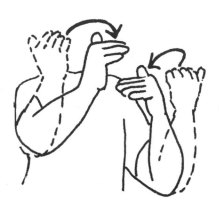

LIMIT

Palm-in bent hands, right higher than left, pivot to point sideways, right above left
(See "MAXIMUM")

LINCOLN

Right L-thumb taps temple

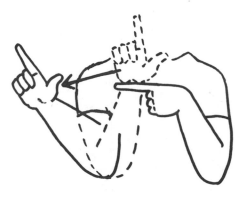

LINE ★

Palm-out L slides along and off side of left index
(See "BAR")

LINGUISTIC

Thumbtips of palm-down L's touch, separate sideways with slight shaking motion, change to palm-out C's
(See "SENTENCE")

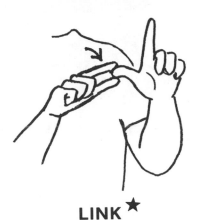

LINK ★

Thumb and index hold thumb of left L

LINOLEUM

L drags across back of left hand

(See "CARPET")

LION

Claw-hand combs backward with a shaking motion over mane

LIP

Index draws under lower lip

LIPSTICK

Thumb and finger apply lipstick

LIQUID

Thumbtip of L pours into left O

LIQUOR

Index and little fingers out, right taps left hand

(See "WHISKEY")

LIST ♔

Bent right hand moves down left palm

LISTEN

Thumb of palm-out L points to ear   (See "SOUND")

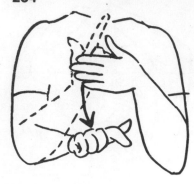

LITTER ★

Palm-in L behind left palm swings under and out to palm-down

(See "NATURE")

LITTLE

L-hands face each other, jerk slightly toward each other; repeat

(See "SMALL")

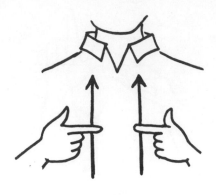

LIVE

Palm-in L-hands move up body

(See "ADDRESS")

LIVER

Thumb and index grasp base of left palm-in L index; shake

(See "MEAT")

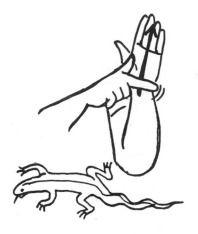

LIZARD

L-hands slides up left palm while L index fingers moves from X to straight several times

LOAD ★

Palm-up L flips to palm-down on left palm-down L

(See "CARGO")

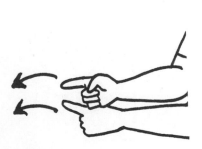

LOAN

Right 1-hand on left 1-hand, both arc forward

(See "LEND")

LOBSTER

Palm-down V-hands, crossed at wrists, move forward and to right while V's scissor

(See "CRAB")

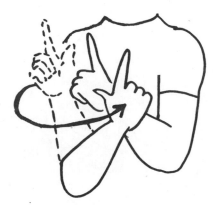

LOCAL

L circles left vertical index

(See "ATMOSPHERE")

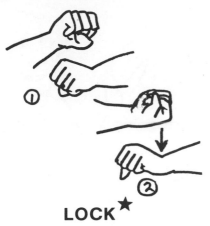

LOCK ★

Palm-down S-hands, right over left; right twists to palm-up, drops on wrist

LOCKER = LOCK + -ER

LOCUST

Palm-out L rides forward on hopping bent-V left hand

(See "GRASSHOPPER")

LODGE ★

Palms-down L's, thumbs touching, right hand lifts off and drops to the right

(See "STAY")

LOG

Little-finger side of L-hand "saws" on back of left hand

(See "SAW")

LOGIC

Palm-left L circles on forehad

(See "REASON")

LOLLIPOP

"Lick" index of L twice

(See "ICE CREAM")

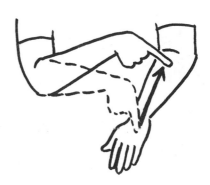

LONE

Palm-in L moves forward

LONELY = LONE + -Y

LONESOME

Index finger moves down chin; may repeat

LONG ★

Index finger slides up left arm

(See "ALONG")

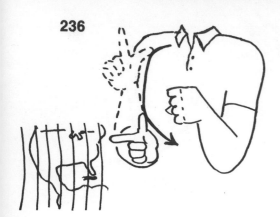

LONGITUDE

L-thumb draws arc downward near knuckles of palm-in S outline longitude

LOOK

Thumb of L at eye; move forward

(See "SEE")

LOOP

Palm-left L circles forward

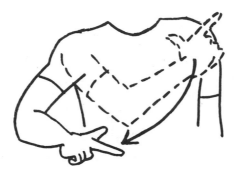

LOOSE

Right claw on left palm-in S; shake (loose) claw

LORD

Palm-in L moves from left shoulder to right hip

(See "CHRIST")

LOSE

Palm-up flat-O's point to each other, drop to palm-down open hands

LOST = LOSE + P. T.

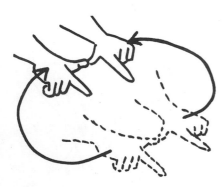

LOT ★

Palm-down L-hands touch thumbtips, circle toward body, and touch again

(See "PLACE")

LOTION

L shakes into left palm

LOUD

Right index at ear opens to 5 and shakes down to right

LOUSE

3-hand throws off nose
LOUSY = LOUSE + -Y
(See "ROT")

LOVE

S-hands cross on heart

LOVELY

Palm-in L circles face
(See "FACE")

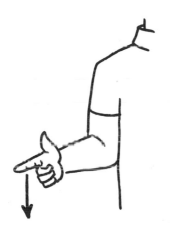

LOW

Palm-left L drops slightly
(See "DOWN")

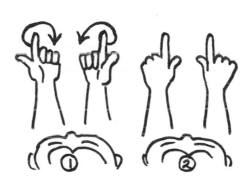

LUCK

Palm-up L's turn to palm-down
LUCKY = LUCK + -Y
(See "HAPPEN")

LUGGAGE

Mime carrying suitcase

LUMBER

Right L-hand shakes while resting elbow on back of left hand
(See "TREE")

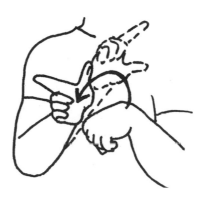

LUMP

Thumb of right L on back of left S arcs to heel of L

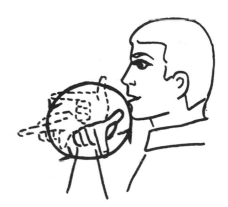

LUNCH

Thumb of L circles in and up near mouth
(See "EAT")

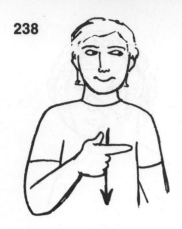

LUST

Palm-in L on chest slides down slowly

(See "HUNGER")

LUTHERAN

L-thumb taps twice on palm-right palm

LUXURY

Thumb of L brushes up middle of chest

(See "FANCY")

LYRIC

Right palm-left L swings back and forth behind bent left arm

(See "MUSIC")

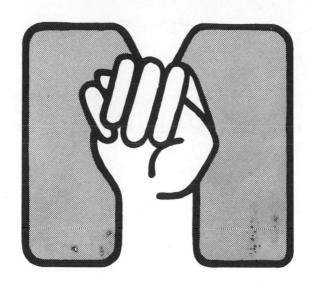

MACARONI

While shaking, M's separate to sides

(See "SPAGHETTI")

MACHINE

Wrists stationary, bent fingers mesh like gear-teeth and shake up and down

MAD

5-hand in front of face contracts to claw

MAGAZINE ♔

Thumb and finger of palm-up hand grasp little-finger side of flat left hand and slide forward and off; may be repeated

MAGIC

S's, palm-down at eye-level, open to 5's and close

MAGNET

Palm-down M's meet at index tips

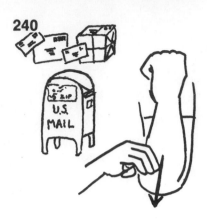

MAIL

Palm-down M brushes down left elbow

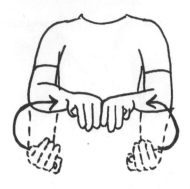

MAIN

M-hands, palm-up, arc up and touch sides, palm down
(See "IMPORTANT")

MAINSTREAM

S's at sides curve together forward, one on top of the other; move forward

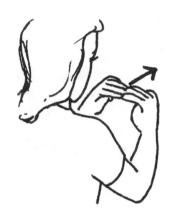

MAINTAIN

Tips of M's touch; move forward together
(See "CONTINUE")

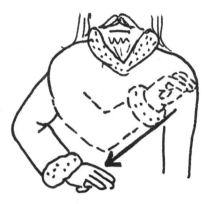

MAJESTY

M touches shoulder and then opposite hip
(See "CHRIST")

MAJOR

Right M on left M; right moves forward
(See "STRAIGHT")

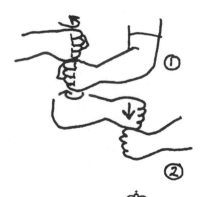

MAKE

Side of S touches on side of S; both twist to palm-in and touch again

MADE = MAKE + P. T.

MALE

Palm-down flat-M slides right across forehead

MASCULINE = MALE + -INE

MAN

Extended-A on temple, then measure height with bent hand
(See "MEN")

240

MANAGE

Palm-up A-hands move alternately forward and back, diagonally

MANE

M-hand passes over head, front to back

MANNER

Palm-down M's move side to side   (See "DO")

MANICURE

A-hand moves back and forth along edge of left fingernails

MANUAL

Sides of open hands slide inward alternately across each other's wrists

(See "HAND")

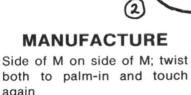

MANUFACTURE

Side of M on side of M; twist both to palm-in and touch again

(See "MAKE")

MANUSCRIPT

M writes forward on palm-up left hand

(See "WRITE")

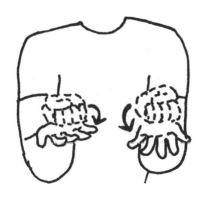

MANY

Palm-up S's spring open into 5's; repeat

MAP

M draws wavy line on back of left hand

(See "CHART")

MARBLE

M's rotate in small circles, one above the other

(See "MIX")

MARCH

With one 5-hand behind the other, swing hands sharply out and repeat

(Alt. 1 for MONTH)

(See "PARADE")

MARCH

(Alt. 2 for MONTH)
M arcs over side of vertical left hand

(See "CALENDAR")

MARGARINE

U flicks back to N off heel of open left M, twice

(See "BUTTER")

MARGIN

G thumb slides down outside of palm-in left hand

MARK

Closed thumb and fingertip jerk toward left palm

MARKET

Flat M-fingertips nod towards side of left C

(See "STORE")

MAROON

M circles on cheek

MARRY

Clasp C-hands, right on left

MARRIAGE = MARRY + -AGE

MARSHMALLOW

M-hand touches top of horizontal left index, then bottom

MARVEL

Palm - out M's make small circle; jerk slightly forward to 5's

MARVELOUS = MARVEL + -OUS
(See "FABULOUS")

MASH

Side of S drops in left palm and twists

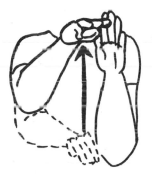

MASK

Palm-in M's before eyes move around to sides

MAST

M, palm-down, slides up vertical left arm

MASTER

M-fingertips on shoulders pivot to palm-out and drop

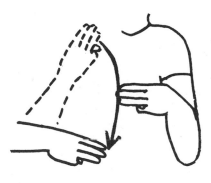

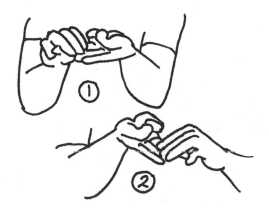

MAT

M drags across back of left hand   (See "CARPET")

MATCH ★

Palm-in M's; tip of right arcs down, striking tip of left

MATE

Both hands' M-fingers rest, palms-facing, first right on left, then left on right
(See "FRIEND")

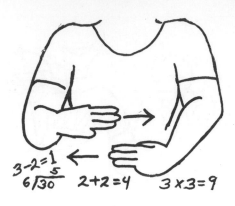

MATERIAL

Palm-up M arcs once to the right

(See "THING")

MATH

Little-finger side of palm-in right M brushes on index finger of palm-in left M twice

(See "ARITHMETIC")

MATTER

Fingertips of open M's alternately slap back and forth

(See "THOUGH")

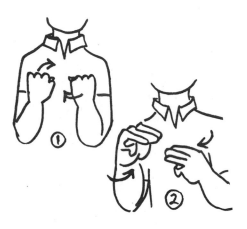

MATURE

Right M brushes inward across top of palm-in S

(See "FULL")

MATZO

Tap left elbow with side of palm-down M

(See "CRACKER")

MAXIMUM

M-hands, palm-in, twist to face each other, right above left

(See "LIMIT")

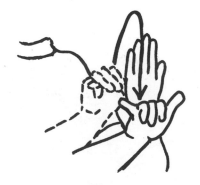

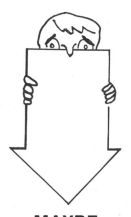

MAY

Palm-up flat hands move alternately up and down

(Alt. 1 for MONTH)

MIGHT = MAY + P. P.

MAYBE = MAY + BE

(See "BALANCE")

MAY

(Alt. 2 for MONTH)

M arcs to Y over side of vertical left hand

(See "CALENDAR")

MAYBE

May + be

MAYOR

M circles by forehead and then touches

(See "GOVERN")

MAYONNAISE

Fingers of palm-down right M brush heel of left palm toward body; repeat

(See "BUTTER")

McDONALDS

M makes the arches

ME

Index points to and touches chest

MEADOW

M on back of left hand circles out and back along left forearm

(See "GROUND")

MEAL

M circles in and up near mouth

(See "EAT")

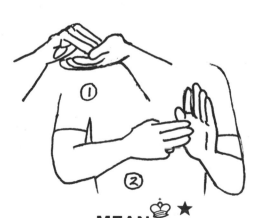

MEAN

Palm-down M touches left flat palm-up; twists and touches again

MEANT = MEAN + P. T.

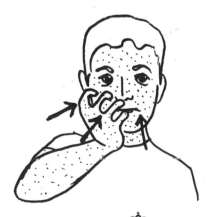

MEASLES

Claw-fingertips spot face several times

MEASURE

Palm-down Y's tap thumbtips; repeat

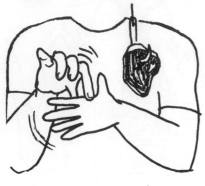

MEAT

Thumb and finger of 9 pinch side of left 5-hand; shake both hands

MECHANIC

With V-fingers, "tighten" left index; repeat

(See "WRENCH")

MEDAL

Fingers of N on left chest close on extended thumb (Pinning on medal)

MEDIC

M fingertips tap left wrist on pulse

MEDICAL = MEDIC + -AL

(See "DOCTOR")

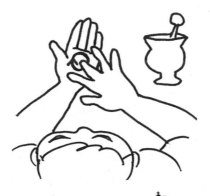

MEDICINE

Tip of bent middle finger rubs circle on left palm

MEDITATE

M circles at temple

(See "REASON")

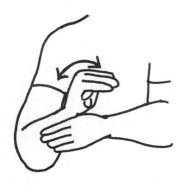

MEDIUM

Right M rocks back and forth on side of palm-in left B

(See "AVERAGE")

MEET

1-hands, palms-facing, meet
MET = MEET + P. T.

MELON

Middle finger snaps on back of left S (as if testing ripeness)

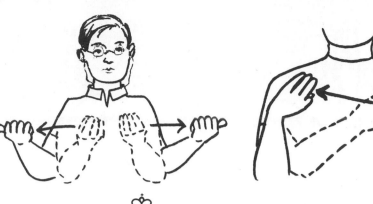

MELT ♔

Palm-up flat -O's separate, changing to palm-up A's

MEMBER ♔

M-fingers touch left shoulder, then right

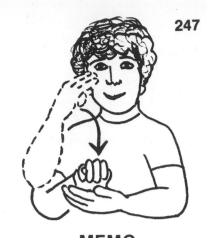

MEMO

M moves from eye to touch left palm

(See "NOTE")

MEMORIZE

Palm-in 5, middle finger on forehead; move forward and down, closing to S

MEMORY

Extended-A thumb on forehead, twist at wrist

MEN

Extended-A on temple, then measure two heights with bent hand

(See "MAN")

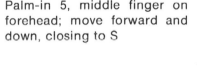

MEND

Fingertips of M's touch and right hand twists

(See "FIX")

MENORAH

Palm-in 4's touch little fingers; separate, rising to sides

(See "HANUKAH")

MENSTRUATE

Knuckles of A against cheek twice

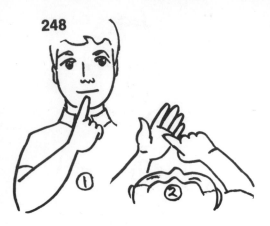

MENTION

Index below mouth drops to
touch palm-up left hand

(See "REPORT")

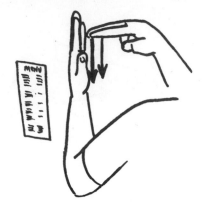

MENU

M-fingertips move down left
palm; repeat (as if scanning
menu)

MERRY

Side of M brushes up chest;
repeat

(See "HAPPY")

MESS

M's, right above left; reverse

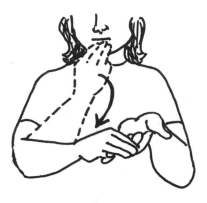

MESSAGE

Fingertips of palm-in M-hand
at mouth drop to touch left
palm-up index finger

MESSENGER = MESSAGE + -ER

(See "LETTER")

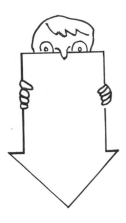

MET

Meet + P. T.

METER

Fingertips of right M slide up
and down left index finger

(See "THERMOMETER")

METAL

Palm-in M arcs right, to palm-
out, after hitting side of left
index

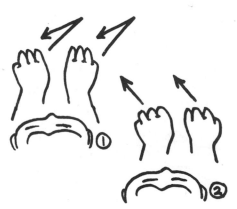

METHOD

Palm-down M's move forward,
right; return; then forward left

(See "SYSTEM")

MEXICO

Index on shoulder drops to
palm-up X

MEXICAN = MEXICO + -AN

MICE

Both index fingers brush past
nosetip twice, alternately
(See "MOUSE")

MICROPHONE

S-hand, by chin as if holding a
microphone

MICROSCOPE

Two S's, right on left, focus
microscope

MID

Fingertips of M fall on left palm

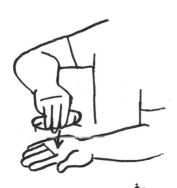

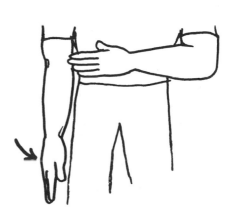

MIDDLE

Fingertips of right M circle
once over left palm, then touch
mid-palm

MIDGET

Palm-down M pats head of
midget; repeat
(See "CHILD")

MIDNIGHT

Flat right hand swings
downward, as you touch inside
of right elbow
(Can be mid + night)

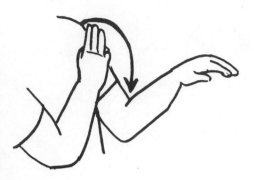

MIGHT
(Power)
M-fingertips draw muscle on left arm
(See "STRONG")

MIGHT
May + P. P.

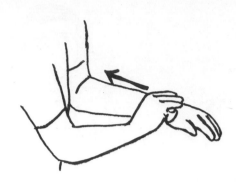

MILE
M brushes up left arm
(See "YARD")

MILITARY
Palms-in right M at left shoulder; left M at left wrist
(See "SOLDIER")

MILK
C to S-hand squeezes in a milking motion

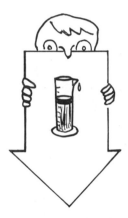

MILLILITER
(ML)
Spell M + L

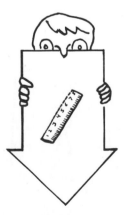

MILLIMETER
(MM)
Spell M + M

MILLION
Fingertips of M hit heel, then fingers, of left hand while both hands move forward
(See "BILLION")

MILWAUKEE
Index finger moves back and forth under lip

MIMEOGRAPH

Side of S circles near left palm
rapidly several times

(See "DITTO")

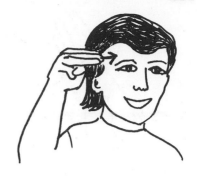

MINCE

Side of flat hand mimes
mincing action on flat left palm

MIND

Tips of M touch temple

(See "THINK")

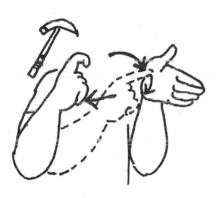

MINE

(Noun or Verb)
Index finger picks at left
vertical palm several times

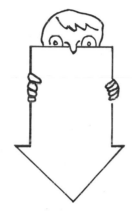

MINE

(Possessive)
My + -ne (-en)

MINIMUM

Right M over left M, right hand
moves down toward left hand

MINIMAL = MINIMUM + -AL
MINIMIZE = MINIMUM + -IZE

MINISTER

Palm-out M near head jerks
slightly forward; repeat

(See "LECTURE")

MINOR

M moves out along little-finger
side of left palm-right hand

(See "STRAIGHT")

MINUS

Side of horizontal index finger
hits on left palm-out hand

(See "NEGATIVE")

MINUTE ♔

Side of palm-out index on left palm twists to point forward

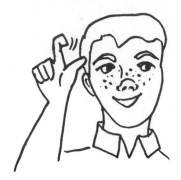

MIRROR

Hand pivots slightly toward face; repeat

MISCHIEF

Thumb on temple; wiggle index

MISCHIEVOUS = MISCHIEF + -OUS

(See "DEVIL")

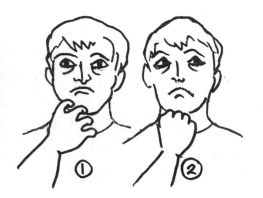

MISER

Palm-in claw-hand on chin; pull down and close to S

MISS ★

Open right hand passes left index finger and changes to S

MISS

(Title)

Fingertips of M on cheek twist forward

(See "GIRL")

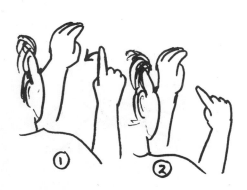

MISSION

Left M at eye-level, right vertical index behind and slightly lower; index drops to point at M

(See "AIM")

MISTAKE

Palm-in right Y taps on chin; repeat

(See "WRONG")

MISTER

Fingertips of M on temple twist forward to palm-out R

(See "HE")

MISUNDERSTAND

Palm-out V on forehead, reverse to palm-in

MITT

Flat palm of right hand draws around edge of left from index finger to little finger

MITTEN = MITT + -EN

MIX

Claw-hands circle, right above left, alternating, in the same direction

MIXTURE = MIX + -URE

(See "MARBLE")

MOAN

M at throat shakes up and out under chin

(See "GROAN")

MODEL ★

Tip of index on palm-up left, make horizontal circle together

(See "DISPLAY")

MODERN

Back of M brushes down, along left palm and up

(See "NEW")

MODIFY

M-hands, palm-to-palm, reverse positions quickly, twice   (See "CHANGE")

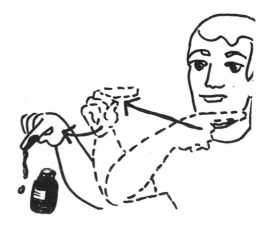

MOLASSES

Index finger brushes across chin and flicks forward, wiping

MOLE

Bent hands rest against cheeks
and "dig", flapping

MOM

M taps near chin
MOMMY = MOM + -Y

(See "MOTHER")

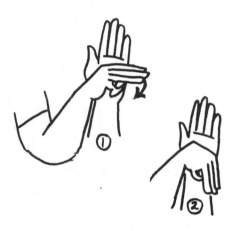

MOMENT

Side of M on left palm, twists to
point downward
(See "MINUTE")

MOMENTUM

Wrist of right M pushes left
index forward
(See "CONTINUE")

MONDAY

Palm-out M circles slightly

MONEY

Back of flat O taps left palm
twice

MONKEY

Scratch sides upwards

MONSTER

Claw-hands rise to sides of
head and claw

MONTANA

Palms-out, M's outline state

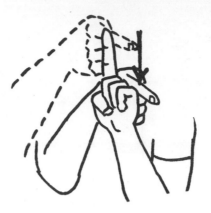

MONTH

Back of right index finger slides down back of left index finger (down the calendar page)

MOOD

M-fingers move up chest once
(See "FEEL")

MOON

One-finger C near right eye

MOOSE

Thumbs of flat hands near temples; move hands out and up   (See "DEER")

MORAL

Side of M on chest near heart, make circle and touch again
(See "CHARACTER")

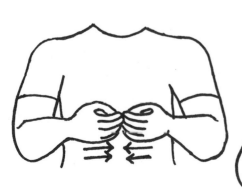

MORE

Palm-in flat 0's bounce tips together twice
(See "EXTRA")

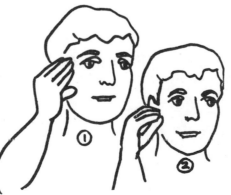

MORMON

Right hand on cheekbone closes to flat O; repeat

MORN

Left hand on right arm by elbow, right palm-up hand rises

MORNING = MORN + -ING

255

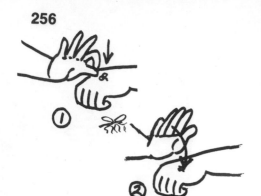

MOSQUITO

9 touches back of left hand; slap hand

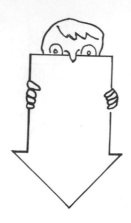

MOST

More + -est

MOTEL

Right cheek rests on back of left hand; right M under palm

(See "BED")

MOTH

Palms-in N's, crossed at wrists, flutter forward

MOTHER

Thumb of palm-left 5 taps jaw near chin

(See "MOM")

MOTIVE

Palm-out M's palms push forward; repeat

(See "ENCOURAGE")

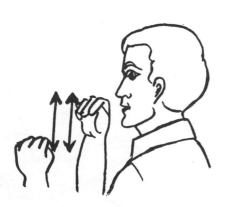

MOTOR

Right M behind left M, move up and down alternately, like pistons

(See "ENGINE")

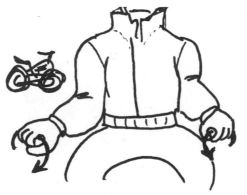

MOTORCYCLE

S-hands hold handlebars and twist inward (rev. up)

MOUND

M arcs through air from left heel to fingertips

(See "AMOUNT")

MOUNTAIN
(Alt. 1)
Right hand draws mountain-tops; left stays still

MOUNTAIN
(Alt. 2)
Right fist raps on left wrist; then push flat hands upward to the right

MOUSE ♔
Index finger flicks past tips of nose; repeat

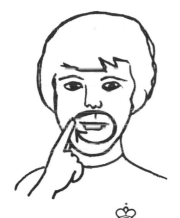

MOUTH ♔
Index circles mouth once
(See "ORAL")

MOVE
Palm-down flat-O's arc to right

MOVIE
Heel of palm-out 5 rests on side of left hand; 5 waves slightly, side-to-side
(See "FILM")

MOW
Push mower several times

MRS.
M on cheek twists forward to palm-out S
(See "GIRL")

MUCH ♔
Cupped 5 hands face each other; arc apart

MUD

M flaps under chin

(See "DIRT")

MUFF

Palms-in, right flat hand moves behind left as if into muff

MUFFIN

Fingertips of flat O on left palm; open to claw-hand

MUG ★

Side of X on left palm; rises off

MULE

Thumb of flat hand on temple, flap hand forward twice

(See "HORSE")

MULTIPLY

Back of palm-in V brushes sideways across left palm

(See "ADD")

MUMPS

Tap claw-hands on sides of neck twice

MURDER

Tips of open M twist diagonally under left palm

(See "KILL")

MUSCLE

Index finger pokes left bicep muscle twice

MUSEUM

Palm-out M's draw house
(See "HOUSE")

MUSHROOM

Bent right hand caps left flat-0

MUSIC

Fingertips pointing toward left palm, flat hand arcs side-to-side behind palm

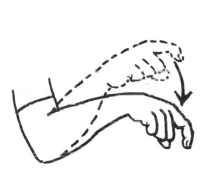

MUST

Palms-down X jerks sharply downward once
(See "NECESSARY")

MUSTACHE

G's on upper lip move sideways to extended-A's

MUSTARD

M-fingertips circle several times on left palm

MY

Flat hand palm on chest
MINE = MY + -EN

MYSTERY

M moves down from chin to under left hand
(See "HIDE")

MYTH

Right M arcs twice off forehead
(See "IDEA")

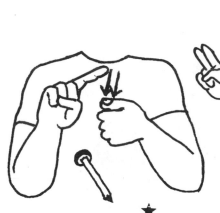

NAG ★

N-fingertips peck vertical left index twice

(See "PECK")

NAIL ★

Index fingertip taps left thumbnail

NAIVE

Palm-in H-fingers cross before chin, open outwards to palm-out   (See "INNOCENT")

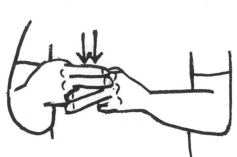

NAKED

N-fingers brush off back of left A-hand

(See "BARE")

NAME ♔

Right H taps on left H twice at right angles

NAP

Open N moves down in front of face, cheek resting on left hand

(See "BED")

NAPKIN

Palm-in A brushes off chin several times

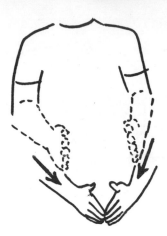

NARROW

Hands converge forward to touch fingertips

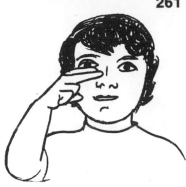

NASAL

N touches side of nose

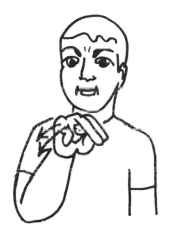

NASTY

N jerks out twice from under chin; repeat

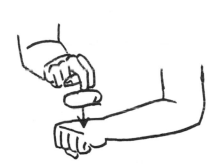

NATION

N circles over, then drops on back of left S

(See "REPUBLIC")

NATURE ♔

Back of A against left palm; A twists down and out under palm to palm-down

NATURAL = NATURE + -AL

NAUGHTY

Open N on mouth swings outward and twists downward

(See "BAD")

NAUSEA

Claw-hand circles on stomach

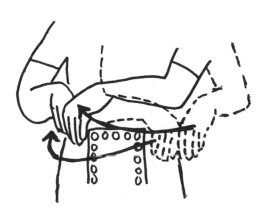

NAVY

B-hands move together from left to right side of waist (buttoning pants)

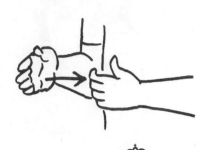

NEAR

Palm of right hand moves nearer back of left hand

NEAT

Heel of N slides across left palm

(See "CLEAN")

NECESSARY

Palm-down N jerks down sharply; repeat

(See "SHALL")

NECK

Fingertips touch neck

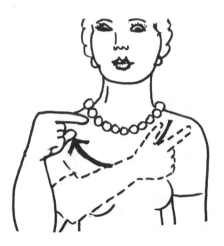

NECKLACE

G-hand outlines necklace on chest

NECTAR

N slides down back of left palm-in S

(See "JUICE")

NECTARINE

N, palm-out to palm-in, circles left S

(See "APRICOT")

NEED

Palm-down N jerks down

(See "MUST")

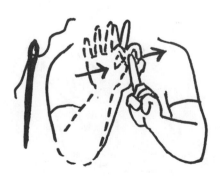

NEEDLE

9-hand threads left fingertip

NEGATIVE

Side of N strikes palm

(See "MINUS")

NEGLECT

Open N flips down and to side from nose

(See "IGNORE")

NEGOTIATE

Index taps left palm each time both move forward and back

NEIGHBOR

Palms together, first 2 H-fingers rest, first right on left, then left on right

(See "FRIEND")

NEITHER

N swings off left L thumb, then E off fingertip

(See "THEN")

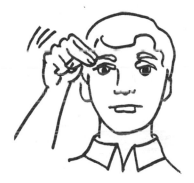

NEPHEW

N shakes near temple

(See "AUNT")

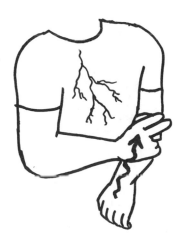

NERVE

N wiggles up left arm (tracing nerve)

NERVOUS

Palm-down 5's shake

NEST

N's, touching, palms up, swing upward to face each other

(See "JAR")

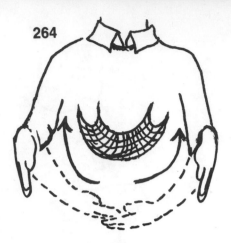

NET

Right 4 on left 4, draw "U" shape

(See "JAR")

NEUTER

N at temple and at jaw

NEUTRAL = NEUTER + -AL

(See "PARENT")

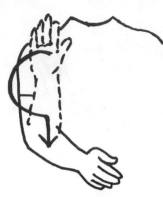

NEVER

Tip of open hand draws large question-mark arc

NEW

Palm-up right hand arcs down, brushes across left palm, and arcs up slightly

NEWS = NEW + S
NEWSPAPER = NEW + S + PAPER

NEW ORLEANS

O brushes off left palm; repeat

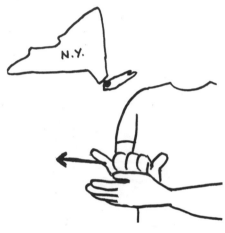

NEW YORK

Palm-down Y slides off left palm

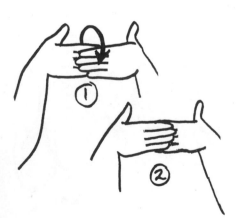

NEXT

Flat hands, palms in; back hand jumps to front

NIBBLE

Thumb + N fingers nibble left index several times

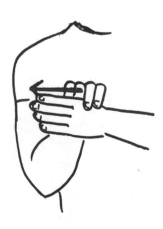

NICE

First 2 fingers of N slides along side of left hand

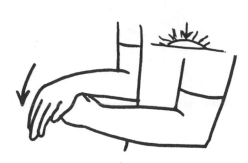

NICKEL
Middle finger of 5 taps temple
once, and pulls away
(See "CENT")

NIECE
N shakes near jaw
(See "AUNT")

NIGHT
Drop bent hand over edge of
left

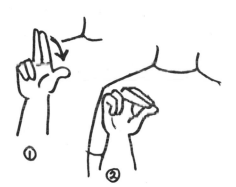

NIP
Thumb and 2 fingers nip left
index finger

NO
First two fingers close onto
thumb

NOBLE
Palm-in N circles, then touches
left shoulder
(See "CHARACTER")

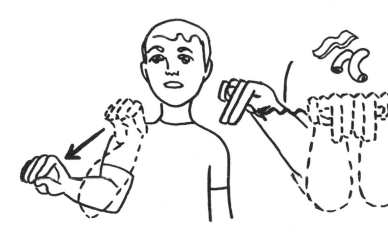

NOISE
Palm-out N shakes up to ear
NOISY = NOISE + -Y
(See "SOUND")

NONE
Palm-out O moves diagonally
right
(See "NOTHING")

NOODLE
Palm-down N's separate and to
sides
(See "SPAGHETTI")

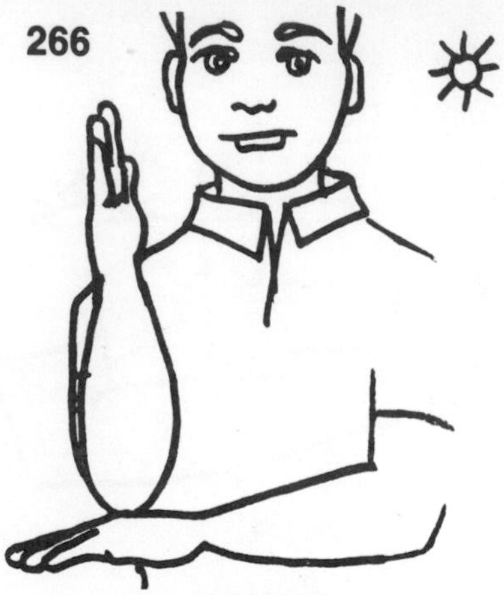

NOON

Right vertical arm rests elbow on back of left hand

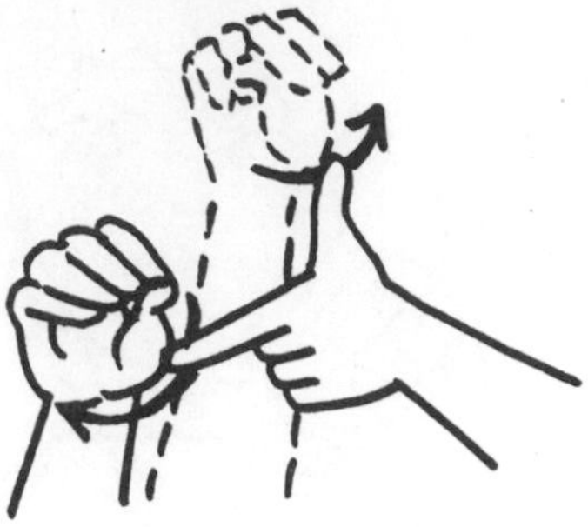

NOR

N off left L-thumb; O off fingertip of index

(See "THEN")

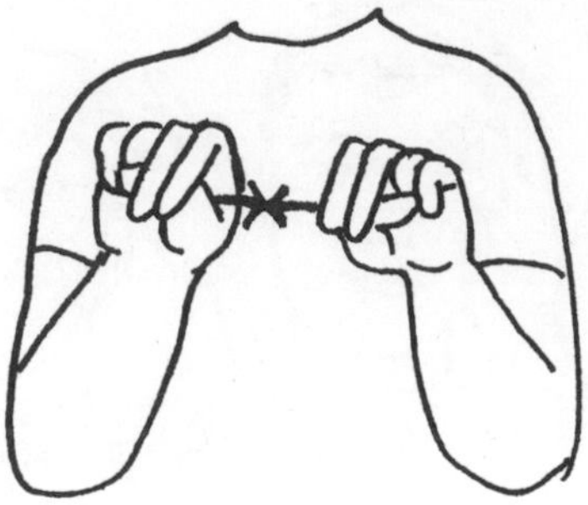

NORM

Palm-out N-hands tap together

NORMAL = NORM + -AL

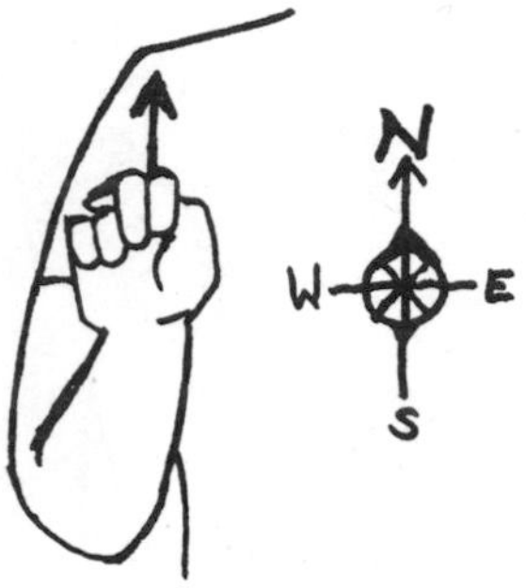

NORTH

Palm-out N moves up

NORTHERN = NORTH + ER + N

(See "UP")

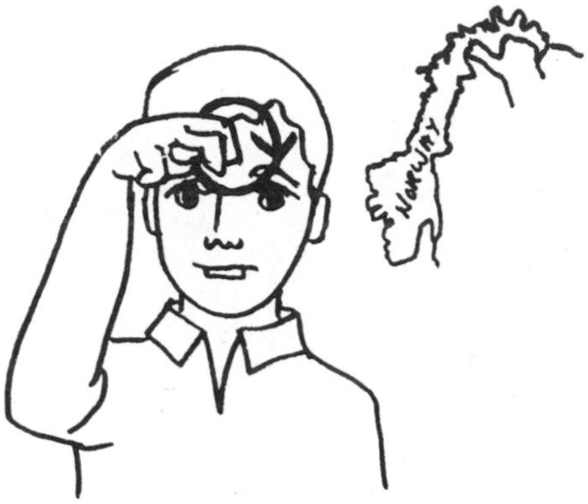

NORWAY

(U.S. Sign)

N circles near forehead

NORWEGIAN = NORWAY + -AN

(See "DENMARK")

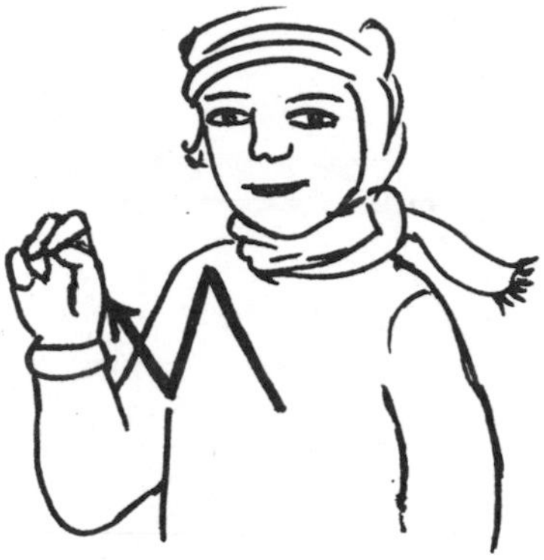

NORWAY

(Norwegian Sign)

Palm-out N draws mountains

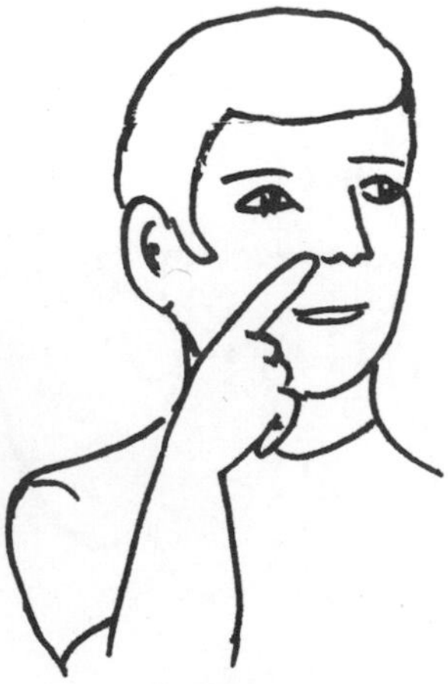

NOSE

Point to nose

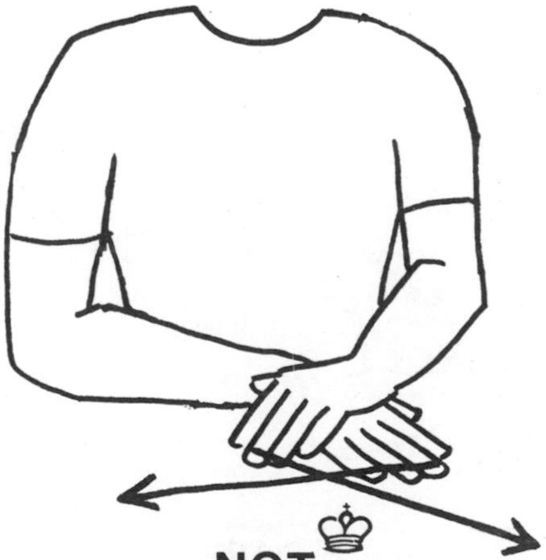

NOT

Palm-down flat hands cross at wrists, separate sideways

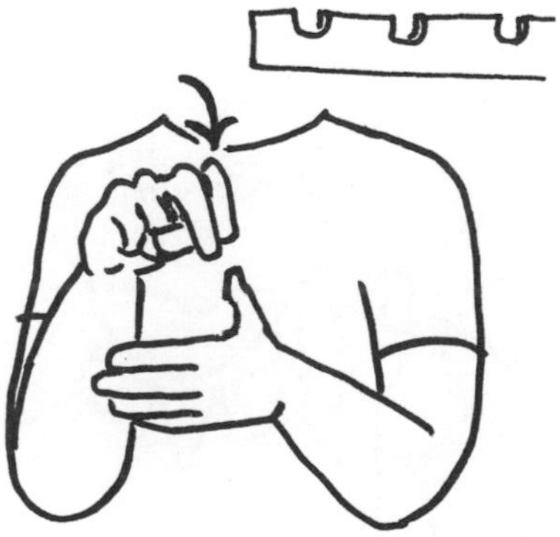

NOTCH

N jerks down toward palm-in left hand

(See "MARK")

NOTE

Palm-in H at eye twists out and
down to touch left palm

NOTICE = NOTE + -ICE

NOTHING

Palm-out O moves right,
opening sharply

(See "NONE")

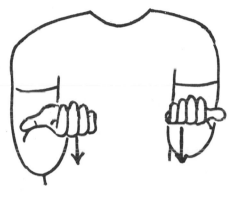

NOUN

Fingertips of N tap side of left H
index

(See "WORD")

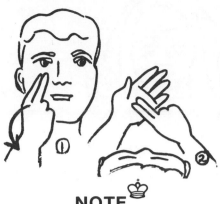

NOVEMBER

(Alt. 1)
N shakes down from under
chin in 3 steps (3 syllables)

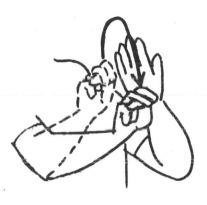

NOVEMBER

(Alt. 2)
N arcs over left vertical hand at
side

(See "CALENDAR")

NOW

Palm-up bent hands slightly
drop

(See "IMMEDIATE")

NUCLEUS

N circles and drops on left
palm

(See "MIDDLE")

NUDE

N brushes off back of left U

(See "BARE")

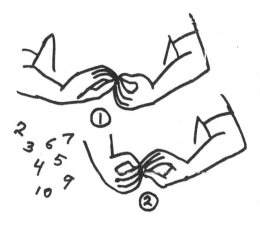

NUMBER

Flat O-tips touch, one palm-up,
one palm-down; reverse;
repeat

NUMERAL = NUMBER + -AL

(See "DIGIT")

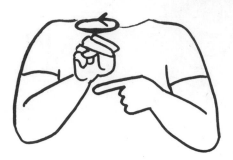

NUMERATOR

N circles above left index

(See "FRACTION")

NUN

N circles over face

(See "VIRGIN")

NURSE

N fingertips tap left pulse twice

NURSERY = **NURSE** + **-ER** + **-Y**

(See "DOCTOR")

NUT

Thumb flips out from under teeth

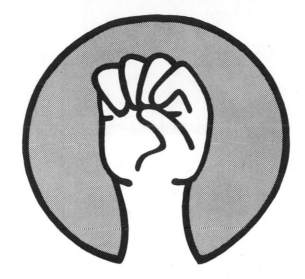

OAR

O-hands row

OAT

O brushes up through left C-hand

(See "GRAIN")

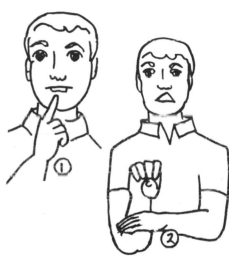

OATH

Index at chin, to palm-out O against left horizontal wrist

(See "PROMISE")

OBEY

Flat O's, left near forehead, right O near chin, both drop down and open

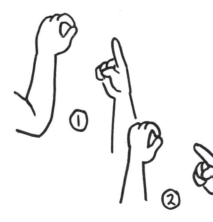

OBJECT

(Noun)

Right index behind left O, finger turns down to point at O

OBJECTIVE = OBJECT + -IVE

(See "AIM")

OBJECT

(Verb)

Side of O hits chest; repeat

OBJECTION = OBJECT + -TION

(See "COMPLAIN")

OBLIGATE

Right O taps back of left hand
OBLIGATION = OBLIGATE + -TION
(See "WORK")

OBSERVE

Palms-facing, O's circle alternately before face

OBSTACLE

Side of right flat hand strikes thumb-side of palm-down left hand
(See "IMPAIR")

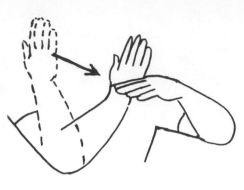

OBVIOUS

Palm-out O's arc sideways, up and out
(See "CLEAR")

OCCUPY

Palm-out O touches left wrist
OCCUPATION = OCCUPY + -TION
OCCUPANT = OCCUPY + -ANT
(See "SET")

OCCUR

Palm-up O's twist to palm-down
(See "HAPPEN")

OCEAN

Palm-down O's move wave-like up and down forward, opening to 5's
(See "SEA")

OCTOBER
(Alt. 1)
O's before eyes, circle back to sides
(See "MASK")

OCTOBER
(Alt. 2)
O arcs over side of left vertical hand
(See "CALENDAR")

OCTOPUS

O sits on left 5-hand, 5 doing "push-ups" from flat-0's to 5's

(See "SQUID")

ODD

Palm-left O arcs in front of nose to palm-down O

(See "STRANGE")

ODOR

O-hand brushes upward at nose

(See "SMELL")

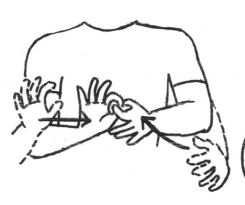

OF

Open hands approach and link thumbs and index fingers of 9's

OFF

Right palm on back of left hand; lift off

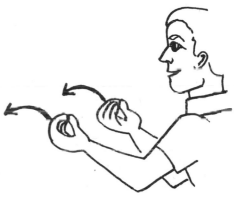

OFFER

Palm-up O's, side by side, arc forward

(See "SUGGEST")

OFFICE

Right O taps right shoulder

OFFICER = OFFICE + -ER

OFTEN

Right bent fingertips touch heel of left palm, then moves to fingertips

(See "FREQUENT")

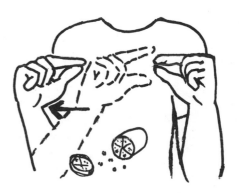

OKRA

Right G-fingers pull off left index and thumb; repeat

OIL

Thumb and middle finger grasp side of left O; slide down and off and shut; repeat

(See "GRAVY")

OLD 👑

C-hand at chin, moves down, closing to S

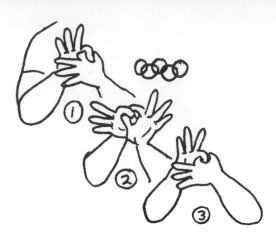

OLYMPICS

9-fingers link alternately three times in the form of a triangle (olympic rings)

OMELET

O's strike fingertips and fall apart

(See "EGG")

OMIT

O's throw down to side, opening palm-down

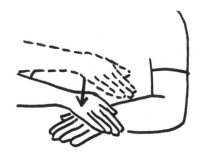

ON

Right palm touches back of left hand

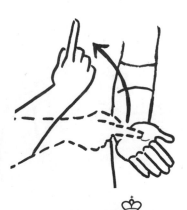

ONCE 👑

Tip of right index finger on left palm twists to pointing upward

ONION

Right X twists at corner of eye; repeat

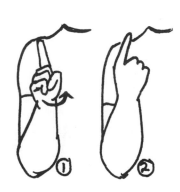

ONLY

Palm-out index twists to palm-in

OPAQUE

V from eye moves forward, is
stopped by left hand

OPEN ♔ ★

Flat hands, palms down and
sides touching, twist apart,
palms facing up

OPERA

O arcs out twice from mouth
(See "SING")

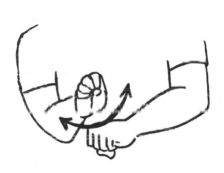

OPERATE

Palm-out O arcs side-to-side,
hitting back of left S
(See "BUSY")

OPINION

O arcs out near forehead
(See "IDEA")

OPOSSUM

Little fingers of right hand
hang from little finger of left
hand

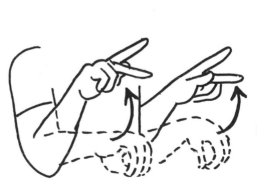

OPPORTUNE

Palm-down O's change to P's
arcing upward
**OPPORTUNITY =
OPPORTUNE + -ITY**
(See "ALLOW")

OPPOSE ♔

Indexes point at each other;
hands jerk apart
OPPOSITE = OPPOSE + -ITE

OPTION

O moves back from index of
palm-in left V
(See "CHOOSE")

OR

Palm-out O off left L-thumb,
then off fingertip

(See "THEN")

ORAL

O circles before mouth

(See "MOUTH")

ORANGE

S squeezes in front of chin;
repeat

ORBIT

Index circles left S-hand

(See "PLANET")

ORCHARD

Elbow of palm-out O on back
of left hand; twist, moving
slightly right

(See "TREE")

ORCHESTRA

O's swing apart, then together;
repeat (conducting the
orchestra)

(See "CONDUCT")

ORDER ★

Palm-in index on chin twists to
palm-out; jerks to point
forward

(See "COMMAND")

ORDINANCE

Palm-out O on fingertips then
on heel of vertical left palm

(See "LAW")

ORGANIZE

Palm-out O-hands circle
horizontally to palm-in
**ORGANIZATION =
ORGANIZE + -TION**

(See "CLASS")

ORIENT

Right O circles left vertical index

ORIENTATION = ORIENT + -TION

(See "ATMOSPHERE")

ORIGIN

Right index fingertip touches wrist of palm-out left O, then twists to palm-in

ORIGINAL = ORIGIN + -AL
ORIGINATE = ORIGIN + -ATE

(See "START")

ORPHAN

O at temple, then at jaw

(See "PARENT")

ORTHODONTIC

Fingertips of O tap at side of mouth

ORTHODONTIST =
ORTHODONTIC + -IST

(See "DENTIST")

OSTRICH

O-hand nods, resting elbow on back of open hand

(See "GULL")

OTHER

Palm-down A-hand, twist over to palm-up

ANOTHER = AN + OTHER

OUGHT

Palm-out O twists to palm-in

(See "SEEM")

OUNCE

O rocks on index finger of H-hand

(See "WEIGH")

OUR

O, on right side of chest, circles to left side

OURS = OUR + -S

(Can be made with open hand)

OUT 👑

Right O-hand pulls out from palm-left C

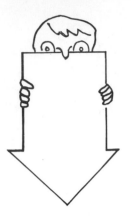

OUTFIT = OUT + FIT

OUTSIDE = OUT + SIDE

OUTWARD = OUT + WARD

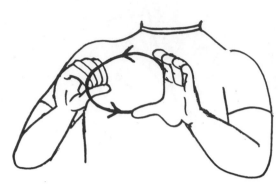

OVAL

O circles behind left C

OVEN 👑

Circle O under left palm

OVER

Palm-down right hand circles over back of left

OVERALLS

O's circle on chest, change to palm-in A's, then to L's, dropping

OWE

Index-fingertip taps heel of palm-up left O; repeat
(See "DEBT")

OWL

C's at eyes

OWN

C-hands approach each other
and link as O-hands

OYSTER

Right hand cups over left palm-
right O; flaps up and down

PACK ★

Flat O's alternately "pack" circularly

PAD ★

Middle finger of P taps pad of left thumb

PADDLE ★

P-hands paddle at side

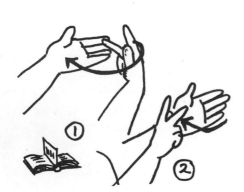

PAGE

P turns page on left palm
(See "RECIPE")

PAIL

P-hand, at side, rises
(See "BUCKET")

PAIN

P-hands point at each other, twist toward each other; repeat
(See "HURT")

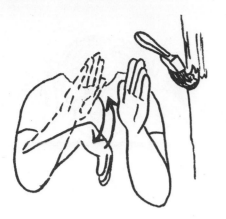

PAINT

Right flat hand fingertips brush up and down vertical left palm

PAIR

Thumb and finger of right hand close left-hand P-fingers together

(See "COUPLE")

PAJAMA

Middle fingers of P's press to chest and brush down; repeat

PAJAMAS = PAJAMA + -S

(See "DRESS")

PAL

L-thumb slides from left side of chin to right side

PALACE

P-hands face each other, arc up several times, closer together each time

(See "CASTLE")

PAMPHLET

P slides along edge of palm-right flat left hand

(See "MAGAZINE")

PAN

Middle P-finger outlines pan-rim and handle

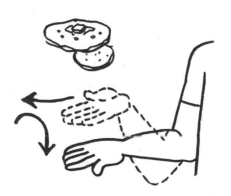

PANCAKE

Flat hand moves out and inverts

(See "FLAPJACK")

PANDA

Palm-in P circles eye

PANEL ★

Palm-out P slides toward elbow from left wrist

(See "BOARD")

PANIC

P's, palm-out, shake downward, slightly, toward body

(See "AFRAID")

PANSY

P middle-finger on each side of nose

(See "FLOWER")

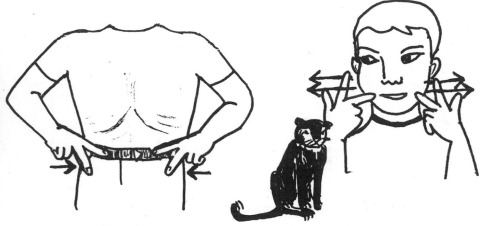

PANT ♛ ★

P's tap at waist twice

PANTS = PANT + -S

PANTHER

3-hands move from side of mouth to side; repeat

(See "CAT")

PAPER ♛

Palm-down right heel brushes across palm-up left heel slightly to left; repeat

PARACHUTE

Palm-up O under open hand swing together downwards

PARADE

P's, left behind right, palm-down, jerk away from body in parallel upward jerks

(See "MARCH")

PARADISE

Right P passes under and around left P above head; P's separate

(See "HEAVEN")

PARADOX

Parallel P's move to cross indexes

(See "CONFLICT")

PARAGRAPH

Thumb and fingertips of C tap vertical left palm; repeat

PARAKEET

Tips of bent index and thumb tap at side of mouth

(See "BIRD")

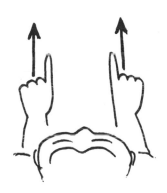

PARALLEL

Palm-down indexes move forward

(See "HALL")

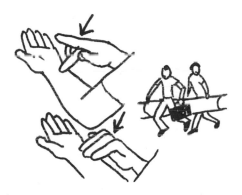

PARAMEDIC

Middle finger of P taps on pulse, then fingers of M tap

(See "DOCTOR")

PARANOID

P-hand stationary, middle P finger flexes and scratches temple; repeat

(See "SUSPECT")

PARAPROFESSIONAL

Middle finger of P taps base of thumb of palm-right left hand, then slides off finger + -ion + -al

PARASITE

Right P middle finger rests on left index; both drop slightly

(See "DEPEND")

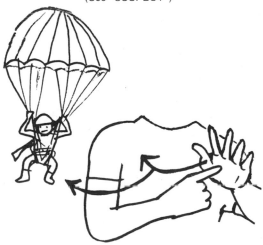

PARATROOPER

Left 5-hand on right index finger, both swing down

PARDON

Middle P-fingertip brushes off
left fingertips; repeat

(See "EXCUSE")

PARE

Back of H brushes inward off
back of left H-hand as if paring

PARENT ♛

Middle fingertip of P-hand
touches temple, then jaw

PARENTHESIS

P's draw parentheses

PARK ★

Palm-left 3 set on left palm

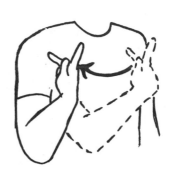

PARLIAMENT

Middle finger of P touches left,
then right, shoulder

(See "MEMBER")

PARROT

Hand beside chin, bent index
and thumb tap each other

(See "BIRD")

PARSNIP

Index finger slices side of left
P; repeat

(See "TOMATO")

PART ★

Middle fingertip of P draws arc
on palm-up left hand

(See "SOME")

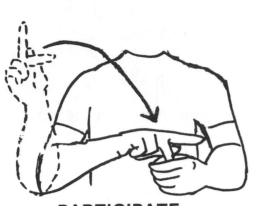

PARTICIPATE

Middle finger of Parcs into left left O

(See "JOIN")

PARTICULAR

Pull up index of left palm-out P

(See "EXCEPT")

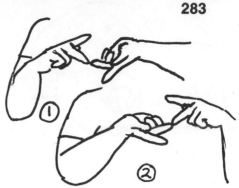

PARTNER

Middle fingers of P's, first right on left, then left on right

(See "FRIEND")

PARTY

P's swing at wrists from side to side rapidly

(See "PLAY")

PASS

Palms facing, right A-hand passes left A

PAST - PASS + T

PASSED = PASS + P. T.

PASSENGER

P middle-finger rides forward on thumb of left C

(See "RIDE")

PASSION

Palm-in C moves down middle of chest several times

(See "HUNGER")

PASTE

Palm-up H turns to palm-down; fingers sweep across left palm

(See "GLUE")

PASTRAMI

Right palm slices side of thumb of left P; repeat

(See "SLICE")

PASTRY

Middle finger of P circles on the back of palm-in S

(See "DOUGH").

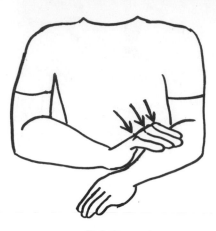

PAT

Pat left arm several times

PATH

Palm-down P's move forward, weaving slightly side-to-side

(See "WAY")

PATIENT

Side of A moves down lips and chin

PATIENCE = PATIENT + -ENCE

(See "TOLERATE")

PATIO

Palm-down P arcs out from horizontal left arm, circling back to fingers (outlining patio)

PATROL

C outlines patrol belt

PAUSE

Palm-down P behind palm-up left hand; flutter left fingers

(See "WAIT")

PAVE

Palm-down right P circles over back of horizontal left hand

PAVEMENT = PAVE + -MENT

PAW

Middle finger of P cuts off left hand at wrist

(See "FOOT")

PAY

Middle finger of P on left palm;
flip up and out

PAID = **PAY** + **P. T.**

PEA

P-index taps across left index

(See "BEAN")

PEACE

P-hands, crossed at chin;
separate downwards

(See "QUIET")

PEACH

5 to flat-O, palm-in,
strokes cheek; repeat

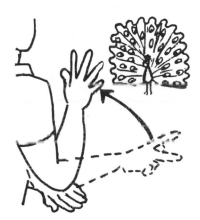

PEACOCK

Right elbow on back of left
hand, palm-down P rises and
opens to 5 (like tail)

PEAK

Index fingers rise to touch

(See "CLIMAX")

PEANUT

P-index and then thumb of A
jerk from under teeth

(See "NUT")

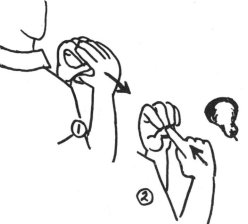

PEAR

Grasp left flat-O; hand slides
off into flat-O, changes to
index and touches left fingers

PEBBLE

Palm-up P taps back of left S

(See "STONE")

PECAN

Index of P flicks from under front teeth

(See "NUT")

PECK

Index and thumb peck at left index finger

(See "NAG")

PEDDLE

Palm-down P's shake out and up twice

(See "SELL")

PEEK

Peek through P-fingers

PEEL

(Alt. 1)
P-middle finger, twisting outward, slides down back of left S-hand and fingers

PEEL

(Alt. 2)
Right 9 peels from back of palm-down left hand

PEN

Middle fingertip of P writes on left palm

(See "WRITE")

PENCIL

Thumb and index finger at mouth, then write on left palm

(See "WRITE")

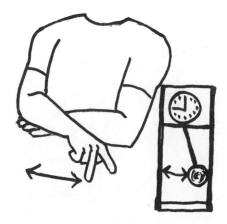

PENDULUM

P-arm down; swing it on the edge of left flat hand

PENETRATE

Index thrusts through middle and third fingers of left hand

PENGUIN

Inside of wrists on hips, hands bent back, tilt body from side to side

PENIS

Right index points down, wrist on horizontal left index; wag slightly up and down

PENNANT

P waves in breeze, left index on arm

(See "FLAG")

PENNY

Middle finger of P taps temple, moves out, then shakes

(See "CENT")

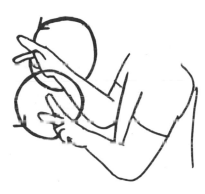

PEOPLE

Palm-out P's circle alternately up and down and forward

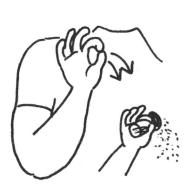

PEPPER

Thumb-side of 9-hand sprinkles

PEPPERMINT

Middle finger of P on chin; move out to M

PERCENT

O moves diagonally up to right, then down

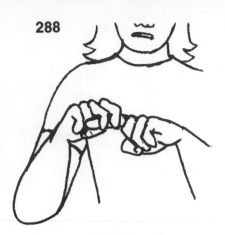

PERCH

Right bent fingers perch on left index

(See "SIT")

PERFECT

Right P circles, facing left P, then touches middle fingertips

(See "EXACT")

PERFORM

P's, palm-out; backs brush alternately down chest

(See "ACT")

PERFUME

9-hand at side of neck tips bottle onto neck

PERHAPS

Palm-down P pivots several times side-to-side

PERIOD

P circles forward once near left palm, then touches palm

(See "HOUR")

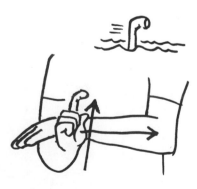

PERISCOPE

X rises outside left forearm and moves slowly toward elbow

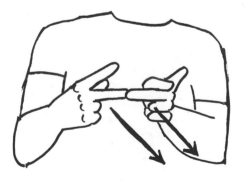

PERMANENT

Middle fingers of P's touch, and both move forward

(See "CONTINUE")

PERMIT

Palm-down P's twist to palm-out

PERMISSION = PERMIT + -TION

(See "ALLOW")

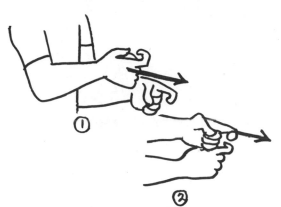

PERSECUTE

Right X hits forward off top of left X, then left X off right X

(See "TORTURE")

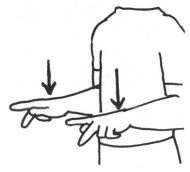

PERSON

Palm-down P's move straight down

PERSONALITY

P circles clockwise then touches on left shoulder

(See "CHARACTER")

PERSPECTIVE

P swings from eye in arc halfway to left P

PERSUADE

Palms facing, X-hands jerk forward twice

(See "URGE")

PERVERT

P's touch forehead and stomach, twisting slightly

(See "SICK")

PEST

P rides forward on wiggling left fingers

(See "ANT")

PET ★

Pet back of left hand

(See "TAME")

PHILADELPHIA

P arcs sharply down to right

(See "CHICAGO")

PHILOSOPHY

P nods down near center of forehead; repeat

(See "WISE")

PHOTO

Side of P moves from cheek to palm of left hand

(See "PICTURE")

PHOTOGRAPH

Right P arcs back against left palm-out palm

PHRASE

Middle P-fingertips shake apart sideways

(See "SENTENCE")

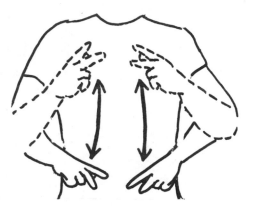

PHYSICAL

P-hands on chest and then on ribs

(See "BODY")

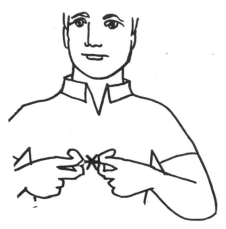

PHYSICS

Bent-V's bump several times

(See "ELECTRIC")

PIANO

Wiggling fingers play piano up and down scales

PICCOLO

Palm-in fingers play back and forth on left index

PICK ★

Palm-down G-hand "picks up" to palm-out 9-hand

PICKLE

Index of G-hand touches chin,
then shakes outward

PICNIC

Palm-in P's circle up towards
mouth alternately
(There are many local signs for
this word)
(See "BANQUET")

PICTURE

C moves from side of eye to
palm of left hand

PIE

Side of right hand draws an X
on left palm (cutting pie)

PIECE

Middle finger of P arcs down,
hitting side of left index
(See "CHIP")

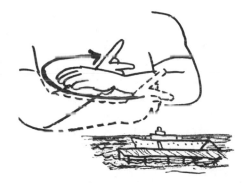

PIER

P circles left hand and arm,
starting at outside
(See "DOCK")

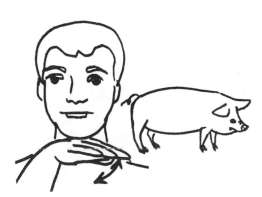

PIG

Fingers together, hand flaps
under chin
(See "HOG")

PIGEON

At chin, close index finger of P
to middle finger; repeat
(See "BIRD")

PIGLET

Right hand palm-down under
chin, flap fingers together,
then drop slightly to stop
above palm-up left hand

PILE

P outlines a pile in left palm
(See "AMOUNT")

PILGRIM

Middle fingertips of P's on chest move to side, then up chest

PILL

Thumb and finger flick toward mouth (popping pill in)
(See "VITAMIN")

PILLOW

Rest head on back of left hand; with right pat underside of invisible pillow
(See "BED")

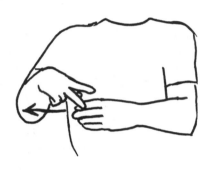

PILOT

Right P middle-finger on index of left open hand, both move diagonally forward
(See "LEAD")

PIMPLE

Index finger flicks repeatedly off thumb as hand moves around face
(See "MEASLES")

PIN

9-hand "sticks" two invisible pins in right shoulder

PINAFORE

4's at side of chest curve down body (ruffles on pinafore)

PINCH

Thumb slips past tip of index while resting on back of left hand (takes a pinch)

PINEAPPLE

Middle finger of P twists at corner of mouth

(See "APPLE")

PINGPONG

Right wrist swings A-hand from side to side (holding paddle)

PINK

Middle finger of P brushes twice down chin

(See "RED,")

PINT

P passes down to T through C

(See "GALLON")

PIONEER

Middle finger of P from eye arcs along left palm and forward

(See "INSPECT")

PIPE ★

Thumb of Y at corner of mouth

PIRATE

Hand covers right eye from above

PITCH

P throws forward from near shoulder

PITCHER = **PITCH** + **-ER (Person)**

(See "THROW")

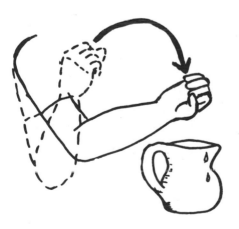

PITCHER

S-hand pours

PITTSBURGH

9 index and thumb brush down right chest rapidly several times

PITY

Right middle finger strokes the air, hand arcing up and down

PIXIE

P's swing off shoulders to sides

(See "ANGEL")

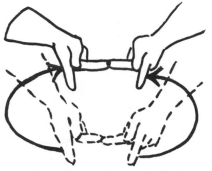

PIZZA

P draws a triangle above left palm

PLACE

P-tips touch ahead of you, circle, then touch nearer you

PLAGIARIZE

P at left elbow moves along arm toward wrist

(See "STEAL")

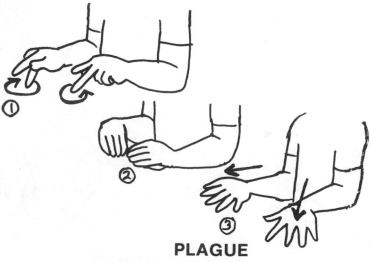

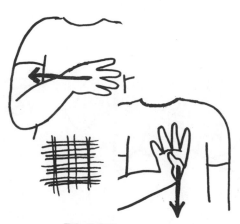

PLAGUE

P's circle, change to flat-O's, spread to 5's with move outward

(See "EPIDEMIC")

PLAID

With 4-hand, draw plaid on chest, palm-in across; palm-out down

(See "SCOT")

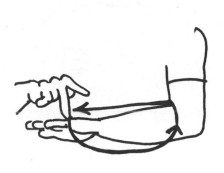

PLAIN

Middle finger of P on back of
left hand circles out and back
to arm, along arm to hand
(See "GROUND")

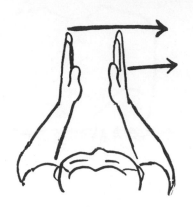

PLAN

Parallel flat hands, palms-
facing, move to right

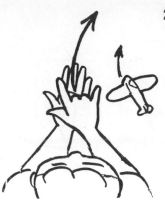

PLANE ★

Palm-down L + I on left palm,
move right hand forward
slightly

PLANET

P vertically circles around
left S
(See "WORLD")

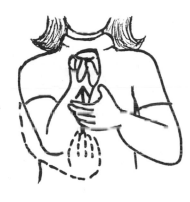

PLANT ★

Flat-O "grows" through C like a
plant into palm-out P
(See "GROW")

PLASTIC

Grip middle finger of left P and
flex back and forth
(See "FLEX")

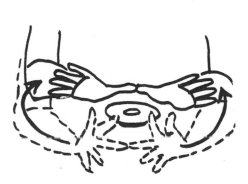

PLATE ★

Middle fingers touch; outline
plate with palms, touch thumbs
(See "DISH")

PLAY ♔ ★

Y-hands face each other;
shake

PLEASE

Palm rubs on chest in circle
PLEASANT = PLEASE + -ANT
PLEASURE = PLEASE + -URE

(See "APPRECIATE")

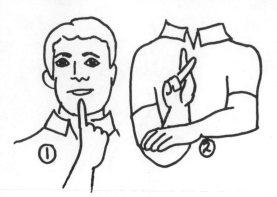

PLEDGE

Index at chin to palm-out P on back of left hand

(See "PROMISE")

PLENTY

Fingers of palm-down 5 on top of left S, move off and forward, fingers fluttering

PLIERS

Invisible pliers "tighten" left index

PLOW

Side of flat hand slides along left palm forward to palm-up

PLUG

Right index and middle finger plug onto vertical left index

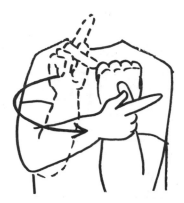

PLUM

Middle finger of right P slices around left palm-in S-hand

(See "APRICOT")

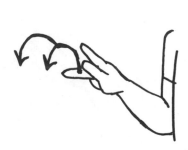

PLURAL

P middle fingertip points at three things in succession, moving right

PLUS

Index fingers form plus sign

(See "POSITIVE")

PNEUMONIA

Fingertips of bent hands rub up and down chest

POCKET ★

Right hand slides into left C wherever pocket is located

POEM

P arcs behind left palm, ending in palm-out M

(See "MUSIC")

POET

P arcs behind left palm, ending in palm-out T

(See "MUSIC")

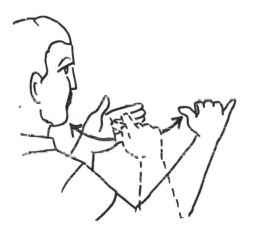

POETRY

P arcs behind left palm, ending in palm-out Y

(See "MUSIC")

POINT

Middle fingertip of P moves to left index fingertip

(See "PRECISE")

POISON

P middle finger rubs in circle on left palm

(See "MEDICINE")

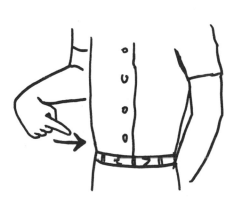

POKE ★

Index pokes self in side

POLAND

A-thumb flicks off nose-tip; repeat

POLISH = POLAND + -ISH

POLE

Palm-in 9's separate, vertically

(See "TUBE")

POLICE

Thumb and index finger show
badge on shoulder

POLICY

P on left fingers, then Y on heel,
of flat hand

(See "LAW")

POLISH

(Verb)
Shaking, P-hand rises off back
of left hand

(See "SHINE")

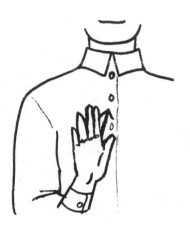

POLITE

Side of thumb of palm-left 5-
hand taps chest

POLITIC

P circles once near temple,
then touches temple

(See "GOVERN")

POLLUTE

P wiggles under chin

(See "DIRT")

PONCHO

Flat hands brush off shoulders
and out

(See "DRESS")

POND

Middle fingers of P's touch,
shake forward in a circle, touch
again   (See "LAKE")

PONDER

Middle finger of P circles on
forehead

(See "REASON")

PONY

Side of P at temple nods from wrist

(See "HORSE")

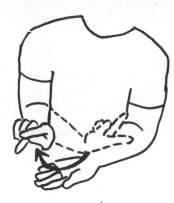

POOL★

Back of P arcs down to right across left palm and up again

POOR

Grasp left elbow; close to flat-O; repeat

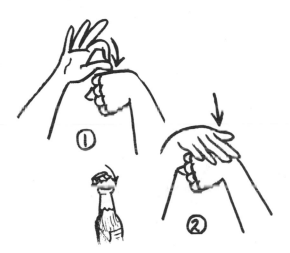

POP

Put 9 inside of left S, then slap top of S with flat hand

POPSICLE

V-fingertips twice stroke down chin

(See "ICE CREAM")

POPULAR

Right claw-hand moves to left vertical index finger and taps side of index

POPULATE

Middle fingertip of P brushes across 5-fingers of palm-in left hand

POPULATION = POPULATE + -TION

(See "DISTRIBUTE")

PORCH

P's outline from of porch
(See "DECK")

PORCUPINE

Back of 4-hand rests against left S. tilted to side; rotates upward like quills rising

PORK

Thumb and finger of 9 grasp
side of left P and shake
(See "MEAT")

PORPOISE

P makes 2 curves left along arm
(See "DOLPHIN")

POSITION

P's touch; sweep out and back
to N's touching
(See "PLACE")

POSITIVE

Index at chin drops to hit left
index

POSSIBLE

P's face each other, twist to
palm down, change to A's and
drop slightly
(See "ABLE")

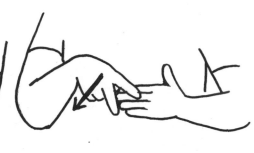

POST ★

P moves from back of left hand
straight forward
(See "AFTER")

POSTER

P's outline poster

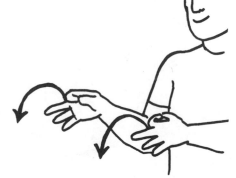

POSTPONE

Palms-facing, horizontal 9's
arc forward

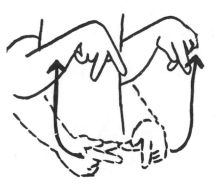

POT ★

Palms-down to palms-facing,
P's make shape of pot
(See "JAR")

POTATO

2 bent fingers tap on back of
left S

(See "IRELAND")

POUCH

H draws pouch under palm-
down left S

(See "BAG")

POUND★

Rock middle finger of P on
index of horizontal left H-hand

(See "WEIGH")

POUR ★

Extended-A lifts and "pours"
into side of left C

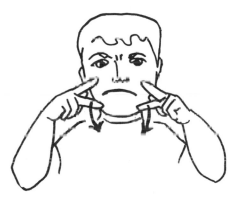

POUT

P's beside mouth pull down

(See "GRIM")

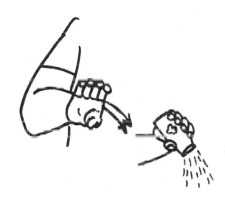

POWDER

C-hand shakes to sprinkle

POWER

Middle finger of P draws
muscle on left arm

(See "STRONG")

POX

Middle finger of P makes spots
on face

(See "MEASLES")

PRACTICE ♔

Palm-down A brushes back
and forth on left index

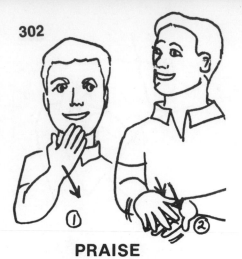
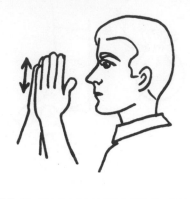

PRAISE

Flat hand on chin, then clap hands

(See "COMPLIMENT")

PRAY

Palms-together, hands move slightly up and down before face

PREACH

Palm-out 9 near side of head jerks slightly forward; repeat

(See "LECTURE")

PRECIPITATE

P's move down in small jerks

(See "RAIN")

PRECIOUS

Palm-down P's arc up to touch sides

(See "IMPORTANT")

PRECISE

Left P, palm-in, right P, palm-out, right jerks slightly toward left and recoils

(See "POINT")

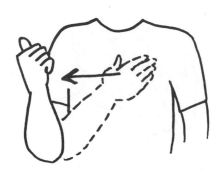

PREDICT

V, from eye, arcs under left hand and up

(See "PROPHECY")

PREFER

Flat hand on chest closes sideways to a palm-in A

PREGNANT

Fingers of 5-hands mesh

PREJUDICE

Middle fingertip of P hits left palm

(See "AGAINST")

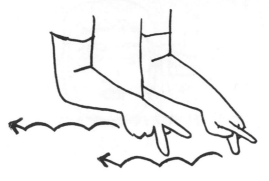

PREPARE

Parallel palm-down P's move to right in small arcs

PRESBYTERIAN

Middle finger of P taps on palm-right palm

(See "LUTHERAN")

PRESCRIBE

Middle finger of palm-in P on chin, twist out and point forward against palm of vertical left hand

**PRESCRIPTION =
PRESCRIBE + -TION**

(See "ASSIGN")

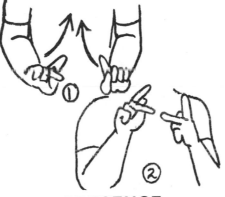

PRESENCE

P's swing up to face each other before chin, not touching, right slightly before left

(See "CONFRONT")

PRESENT

(Noun, Adj.)

P-hands, palms facing but turned slightly upwards drop slightly

PRESENT

(Verb)

P's, left behind right, with forefingers pointing forward, arc forward and a bit up

(See "SUGGEST")

PRESIDENT

Palm-out C's at temples rise to sides, closing to S's

(See "SUPER'INEN'D'ENT")

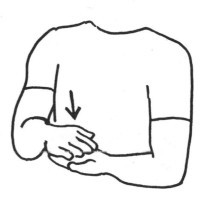

PRESS ★

Palms press together, right hand on top

PRETEND

Side of P brushes across chin; repeat

(See "FALSE")

PRETTY

Middle fingertip of P circles face

(See "FACE")

PRETZEL

Palm-down P draws a figure-8

PREVENT

Crossed flat hands move forward together

(See "GUARD")

PRICE

Middle fingertip of P strikes downward on left palm

(See "COST")

PRIDE

Middle finger of P draws up chest

(See "FEEL")

PRIEST

Side of G-hand slides across neck

PRIME

P circles under left palm

PRIMARY = PRIME + -AR + -Y

(See "BASE")

PRINCE

Middle P-fingertip touches left shoulder, then right side of body

PRINCESS = PRINCE + -ESS

(See "CHRIST")

PRINCESS

P-hand arcs from right to left shoulder, then drops down trunk

(or Prince + -ess)

PRINCIPAL

Right P circles over, drops on back of left S

PRINCIPLE

Side of P on left fingers, then on heel

(See "LAW")

PRINT ★

Right G-hand, slightly above left palm, drops and closes on left palm

(See "IMPRINT")

PRIOR

Middle finger of P taps extended thumb of left A

(See "FIRST")

PRIORITY

Palm-in left 5, pointing right; middle finger of palm-out right P bounces off thumb, index, and middle fingers

(See "CRITERIA")

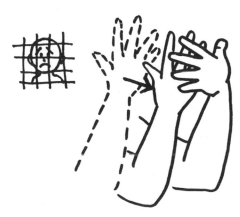

PRISON

Palms-in right 5 behind left 5; right hits left

(See "JAIL")

PRIVATE

Index of palm-out P taps lips

(See "SECRET")

PRIZE

X-hands, palms facing, right ahead of left, drop to the right

(See "GIFT")

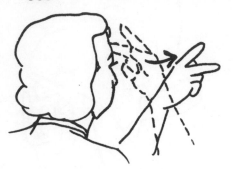

PRO

Middle fingertip of P on forehead twists to palm-out

(See "FOR")

PROBABLE

Horizontal P-hands face each other; raise and lower alternately

PROBABLY = PROBABLE + -LY

(See "BALANCE")

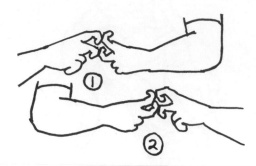

PROBLEM

Bent-V knuckles hit, separate; right bent-V rotates forward, left rotates back; knuckles hit again

(See "HARD")

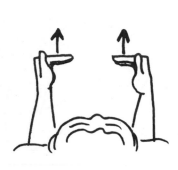

PROCEED

Palms-facing bent hands move forward

PROCLAIM

From corners of mouth, P's swing out

(See "ANNOUNCE")

PROCRASTINATE

9's palms facing, arc forward several times

(See "POSTPONE")

PRODUCE

Touch right P on left, twist hands to palm-in and touch again

PRODUCT = PRODUCE + -T

(See "MAKE")

PROFANE

Middle finger of palm-in P touches lips, twists out and throws down

(See "BAD")

PROFESS

Middle fingertip of P slides forward on side of left flat hand

PROFESSION = PROFESS + -ION

PROFESSOR = PROFESS + -ER

(See "STRAIGHT")

PROFILE

Index finger traces profile
(See "HANDSOME")

PROFIT

Side of 9 on body near waist;
slide down

PROFOUND

Side of right P slides down left
vertical palm
(See "DEEP")

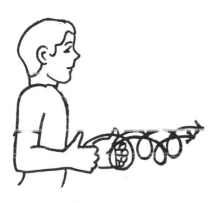

PROGRESS

Bent hands circle over each
other several times while
moving forward

PROGRAM

Middle fingertip of P moves
down palm-in left hand, then
down back of hand
(See "PROJECT")

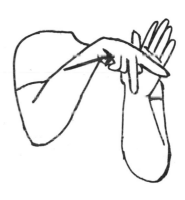

PROHIBIT

Side of P strikes sharply
against left palm
(See "FORBID")

PROJECT

(Verb)
Flat O against left palm, moves
forward and opens
PROJECTOR = PROJECT + -ER

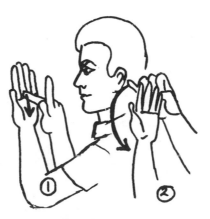

PROJECT

(Noun)
P moves down left palm, then
makes J back of vertical left
hand   (See "PROGRAM")

PROLOGUE

P's swing inward to touch
middle fingertips
(See "INTRODUCE")

PROMISE ♔

Index from chin, to rest flat hand against top of left hand

PROMOTE

Bent hands, face each other; arc in and up

PROMOTION = PROMOTE + -TION

(See "ADVANCE")

PRONOUN

PRO + NOUN

PRONOUNCE

Palm-down P (Pointing left) circles out from mouth

PRONUNCIATION = PRONOUNCE + -TION

PROOF

Back of F drops onto left palm

(See "PROVE")

PROPAGANDA

P in front of left S; P shakes forward

(See "EXAGGERATE")

PROPER

Right 1-hand above left, both pointing forward; hit several times, moving forward

PROPHECY

P from eye arcs under left P and up

PROPHET = PROPHECY + -T

(See "PREDICT")

PROPORTION

Parallel P's move slightly down, back up and to other side, and slightly down again

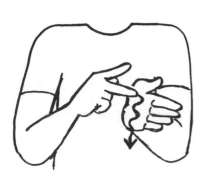

PROSE

Middle finger of P moves in wavy motion down across left palm   (See "READ")

PROTECT

Left P behind right P, both move forward, not touching   (See "GUARD")

PROTESTANT

Bent V-knuckles tap twice on palm-right left palm   (See "LUTHERAN")

PROUD

Palm-down right A-thumb draws up chest   (See "FEEL")

PROVE

Back of V drops onto palm

PROVERB

P's together; slide out to bent-V's that twist   (See "QUOTE")

PROVIDE

P rises out of pocket and twist forward to palm-up   (See "CONTRIBUTE")

PRUNE

P draws across chin, index crooking   (See "DRY")

PSYCHIATRY

Middle finger of right P taps left wrist

PSYCHIATRIST = PSYCHIATRY + -IST

(See "DOCTOR")

PSYCHOLOGY

Flat right hand taps left thumb-
joint from behind; repeat

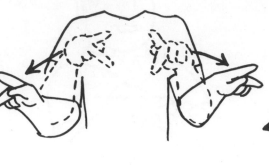

PUBLIC

P's move out and forward

(See "BROAD")

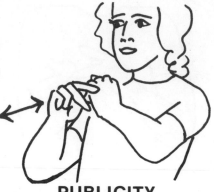

PUBLICITY

P in front of S; P pushes
forward like a trombone;
repeat rapidly

(See "ADVERTISE")

PUDDING

P-hand ladles up to mouth
twice from left palm

(See "SOUP")

PUDDLE

P outlines puddle in wavy
circle on back of left hand

PUFF ★

P at mouth moves out to F

PULL ♔

Palm-up A-hands pull toward
body

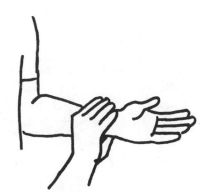

PULSE

Grasp left pulse, thumb on
bottom (See "DOCTOR")

PUMP

Inverted A pumps up and down

PUMPKIN

Middle finger of P taps on back of left S

(See "MELON")

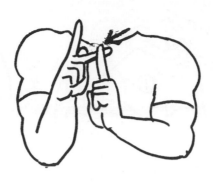

PUNCH ★

P, slightly behind left index, moves forward to hit index with middle finger

(See "BEAT")

PUNCTUATE

Fingertips of P-hand jerks toward left palm

(See "MARK")

PUNISH

Index finger strikes down on left elbow

PUPIL

Side of P brushes off left palm twice

PUPPET

Closed X-hands, palm-down, move alternately up and down (pulling puppet)

PUPPY

Right P-thumb is rubbed by right middle finger

(See "DOG")

PURCHASE

Right palm-in P moves forward off left palm

(See "BUY")

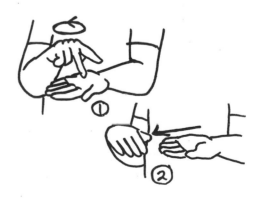

PURE

P circles over left palm, then flat hand wipes off left palm

(See "HOLY")

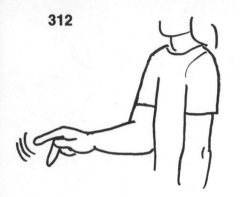

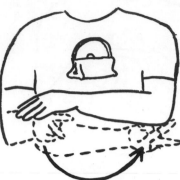

PURPLE

P shakes from wrist
(See "BLUE")

PURPOSE

P on left palm, twist and touch
again   (See "MEAN")

PURSE

P draws bag under left arm
(See "BASKET")

PURSUE

Right P behind left A, both
move forward left, P circling
slightly (See "CHASE")

PUSH

Palm-out flat hands push
forward

PUT

Flat-O moves forward to put
something down

PUZZLE

Palm-out index finger jerks
back to and X on forehead

QUAKE ★

Q's shake side to side

QUARREL

Index fingers point to each other, move rapidly side-to-side   (See "WAR")

QUART

Q passes to T down through C
(See "GALLON")

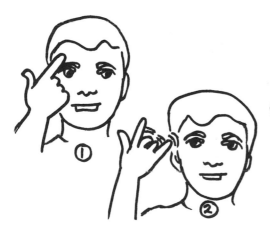

QUARTER

Index at temple move L out slightly, flutter last 3 fingers together in palm-in 25
(See "CENT")

QUEEN

Right Q on left shoulder, then on right side of body
(See "CHRIST")

QUEER

Right palm-left Q arcs on front of eyes to palm-down
(See "STRANGE")

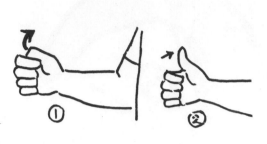

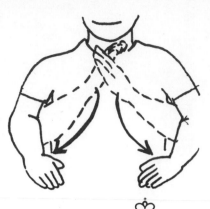

QUESTION ♔

Flick a question-mark: 1 back to X, and forward to point with index finger

QUICK

Thumb inside right fist, snaps out

QUIET ♔

Flat hands cross under chin and separate downwards

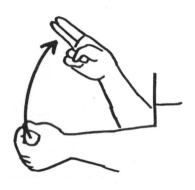

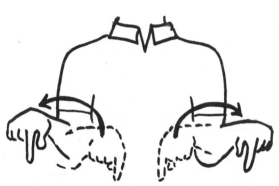

QUIT

H-fingertips in Q; pull out and up

(See "OUT")

QUITE

Palm-down Q's arc to the sides

(See "MUCH")

QUIZ

Flick "question" 1 to X to 1 with both hands

(See "QUESTION")

QUOTE ♔

Bent V's twist slightly, outlining quotation marks; may repeat

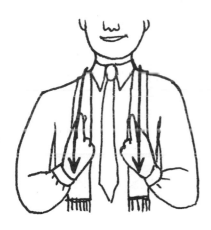

RABBI

R-hands outline prayer-shawl down chest

RABBIT

Palm-in U-fingers at temples wiggle backward together

RACE

Vertical R-palms face each other; move alternately forward and back

(See "COMPETE")

RACCOON

R's outline bottom of mask

RADIO

R rises from side to ear, shaking slightly

(See "SOUND")

RADISH

R shakes down from fingertips of left flat-O

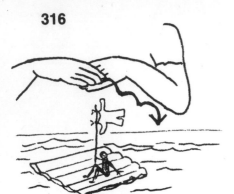

RAFT

Right flat hand on left floats forward with wavy motion

(See "DRIFT")

RAG

R-fingertips rub on chest near shoulder

(See "CLOTH")

RAGE

Palm-in R near stomach jerks up to near shoulder

(See "ANGER")

RAIL ★

One palm-down V-hand slides forward off the other palm-down V-hand

(See "TRACK")

RAIN

Palm-down claw-hands drop sharply; repeat

(See "SNOW")

RAINBOW

Rain + Bow

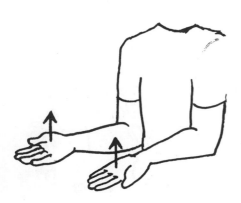

RAISE ★

Palm-up flat hands rise

RAISIN

R hops down back of S-hand

(See "GRAPE")

RAKE

Claw-hand rakes several times

RAM ★

R's circle back like horns from temples

RAN

Run + P. T.

RANCH

Extended thumb of R moves under chin, left to right

(See "FARM")

RANGE

R circles over left arm

(See "GROUND")

RAPE

Palm-out C's; right slides past left as both close to S's

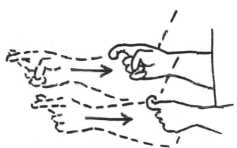

RAPID

Horizontal R's, left ahead of right, jerk back into X's

(See "FAST")

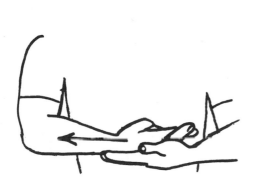

RARE

Back of R slides off left palm toward the right

RASH ★

Horizontal palm-in R brushes down lips, slightly inward to touch chest

RAT

R brushes past nose; repeat

(See "MOUSE")

RATHER

Palm-out R off left L-thumb, then to fingertip

(See "THEN")

RATTLE

R shakes

RAW

R arcs left across palm

(See "NEW")

RAZOR

Side of slightly bent R-fingers brush off cheek (shaving motion); repeat

(See "SHAVE")

REACH

Back of R approaches left palm

(See "ARRIVE")

READ ♔

Left palm in; right palm-down V-fingertips move down past left palm with wavy motion

READ (Past tense) = **READ** + **P. T.**

READY

Horizontal, parallel R-hands move to the right

REAL

(Alt. 1)

Fingertips of R slide down palm-up left hand

REALLY = **REAL** + **-LY**

(See "HONEST")

REAL

(Alt. 2)

R at lips arcs up and forward

REALLY = **REAL** + **-LY**

(See "CERTAIN")

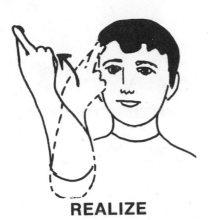

REALIZE

R on forehead twists up and
forward from wrist, remaining
palm-in

(See "UNDERSTAND")

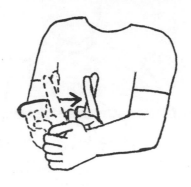

REAR ★

Palm-out R, next to left A, arcs
back and to the side sideways
back to end behind A

(See "HIND")

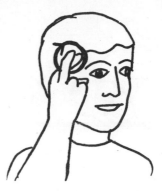

REASON ♔

R-fingertips circle near temple

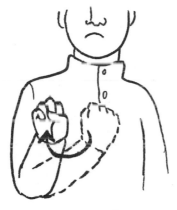

REBEL ♔

(Verb)
Palm-in S turns to palm-out S
REBELLIOUS = REBEL + -OUS

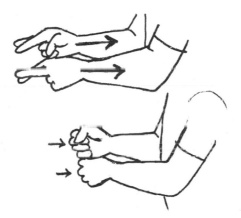

RECEIVE

Right R on left, pull both
toward body, closing to S's

(See "GET")

RECENT

Side of X-hand on cheek, palm-
in; wiggle finger

RECESS

R-hands face each other and
swing back and forth, pivoting
at wrists

(See "PLAY")

RECIPE

Palm-up R on left palm flips to
palm-down

(See "PAGE")

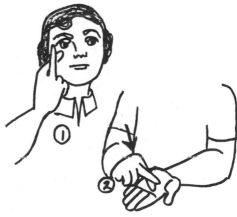

RECOGNIZE

R at eye drops to palm of left
hand

(See "NOTE")

320

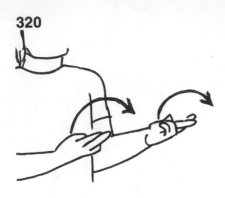

RECOMMEND

R's, palm-up, move forward and slightly up

(See "SUGGEST")

RECORD

(Verb)

R-fingers write across left palm

(See "WRITE")

RECORD

(Noun)

Tip of R circles above, drops on left palm

RECRUIT

V-hands bent fingers grab index

RECTANGLE

R's outline rectangle

(See "SQUARE")

RED

Palm-in, index finger touches chin, brushes down and closes

(See "PINK")

REDUCE

Right flat hand descends in stages above left

REEL ★

R circles around left S

(See "SPOOL")

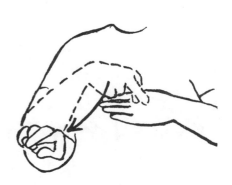

REFER

Palm-down R on back of left hand swings outward

REFERENCE = REFER + -ENCE

(See "SEND")

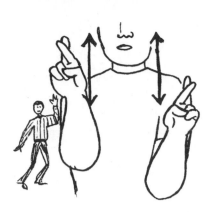

REFEREE

Palm-out R's move alternately up and down

(See "BALANCE")

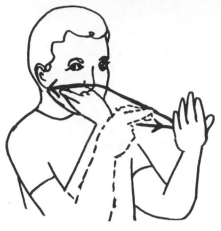

REFLECT

Palm-out R hits left palm and reflects back, palm-in

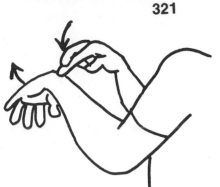

REFLEX

R taps on wrist of limp left hand causing a reflex up-flip

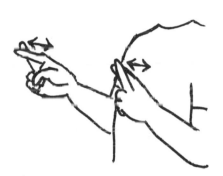

REFRIGERATE

R's move back and forth toward each other in shivering motion

REFRIGERATOR = REFRIGERATE + -ER

(See "COLD")

REFUSE

S-hand jerks back toward shoulder

REGION

R curves around vertical left index

(See "ATMOSPHERE")

REGISTER

Right R-fingertips hop backwards along left palm

REGRESS

Right R moves down in hopping motion on left arm

(See "DETERIORATE")

REGRET

Right R circles on chest

(See "SORRY")

REGULAR

Right index above left, both pointing forward; right makes small clockwise circles, hitting left on each cycle

REHABILITATE

R on left palm; both rise
(See "HELP")

REHEARSE

Heel of R brushes back and forth on left index
(See "PRACTICE")

REIGN

R's move alternately forward and back
(See "MANAGE")

REINDEER

Thumbs of R's on temples, move out and up
(See "DEER")

REINFORCE

R taps bottom of palm-in left S
(See "HELP")

REJECT

Side of flat right hand sweeps forward sharply off left palm
(See "RID")

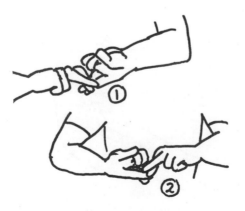

RELATE

R-fingers rest first right on left, then left on right
RELATIVE = RELATE + -IVE
RELATION = RELATE + -TION
(See "FRIEND")

RELAX

Crossed R's rest on chest

RELAY

Palm-up flat-O arcs in and over to body, then arcs out to palm-up on opposite side of body

(See "TRANSFER")

RELEASE

Linked thumbs and indexes of 9's open and separate sideways

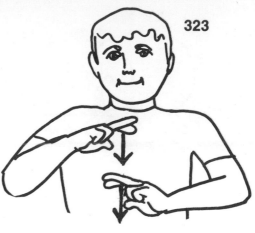

RELIEVE

Right R above left R on chest, both move down

RELIEF = RELIEVE + -F

(See "SATISFY")

RELIGION

R on heart arcs down and forward to palm-out

RELIGIOUS = RELIGION + -OUS

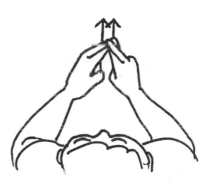

RELY

Palm-down R's cross at fingers and move slightly down

(See "DEPEND")

REMAIN

Right R-fingers on left R-fingers; both move forward

(See "CONTINUE")

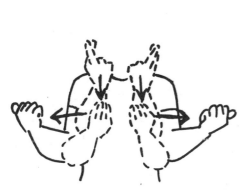

REMEDY

Palm-in R's close to palm-up flat-O's, which close to A's as they separate

(See "MELT")

REMEMBER

Thumb of A on forehead; drops to touch left A-thumbnail

REMIND

Right R-fingers tap forehead

(See "THINK")

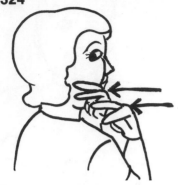

REMINISCE

Palm-in vertical V's in front of face swing back over right shoulder

REMOVE

Fingertips of flat-O on left palm arc off to throw open hand down

(See "WASTE")

RENT

R on R, arc back toward body

(See "BORROW")

REPAIR

R-tips touch; twist in opposite directions and touch again

(See "FIX")

REPEAT

Palm-up R turns over and strikes left palm; repeat

(See "AGAIN")

REPEL

Palm-out R hits palm-in left vertical hand and bounces back

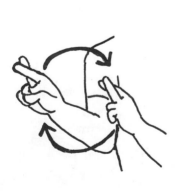

REPLACE

Horizontal R-hands, right in front of left, circle each other once

(See "EXCHANGE")

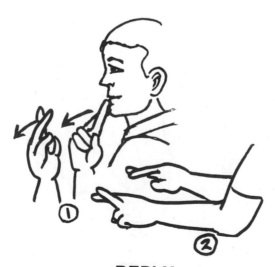

REPLY

Palms-in, right R near lips, left R ahead to left; both hands turn palm-down, left one ahead

(See "ANSWER")

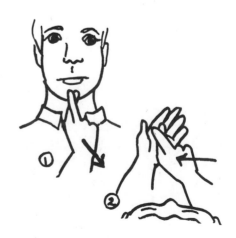

REPORT

Palm-in R on lip twists to palm-down R on left palm

(See "MENTION")

REPRESENT

Tip of R on left palm, move both forward

REPRESENTATIVE =
REPRESENT + -IVE

(See "SHOW")

REPTILE

R circles forward from under chin

(See "SNAKE")

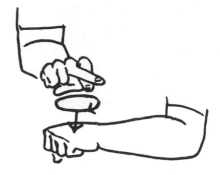

REPUBLIC

Palm-down R circles over, then drops on back of left S

(See "NATION")

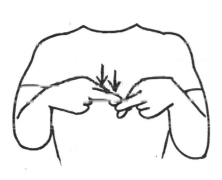

REPUTE

Right R taps left, both horizontal

REPUTATION = REPUTE + -TION

(See "NAME")

REQUEST

R's, touching, arc toward self

(See "ASK")

REQUIRE

Tip of X on left palm, both arc together toward body

RESCUE

Separate palm-in crossed R's to sides, twisting to palm-out

(See "FREE")

RESEARCH

R at eye swings to palm-down; fingertips brush forward twice off left palm

(See "INSPECT")

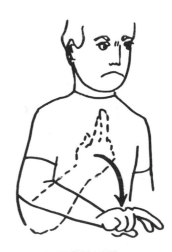

RESENT

Palm-in R on chest twists sharply out and throws palm-down

(See "HOSTILE")

RESERVE

(Alt. 1)

R-fingertips tap back of left S-hand

RESERVATION = RESERVE + -TION

(See "SAVE")

RESERVE

(Alt. 2)

R circles over back of left S and drops onto S

(See "APPOINT")

RESIDE

Palm-in R's slide up body

RESIDENCE = RESIDE + -ENCE

RESIDENT = RESIDE + -ENT

(See "ADDRESS")

RESIGN

R-fingertips arc back out of left O

(See "OUT")

RESIST

S-hand, palm-out elbow-out, jerks slightly forward and right from chest

RESPECT

Palm-left R arcs in and down near forehead

(See "GOD")

RESPONSIBLE

Both R-hands on right shoulder

RESPONSIBILITY = RESPONSIBLE + -ITY

(See "BURDEN")

REST

Right R behind left; both move slightly down

RESTAURANT

R touches on each side of mouth

(See "CAFE")

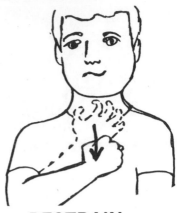

RESTRAIN

Right claw at neck drops slightly down to S

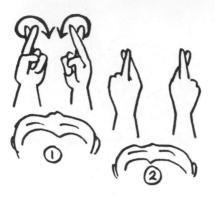

RESULT

(Alt. 1)

Palm-up R's twist to palm-down   (See "HAPPEN")

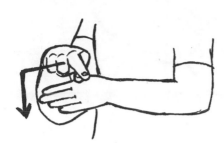

RESULT

(Alt. 2)

R-fingers on side of palm-in flat left hand slide along hand to end and down

(See "FINISH")

RETARD

R-hand draws up back of left hand and wrist

(See "SLOW")

RETIRE

Extended R-thumbs tap front of shoulders

(See "LEISURE")

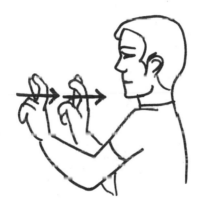

RETREAT

Palm-out vertical R's, right behind left, move back toward body

RETURN

R's point at each other, circle alternately toward body

REVEAL

Palm-down R's open outward

(See "OPEN")

REVENGE

X-hands hit each other sharply and separate

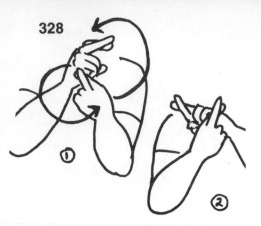

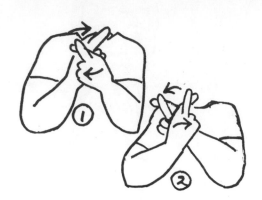

REVERSE

R-hands, palm-to-palm, reverse position

(See "CHANGE")

REVIEW

R sweeps up across fingers of left palm-in horizontal 5

(May be signed Re + View)

REVISE

R-hands, palm-to-palm, reverse positions quickly twice

(See "CHANGE")

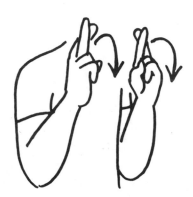

REVOLT

Palm-in R twists back toward shoulder to palm-out

(See "REBEL")

REVOLVE

Vertical R's point at each other; revolve around each other while moving right

REWARD

Vertical R's, one slightly behind the other, both arc forward

(See "GIFT")

RHINOCEROS

C-hand from nose up to S

RHUBARB

Flat O slides up through left C twisting to palm-out R

(See "GROW")

RHYME
(Alt. 1)
R-fingertips touch left thumb
and middle and little fingertips
(alternate rhyming lines)

RHYME
(Alt. 2)
Palm-down R's tap sides
(See "SAME")

RHYTHM
Palm-down R swings side-to-
side behind left palm
(See "MUSIC")

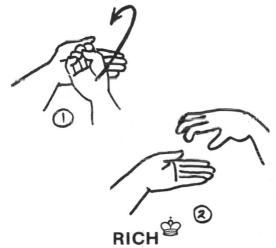

RIBBON
Right palm-in I wiggles away
and slightly down from palm-
out R
(See "CORD")

RICE
R-hand ladles up to mouth
twice from left palm
(See "SOUP")

RICH
Palm-up flat-O on left palm
turns over and opens above
palm to a claw

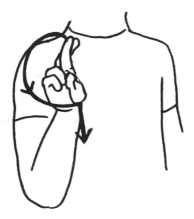

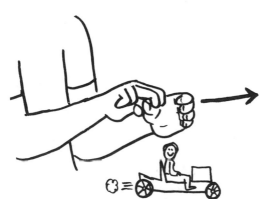

RID
Side of R sweeps forward
sharply off left palm
(See "REJECT")

RIDDLE
Palm-out R draws question-
mark
(See "QUESTION")

RIDE
First two fingers sit on thumb
of horizontal palm-right C-
hand; both move forward
(See "PASSENGER")

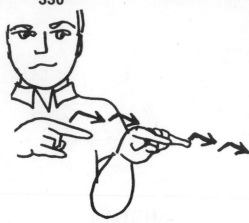

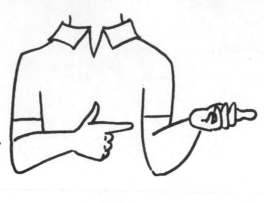

RIDICULE

Index and little fingers extended, right behind left, jerk hands diagonally left; repeat

RIFLE

Right index, thumb extended, points left toward palm-up bent hand (holding rifle)

RIGHT

Palm-out R moves slightly right

RING ★

R shakes away from left ring finger

RANG = RING + P. T.
RUNG = RING + P. P.

(See "DIAMOND")

RINSE

Inverted R's rise and fall simultaneously twice

(See "DIP")

RIPE

Horizontal right R moves inward, brushing across left S

(See "FULL")

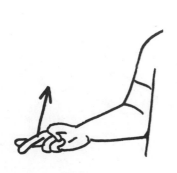

RISE ★

Palm-up R rises

(See "UP")

RIVER

Palm-down R's ripple forward to left up and down

(See "BROOK")

ROACH

R rides forward on back of wiggling fingers of left hand

(See "ANT")

ROAD

Palm-down R's move forward, weaving slightly side-to-side

(See "WAY")

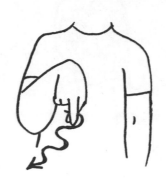

ROAM

R, pointing down, moves forward in a wavy path

(See "WANDER")

ROAR

R's face each other, right above left at chin; move outward, separating vertically with wavy motions

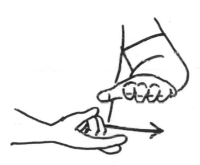

ROAST

Slide palm-up R forward under left palm

(See "BAKE")

ROB

R slides along under left arm, from elbow to wrist

(See "STEAL")

ROBE

Palm-in R-hands arc inward on chest

(See "COAT")

ROBIN

R-fingers open and close on thumb by mouth

(See "BIRD")

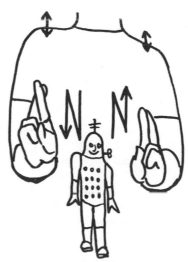

ROBOT

Palm out R's; hands and shoulders move up and down alternately

ROCK ★

Back of R raps on back of left S; may repeat

(See "STONE")

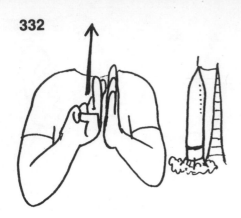

ROCKET

Side of R on left palm, R moves upward

(See "ASTRONAUT")

RODENT

Brush tip of nose alternately with R's

(See "MICE")

ROLE

R circles near and then touches vertical left palm

ROLL★

R's, palms facing, roll forward around each other alternately from chest

ROME

R-fingertips touch forehead, then nose

ROMAN = ROME + -AN

(See "LATIN")

ROOF

R's outline roof

ROOM

R-hands box in a room

(See "BOX")

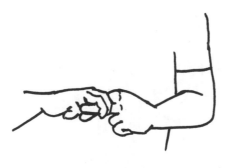

ROOST

2 fingers roost on left R

(See "SIT")

ROOSTER

Thumb of palm-left 3 taps on forehead

ROOT

Flat-O "grows" down through left C to a 5

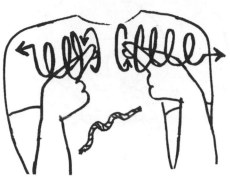

ROPE

Palm-in R-hands point at each other, separate in spiral movement

ROSE

R touches on each side of nose (smelling rose)

(See "FLOWER")

ROT

Thumb of R flings off nose to the left

ROTTEN = ROT + - EN

(See "LOUSE")

ROTATE

R, pointing down, rotates

(See "SPIN")

ROUGH

Fingertips of right claw on left palm; move claw sharply forward and off

ROUND ★

Palm-out R circles once

(See "CIRCLE")

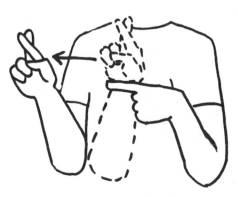

ROW

Heel of palm-out R slides along and off side of left index

(See "BAR")

ROYAL

R at left shoulder then at right waist

(See "CHRIST")

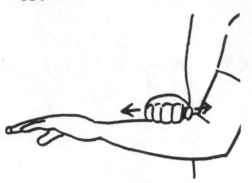

RUB

Palm-down A rubs on back of left arm

RUBBER

Side of X-finger slides down cheek; repeat

RUBBERS = RUBBER + -S

RUBELLA

R-fingers spot face

(See "MEASLES")

RUDE

R on chin; twist to palm-out and throw down

(See "BAD")

RUG

R drags across back of left hand

(See "CARPET")

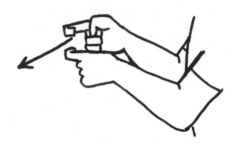

RUIN

Right X on left X; right X (only) moves sharply forward

RULE

Side of R on the fingers, then moves to the heel of left palm

(See "LAW")

RUMOR

R-fingertips touch near chin, circle horizontally out shaking, to touch again

(See "GOSSIP")

RUN ★

Palm-down L-thumbtips touch; hands move forward, index fingers flicking in and out rapidly

RAN = RUN + P. T.

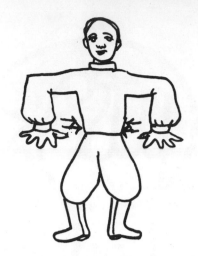

RUSH

Parallel R-hands shake forward

(See "HURRY")

RUSSIA

Thumbs of horizontal 5-hands tap waist; repeat (as in Russian dance)

RYE

R brushes up through left C-hand; repeat

(See "GRAIN")

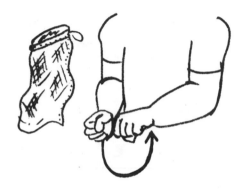

SABBATH

F-hand sets past horizontal left arm

SACK

S draws bag under palm-down left S

(See "BAG")

SAD

Open hands pull down in front of face

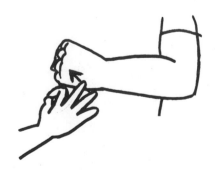

SADDLE

Fingers hook over flat left hand like a saddle

SAFE

Fingertips of F tap back of left S

SAFETY = SAFE + -T + -Y

(See "SAVE")

SAID

Say + P. T.

SAIL

Side of 3 on flat palm; both hands move forward in slight up-and-down motion

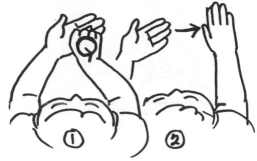

SAINT

Palm-down S circles above left palm, then flat hand slides off end of palm

(See "HOLY")

SALAD

V's toss salad

(See "COLE SLAW")

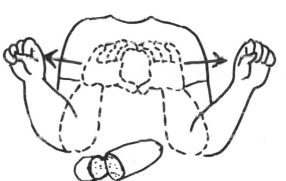

SALAMI

Palm-out C's separate to S's

SALE

Flat-O, palm-down above left palm, flips up at wrist several times

(See "SELL")

SALT

Index and middle fingers tap alternately on left U-fingers

SALUTE

B at forehead, palm-out

(See "SCOUT")

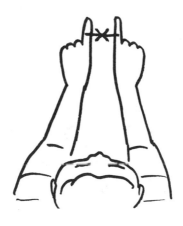

SAME

Palm-down fingers touch sides together

(See "RHYME")

SAMPLE

Palm-out open-9-hands; alternately pull back to 9-hands, while moving slightly to the right

SAND ★

S-palms up; rub thumbs across back of fingers

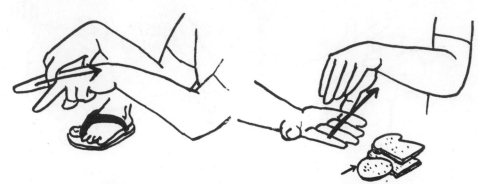

SANDAL

Index finger hooks in left V, then draws back across stationary hand

SANDWICH

Right hand, palm-up, inserts filling between palm-down thumb and fingers of left; repeat

SANG

Sing + P. T.

SANK

Sink + P. T.

SANTA CLAUS

Palm-in C at chin curves down to touch chest, palm-up

SARCASM

Index of right 1-I- hand at corner of mouth arcs out and left past bottom of palm-in 1-I- hand **SARCASTIC = SARCASM + -IC**
(See "TRICK")

SAT

Sit + P. T.

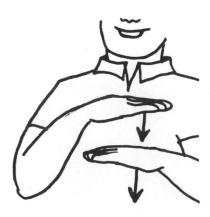

SATISFY

Open, palm-down B-hands resting on chest; both move downward

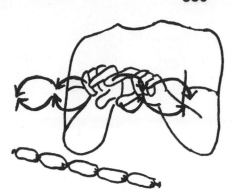

SATURDAY

Palm-out S-hand circles slightly

(See "MONDAY")

SAUCE

Palm-down extended-A hand rotates above left palm as if pouring

SAUCER = SAUCE + -ER

SAUSAGE

G's, moving sideways, open and close fingers to outline sausages

(See "BALONEY")

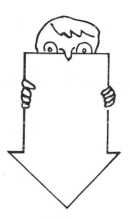

SAVE ♛

Fingers of V tap back of left S

SAVER

Save + R

SAVIOUR

Palm-in S-hands, crossed at wrists, separate and twist to palm-out, then parallel flat hands move down sides of body

(See "FREE")

SAW

Edge of right hand saws on back of left

(May be done with right S-hand)

(See "LOG")

SAW

See + P. T.

SAY

Index circles up and outward near mouth

SAID = **SAY** + **P. T.**
(See "IMPLY")

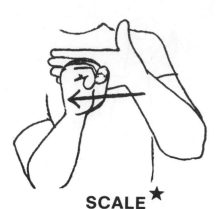

SCALE ★

Side of S slides across the back of palm-in flat left hand

SCARE

S-hands, palms-in, move toward each other, opening to palm-in 5's
(See "FRIGHT")

SCARF ★

Both hands draw scarf around neck and tie at side, finishing in flat-O's
(See "BONNET")

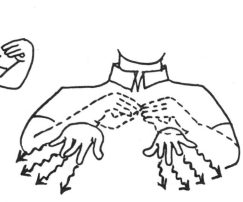

SCATTER

Flat-O tips together; open to palm-down 5's that separate, fluttering fingers

SCHEDULE

Palms-in right 4 behind left, right drops down

SCHEME

Palm-in S at side of forehead rises up and away in nodding motion

(See "DREAM")

SCHIZOPHRENIC

Palm-in bent hand outlines crack down midline

SCHOOL

Clap hands

SCIENCE ♔

Palm-out extended-A hands alternately pour in circles

SCISSOR

Horizontal index and middle finger scissor forward

SCISSORS – SCISSOR + -S

(See "CUT")

SCOLD

Shake index finger at someone

SCOOP ★

Palm-out right S on left palm twists to palm-up right P

SCOOT

S-hand, palm-down, flicks up sharply to palm-out S

SCOOTER = SCOOT + -ER

SCORE ★

Thumb and index check off left 2-fingertips

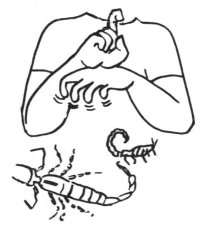

SCORPION

X rides forward on back of wiggling fingers of left hand

(See "ANT")

SCOT

4 fingers draw a cross on left upper arm **SCOTTISH = SCOT + -ISH**

SCOTLAND = SCOT + LAND

SCOTCH = SCOT + -H

(See "PLAID")

SCOUT ★

Three fingers of palm-out hand salute

(See "SALUTE")

SCRAMBLE

Palm-down S circles over left cupped hand like scrambling eggs

SCRAPE

Palm-down S scrapes off back of palm-down left claw several times

SCRATCH ★

Claw scratches left palm

SCREAM

Palm-in claw shakes up and diagonally forward from chin, rapidly

(See "HOLLER")

SCREEN ★

Palms-in, right vertical 4 falls inside left horizontal 4, both palms-in

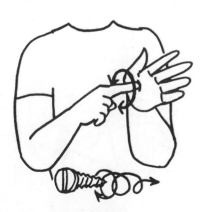

SCREW

Index fingers twists in middle of left palm

SCREWDRIVER

H-fingers twist in palm of left hand

SCRIPT

Right palm-out S moves down behind vertical palm-in left hand

SCRUB

A-hand knuckles scrub together, one on the other

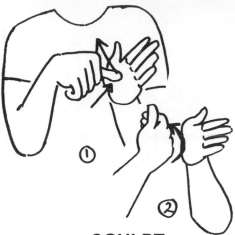

SCULPT

Extended thumb of A sculpts on palm; repeat

SCULPTURE = SCULPT + -URE

SEA

Palm-down S's sweep up and down forward, opening to 5's

(See "OCEAN")

SEAL ★

Right on left bent hand, close right flat hand on left; repeat

SEARCH

Palm-left C-hand makes several circles in front of eyes

SEASON ★

Palm-out S moves downward with a wavy motion

(See "WEATHER")

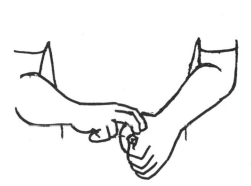

SEAT

2 fingers sit on side of left S-hand

(See "SIT")

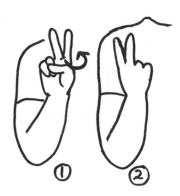

SECOND

Palm-out 2 twists to palm-in

SECONDARY = SECOND + -AR + -Y

(See "THIRD")

SECRET

A-thumb taps chin; repeat

(See "PRIVATE")

SECRETARY

H takes pencil from ear and writes across left palm

(See "WRITE")

SECTION

Side of right S arcs toward body on palm-up left hand

(See "SOME")

SEE

Palm-in V from eye outward

SAW = SEE + P. T.

SEEN = SEE + P. P.

SEED

Palm-down thumb of flat-O rubs fingers, hand moving right (sowing seeds)

SEEM

Bent hand pivots at wrist to palm-in; repeat

(See "OUGHT")

SEESAW

Palm-down bent - V hands alternately rise and drop

SELECT

Heel of S rests on index of left V, then pulls back toward chest; left is stationary

(See "CHOOSE")

SELF

Thumb-up extended - A hand moves forward

SELVES = SELF + -S

(Use for all -self's except myself, ourselves, oneself, in which A turns to face in and touches own chest)

SELFISH

Palm-down V's pull back to bent V's

SELL

Palm-down flat-O's flip up at wrist; repeat

SOLD = SELL + P. T.

(See "PEDDLE")

SEMESTER

Side of S circles once on left palm

(See "HOUR")

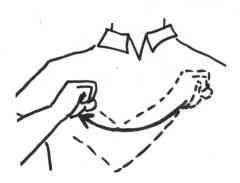

SENATE

S on left shoulder, then on right

(See "MEMBER")

SEND ♔

Right palm-in fingertips on back of palm-in left hand flip forward to palm-down

SENT = SEND + P. T.

SENIOR

Index taps vertical thumb of left 5

(See "FRESHMAN")

SENSE

Bent middle finger taps behind ear; repeat

SENSIBLE = SENSE + -ABLE

(See "CONSCIOUS")

SENSITIVE

Middle finger on heart turns sharply outward

(Can be Sense + -ive)

SENTENCE ♔

9-hands touch at index and thumb-tips; separate, shaking slightly

SEPARATE

Palms-down, backs of bent hands together; separate hands   (See "ISOLATE")

SEPTEMBER

(Alt. 1)

Palm-down S brushes down left elbow twice.

(See "AUTUMN")

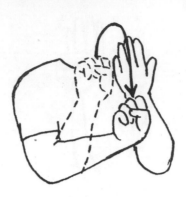

SEPTEMBER

(Alt. 2)

S arcs over side of vertical left hand

(See "CALENDAR")

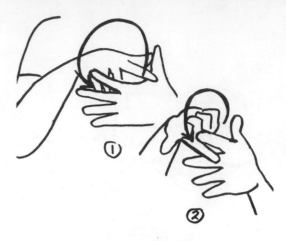

SEQUENCE

Index of palm-down L between left thumb and index; turn to palm-up between index and middle fingers

SEQUIN

Side of S taps across left palm, like sequins

(See "BEAD")

SERGEANT

3-hand index and middle fingers draw chevron on left shoulder

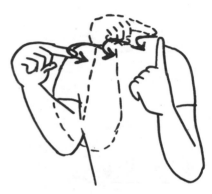

SERIES

Right index on left palm-in vertical index; right index dots off to right; left is stationary

SERIOUS

Palm-left S-hand moves forward from chin

(See "CERTAIN")

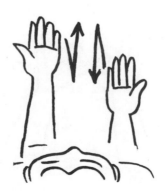

SERVE

Palms-up, move hands alternately to and from body

SERVANT = SERVE + -ANT

SERVICE = SERVE + -ICE

SET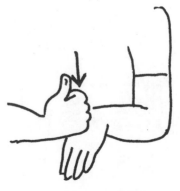

Palm-in extended-A is set on back of left hand

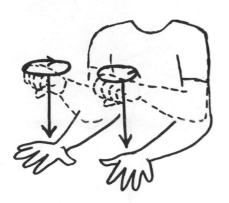

SETTLE

Palm-down S's circle and drop to palm-down 5's

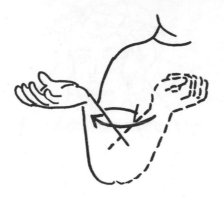

SEVERAL

A moves sideways to open palm, one finger at a time

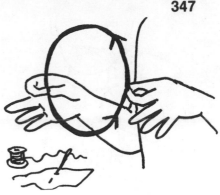

SEW

Right 9 sews left thumb and fingertip of 9

(See "TAILOR")

SEX

Palm-out X at temple, then on jaw

(See "PARENT")

SHADE

Both palm-out S-hands fall and cross at wrists

SHADOW = SHADE + -W

(See "DARK")

SHAKE

Shake palm-left 5-hand

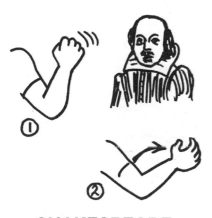

SHAKESPEARE

Right hand shakes and throw and spear

SHALL

(Alt. 1)
Palm-down X nods several times   (See "SHOULD" Alt. 1)

(See "NECESSARY")

SHALL

(Alt. 2)
S-hand at side of face moves forward to L, (palm-left)
(See "SHOULD" Alt. 2)

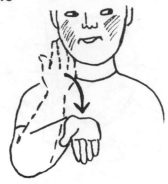

SHAME

Flat hand brushes up cheek, over and out, from palm-in to palm-up

SHAMPOO

Both hands make washing motion on head

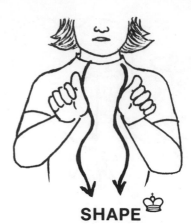

SHAPE

Palm-out A-thumbs outline shape

SHARE

Side of right hand arcs from side to side, on side of palm-in left hand

SHARK

Flat-hand fingertips between left ring and middle fingers; swim forward

(See "FISH")

SHARP

Middle finger pulls away from left index tip, turning palm-down

SHARPEN = SHARP + -EN

(See "BLADE")

SHAVE

Thumb of Y draws along cheek, palm-out; repeat

(See "RAZOR")

SHE

Palm-out E slides along jawline and forward

(See "GIRL")

SHEEP

Palm-up V clips wool off left arm

SHEPHERD = SHEEP + HERD

(See "LAMB")

SHEET

Right arm bends in and up, over left hand near chest

SHELF

Fingertips of bent hands touch at eye-level, then separate

SHELTER

Right palm-in S arcs over left palm-down, flat hand

SHH

Index finger shushes lips

SHEPHERD

Sheep + Herd

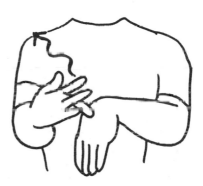

SHINE

Bent middle finger rises off back of left hand, shaking

SHIP

Palm-out S on left palm; both move forward

SHIRT

Palm-out S-hands on chest, arc inward, downward
(See "COAT")

SHOCK

Index touches forehead, then drop hands into claws, palm-down

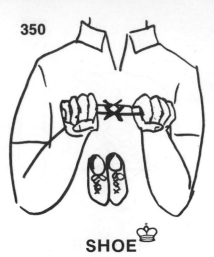

SHOE

S-hands bump together; repeat

SHOES = SHOE + -S

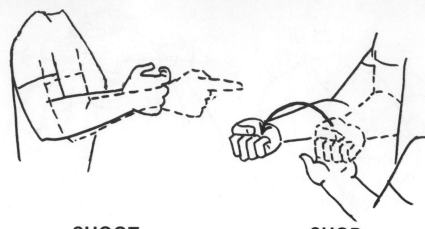

SHOOT

Index jerks back to X (pulling trigger)

SHOT = SHOOT + P. T.

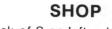

SHOP

Back of S on left palm; S arcs forward

(See "BUY")

SHORE

Fluttering fingers of palm-down 5 sweep, wave-like, onto and back from left palm-down hand   (See "TIDE")

SHORT

Side of right H rubs back and forth on side of left H

SHORTEN = SHORT + -EN

SHOULD

(Alt. 1)
Palm-down X nods, then flat hands, palms facing, drop to palms-down

SHOULD

(Alt. 2)
Palm-out S-hand, at side of face, moves forward to D

SHOULDER

Pat opposite shoulder

SHOUT

C before chin jerks up and forward, right

(See "CALL")

SHOVEL

Back of right hand slides forward in palm of left hand and flips up

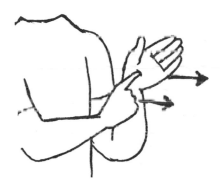

SHOW ♚

Index on left palm; both move forward

SHOWER

From above, claw-hand jerks toward and away from head, fingers remaining curved

SHRIMP

Wrists of palm-down I's crossed, move to front and right, wiggling I-little fingers

(See "CRAB")

SHUT

Side of palm-in right hand drops on side of palm-in left B

SHY

Bent hand, palm-in, moves up cheek

SICK

Bent middle fingers touch forehead and stomach

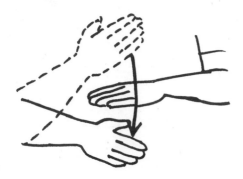

SIDE

Palm-in right hand brushes down past side of palm-down left hand

SIGH

Both hands in S, on chest, right above left; move out and in again

(See "BREATH")

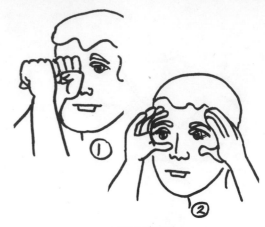

SIGHT

S-hands before eyes, left before right, separate sideways opening to C's

SIGN

Palm-out indexes circle alternately and vertically (sign language)

SIGN ★

U fingers touch palm, circle to side, touch palm again

SIGNATURE = SIGN + -URE

SILENT

S-wrists cross before chin, separate downward

SILENCE = SILENT + -ENCE

(See "QUIET")

SILLY

Y-hand shakes in front of eyes

SILVER

S at ear shakes down to the right

(See "CALIFORNIA")

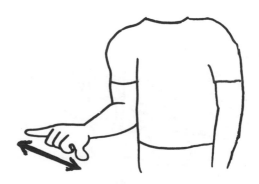

SIMILAR

Palm-down Y moves slightly from side to side

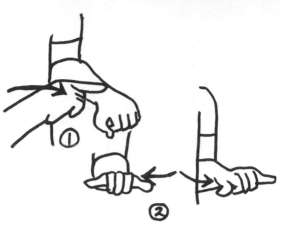

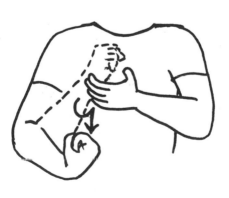

SIMPLE

S brushes up back of left bent fingers twice

SIMPLICITY = SIMPLE + -ITY

(See "EASE")

SIMULTANEOUS

Index touches left wrist; then separate to palm-down Y's

SIN

Palm-in indexes point at each other, arc toward each other in front of body; repeat

SINCE

Palm-in indexes on right shoulder, arc up and out to point forward

SING

Palm-out H from corner of mouth arcs forward and out, slightly to the side

SANG = SING + P. T.
SUNG = SING + P. P.

(See "OPERA")

SINGLE

(Alt. 1)

Right index, palm-in circles slightly horizontally

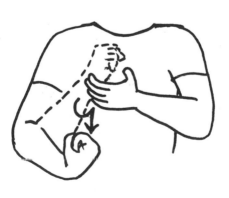

SINGLE

(Alt. 2)

S-hand arcs from left side of mouth to right side

(See "BACHELOR")

SINK ★

(Alt. 1)

Drop palm-left 3 down from palm-right left hand

SANK = SINK + P. T.
SUNK = SINK + P. P.

SINK

(Alt. 2)

Palm-out right S rotates down through horizontal left C-hand

(See "DRAIN")

SIR

S at temple goes forward to palm-out R

(See "HE")

SIREN

Flat-O repeatedly opens and closes as it revolves within left C

SISTER

Extended A-hand moves down jawline; drops to index fingers together

(See "BROTHER")

SIT

Right U sits 2 fingers on left palm-down U

SAT = SIT + P. T.

SITUATE

Palm-out S-hands touch, circle horizontally toward body, and touch again

SITUATION = SITUATE + -TION
(See "PLACE")

SIZE

S moves from little finger to thumb of palm-down left Y

SKATE

Palm-up bent-V's move back and forth alternately

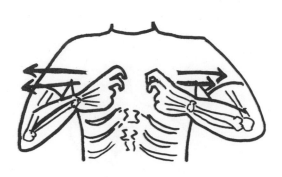

SKELETON

Bent-V's scratch outward on chest; repeat

SKEPTIC

Palm-in V, in front of face, bends fingers several times

SKETCH

Right 1-hand points little fingers at left palm and moves quickly up and down several times

(See "ART")

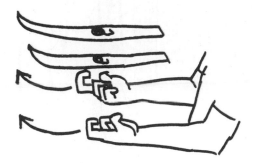

SKI

Palm-up X's arc forward

SKILL

Right hand grasps side of left S; slide off forward into A

(See "EXPERT")

SKILLET

Palm-down S circles horizontally once, then pulls back toward body

(See "PAN")

SKIN

Pinch skin on back of left hand

SKIP

Right middle to index of K skip upward on left flat palm

(See "JUMP")

SKIRT

Thumbs of 5-hands brush down and out from waist

SKULL

Wrists of bent V-hands cross below neck

SKUNK

K moves back across middle of head

SKY

Palm-down flat hand at left arcs to palm-up hand at right

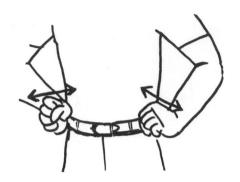

SKYSCRAPER

1-hands alternately move up and down, moving hands to right

SLACK

S-hands tap waist

SLACKS = SLACK + -S

(See "PANT")

SLANG

S's together, palm-out, separate to bent-V's that twist slightly down

(See "QUOTE")

SLAP

Open hand slaps left index

(See "BEAT")

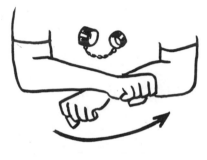

SLAVE

S's , crossed at wrists, palm-down swing to side

SLED

Back of bent-V on left palm; both arc forward

(See "TOBOGGAN")

SLEEP

Before face, 5-hand drops to flat-O, palm-in

SLEPT = SLEEP + P. T.

SLEEVE

C-hand moves from left elbow to grip wrist

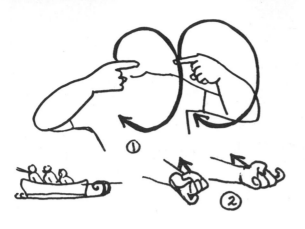

SLEIGH

Palm-in 1-hands circle forward to palm up X-hands that pull back

SLICE ♔

Palm slices side of left S

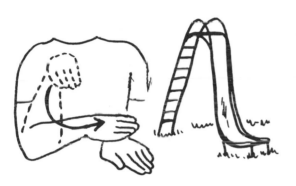

SLIDE ★

Right palm-down hand slides down and outward over back of left hand

SLIM

Near body, palms facing each other, hands curve in and down

(See "DIET")

SLIP ★

Flat hand arcs out along left palm

(See "LAP")

SLIPPER

Palm-down flat hand slides in and out of palm-up left C

SLOP

Thumb under chin, 5-hand moves to right under chin, fingers fluttering

SLOPPY = SLOP + -Y

SLOPE ★

S-hand outlines slope up and to the right

SLOW

Palms-down, right hand moves slowly up back of horizontal left hand

(See "RETARD")

SLUG ★

Palm-up S moves along left arm

(See "CATERPILLAR")

SMALL ♔

Flat hands with extended thumbs face each other, jerk slightly toward each other; repeat

SMART

Palm-in, bent middle finger on forehead snaps off and twists to palm-out

(See "WIT")

SMELL ♔

Palm-in hand near nose brushes with the "fumes"; repeat

SMILE ♔

Index-finger side of bent hands curves corners of mouth up

SMOG

Palm-in open hand and palm-out S-hand pass each other in front of face

(See "DARK")

SMOKE

Palm-in V moves forward from corner of mouth

SMOOTH

Palm-up flat-O's both move forward diagonally, closing to palm-up A's

SNACK

Middle finger snaps up to G at mouth

SNAIL

Heel of bent-V slides up left forearm

(See "CATERPILLAR")

SNAKE

Bent-V circles forward from under chin

(See "REPTILE")

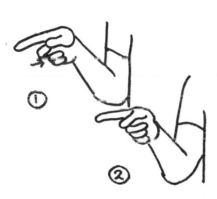

SNAP

Middle finger and thumb tips together, index extended, snap outward to G

SNATCH

Palm-in V jerks right to bent-V

(See "STEAL")

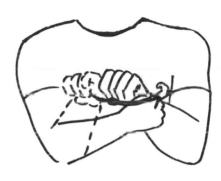

SNEAK

X sneaks around left S to peek at little finger of left hand

SNEAKERS = SNEAK + -ER + -S

SNEEZE

Index finger under nose, jerk head back and then forward slightly

SNIFF

X against nose, sniff with head moving slightly up

SNIP

First two fingers snip corner of first knuckle of left S, palms down; may repeat

(See "CUT")

SNOB

Index finger on nose tilts head back, little finger out

SNORE

Index zig-zags out from mouth

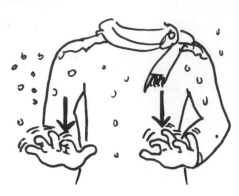

SNOW

Hands drops slowly, palm-down, fluttering fingers

(See "RAIN")

SO

Right S moves sharply down, striking side of left S in passing

SOAP

Flick fingers of bent hand back off left palm; repeat

SOCCER

Side of flat right hand kicks side of palm-in left hand several times

(See "KICK")

SOCIAL

Right S curves around vertical left index

SOCIETY = SOCIAL + -ITY

(See "ATMOSPHERE")

SOCK ★

S hits forward along side of palm-down left index finger

SOCKS = SOCK + -S

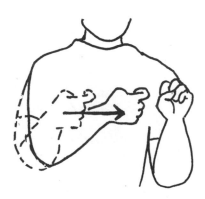

SOCKET

Palm-in right X taps palm-out left S

(See "ELECTRIC")

SODA

Fingers of palm-down hand flutter up from palm-right left S-hand

SOFA

First two fingers sit on middle finger of left F-hand

(See "SIT")

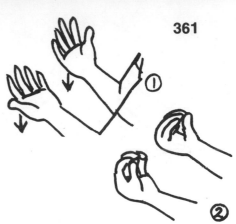

SOFT

Palm-up open hands drop slightly, closing to flat-O's; repeat

SOIL

Flat-O thumb rubs on balls of fingers

SOLAR

Right S behind left, palms-out; right circles around left to palm-in

(See "EQUATOR")

SOLD

Sell + P. T.

SOLDER

Index, thumb extended, circles near left S

(See "WELD")

SOLDIER

A's tap at shoulder and side; repeat (Holding gun)

(See "MILITARY")

SOLE ★

Palm-up index finger slides backwards under horizontal left palm

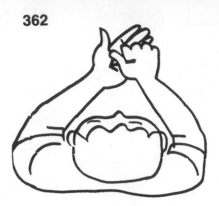

SOLID

Right A knocks on left palm

SOME ♔

Side of right hand draws small arc across left palm

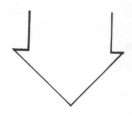

SOMEBODY = SOME + BODY

SOMEHOW = SOME +HOW

SOMEONE = SOME + ONE

SOMETHING = SOME + THING

SOMEWHERE = SOME + WHERE

SOMERSAULT

S somersaults twice off left palm, twisting

(See "TUMBLE")

SOMETIMES

Index touches left palm, moves toward body, circles back to palm; repeat

(Can be some + time + -s)

SON

Right A-hand at temple drops in an arc to open palm-up on palm-up left hand

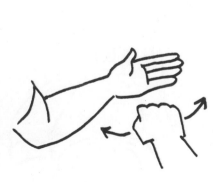

SONG

S arcs from side to side behind left palm

(See "MUSIC")

SOON

Side of palm-out S on left palm; twists to palm-down

(See "MINUTE")

SOPHISTICATE

Thumb of 3 brushes off chin; repeat

**SOPHISTICATION =
SOPHISTICATE + -TION**

SOPHOMORE

Index taps middle finger of left 5

(See "FRESHMAN")

SORE ★

S twists on chin; repeat

(See "SOUR")

SORRY

A circles on chest
SORROW = SORRY + W
(See "REGRET")

SOUL

9-hand rises, shaking, from flat-O near heart

SOUND ♔

Palm-out 5 moves to ear, closing to flat-O

SOUP ♔

H-hand ladles twice from palm to mouth

SOUR ♔

Index finger on chin, twist to palm-in

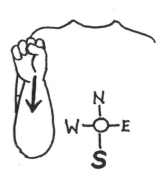

SOUTH

Palm-out S moves down
SOUTHERN = SOUTH + -ER + -N
(See "DOWN")

SPACE

S arcs up in front of face

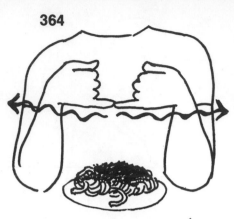

SPAGHETTI

Tips of I's touching, palm-in, separate with a shaking movement

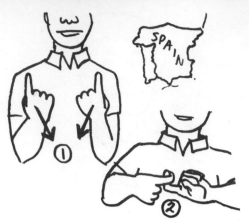

SPAIN

Index fingers on shoulders drop to interlocking X's (Fastening cape)

SPANISH = SPAIN + -ISH

SPANK

Flat hand spanks vertical flat hand

SPARK

Right index flicks up alongside left index; repeat

SPEAK

Palm-left 4 at chin moves forward, fluttering fingers; repeat

SPOKE = SPEAK + P. T.
SPOKEN = SPEAK + P. P.

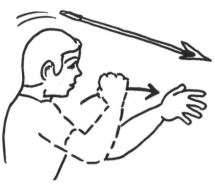

SPEAR

Mime throwing a spear

SPECIAL

9 pulls middle finger of palm-in 5 upward

(See "EXCEPT")

SPECIFIC

Tip of palm-in 1-hand makes small circle then jerks toward left vertical index

SPECIFY = SPECIFIC + -Y

(See "EXACT")

SPEECH

Bent V circles in front of mouth

(See "MOUTH")

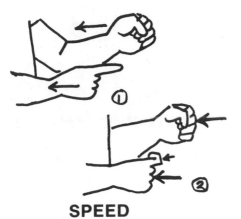

SPEED

Left S ahead of right index, jerk both toward body, closing index to X

(See "FAST")

SPELL★

Palm-down hand moves right, fingers waving alternately

SPEND

Back of flat-O on left palm slides off, closing to A

SPENT = SPEND + P. T.

SPICE

Right index and middle finger alternately tap left palm-out S

(See "SALT")

SPIDER

Little fingers interlock and wiggle forward

SPILL

C-hand tips forward off left palm

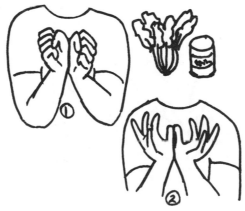

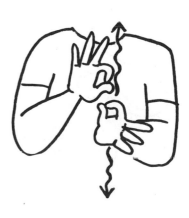

SPIN ♛

Index points down and spins

SPINACH

Palms up and heels together, S-hands open

SPIRIT

9-hand's palms-facing, separate up and down in wavy motion (See "GHOST")

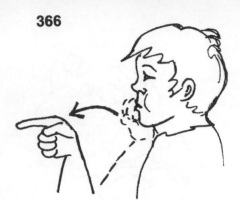

SPIT

S at mouth, index snaps out, pointing forward

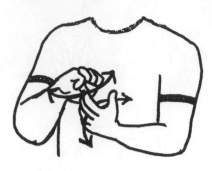

SPITE

Palm-in left hand and right S brush back and forth forward and back

(See "THOUGH")

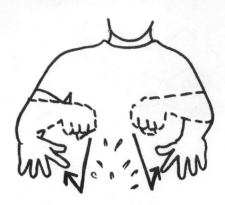

SPLASH

Palm-down S's drop; 5's splash up

SPLINTER

Index is splinter that goes into left palm

SPLIT

Flat hands, right on left at right angles; drop, separating to sides

SPONGE

Hold sponge between claw-hands, all fingertips touching and move fingers downward in squeezing motion

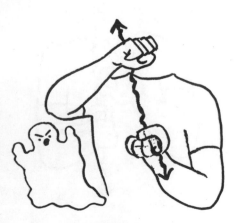

SPOOK

Palms-facing, S rises above S in wavy motion

(See "GHOST")

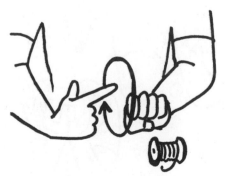

SPOOL

Fingertip of L circles around side of left S

(See "REEL")

SPOON

H circles up from left palm

(See "SOUP")

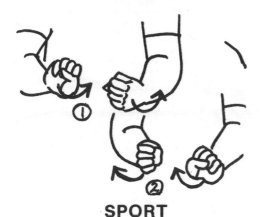

SPORT

S-hands swing side to side
(See "PLAY")

SPOT ★

Side of F placed wherever
spot is

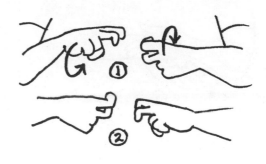

SPRAIN

Bent V's near each other twist
sharply in opposite directions
(See "TWIST")

SPRAY

Thumb pushes aerosal spray
knob, moving the "can" left and
right

SPOKE

Speak + P. T.

SPREAD

O-hands, palms-down, spread
to palm-down 5's

SPRING ★

Flat-O "jumps" upward
through C to 5; repeat

SPRANG = SPRING + P. T.
SPRUNG = SPRING + P. P.
(See "GROW")

SPRINKLE

Palm-down 5 circles horizontally, fluttering fingers

SQUARE

Indexes draw a square
(See "RECTANGLE")

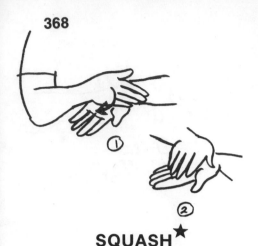

SQUASH ★

Right palm twists on left palm
(squashing)
(See "CRUSH")

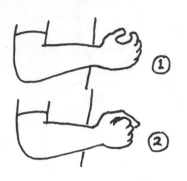

SQUEEZE

Hand squeezes from claw to S

SQUID

S sits on 5; 5-hand does push-ups
(See "OCTOPUS")

SQUIRM

Back of bent-V on left open palm squirms from side to side

SQUIRREL

At chin, tap bent-V fingertips together, heels together

STAB

Fist stabs left palm

STACK ★

Palm-up S arcs over to palm-down on back of left hand
(See "CARGO")

STAGE

Heel of S slides across left arm
(See "BOARD")

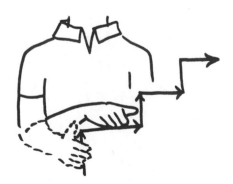

STAIR

Right palm describes stair-steps

STALE

X-finger draws across fingers
of S   (See "DULL")

STAMP ★

Side of S-fist hits left palm

STAND

V-fingertips stand on left palm
STOOD = STAND + P. T.

STANDARD ♔

Palm-down Y's move in circle
horizontally together

STAPLE

Heel of A-hand presses stapler
on the heel of the left hand

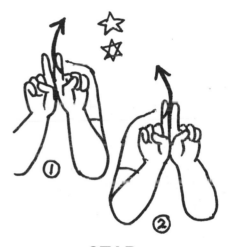

STAR

Side of right index finger
strikes upward against left
index finger; left strikes
upward against right
   (See "CONSTELLATION")

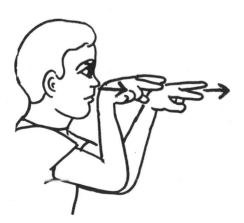

STARE

Both V-hands, palm down near
eyes, right behind left; move
forward slightly

START

(Alt. 1)
Index fingertip on wrist of left S
twists

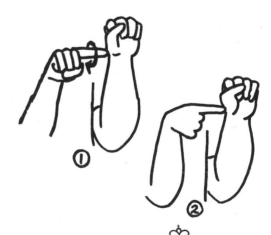

START ♔

(Alt. 2)
Right index between left index
and middle finger; twist right
hand

STARTLE

S's at sides of eyes spring open to 5's

STARVE

Both palm-in C-hands, one above the other, move down middle of chest once

(See "HUNGER")

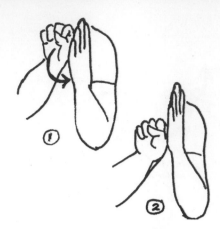

STATE

Side of S on fingertips of left flat hand arcs down to heel

(See "LAW")

STATION

Palm-out S's touch, then outline roof and sides

(See "HOUSE")

STATUE

Palm-out S's outline statue

(See "SHAPE")

STAY

Palm-down Y-thumbs together; right arcs slightly down to right

(See "LODGE")

STEAD

Side of S hits heel of left hand

STEADY = STEAD + -Y

STEAK

Right hand pinches thumb-knuckle of left S; shake both hands

(See "MEAT")

STEAL

V-hand pulls to bent-V from left elbow

STOLE = STEAL + P. T.
STOLEN = STEAL + P. P.

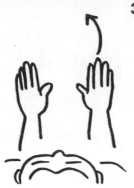

STEAM

W spirals upwards from chin

STEEL

Palm-in S arcs right, hitting side of left index, ending palm-out

(See "METAL")

STEP

Flat hands, palms down, one hand steps forward

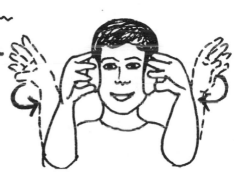

STEREO

(Alt. 1)
Both S's wiggle to ears from sides

STEREO

(Alt. 2)
5-hands swing from outward to facing toward ears

STETHOSCOPE

Indexes and thumbs grip at ears; drop hands to meet on chest; then right hand touches chest at left and right

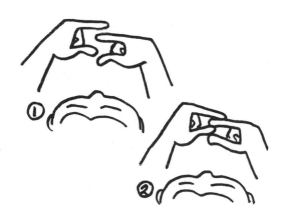

STEW

Right S pointing down above left C opens to 5; repeat

STICK ★

G's close on each other
STICKY = STICK + -Y
STUCK = STICK + P. T.

STILL ★

Y-hand swings down and then up, forward

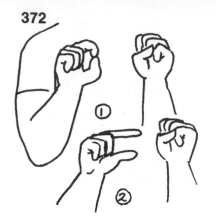

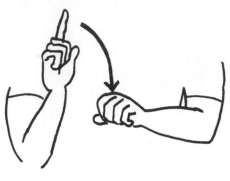

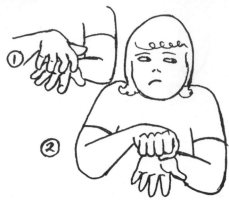

STIMULUS

Index of right S repeatedly flicks toward left S

STIMULI = STIMULUS + -I

STING

Index finger hits back of S sharply

STUNG = STING + -P. T.

STINGY

Claw on left palm scrapes closed to S

STINK

Pinch nose

STIR ★

A-hand stirs, thumb pointing down

STITCH ★

X-fingertip taps forward on left palm

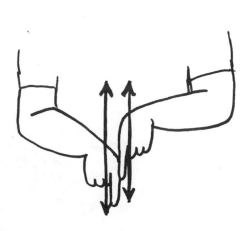

STOCKING

Pointing downwards, index fingers slide back and forth against each other

(See "HOSE")

STOLE

Steal + P. T.

STOMACH

Fingertips of bent hand pat stomach

STOMACHACHE = STOMACH + ACHE

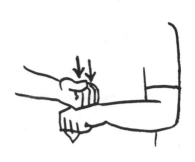

STONE ♔

Back of S raps back of left S; repeat

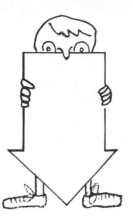

STOOD

Stand + P. T.

STOP ♔

Side of right flat hand strikes left flat palm

STORE ♔ ★

Flat-O behind left C, nod rapidly toward and away from side of C

STORAGE = STORE + -AGE

STORM ♔

Claw hands circle alternately over head

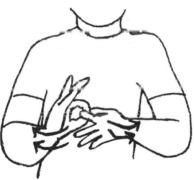

STORY

Open 9-hands approach, link, and separate still closed; repeat

STOVE

Thumb and bent-V turn on 2 burners of the stove, along left arm

STRADDLE

Inverted V straddles side of flat left hand and rocks side to side

STRAIGHT ♔

Side of right B slides forward on side of left B

STRANGE

Right palm-left C arcs in front of nose to palm-down C

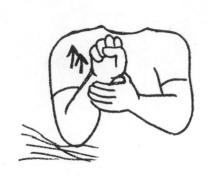

STRAW

Palm-out S brushes up through C; repeat

(See "GRAIN")

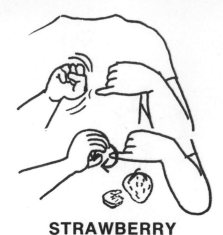

STRAWBERRY

(Alt. 1)

S shakes by little finger of palm-in horizontal left I; then add "berry"

STRAWBERRY

(Alt. 2)

Palm-in 9 at lips moves out

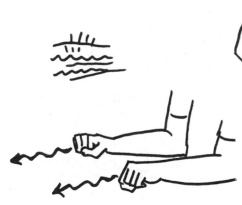

STREAM

Palm-down S's ripple forward to left, up and down

(See "BROOK")

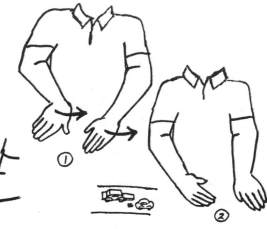

STREET

Palms-in, hands pointing down with right slightly before left, hands sweep to the left

STRENGTH

Strong + -th

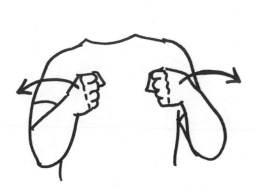

STRETCH

S's pull apart, palms-in

STRICT

Side of bent-V hits bridge of nose lightly

STRIKE

Right palm-in S-hand strikes palm-out vertical left index

(See "BEAT")

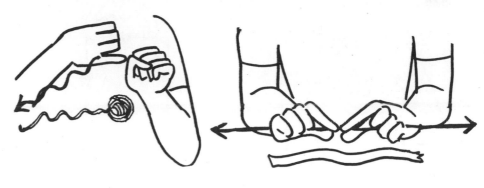

STRING

I-fingertip shakes to side and down from left S

(See "CORD")

STRIP ★

G fingertips together, pull to sides and close thumb and finger

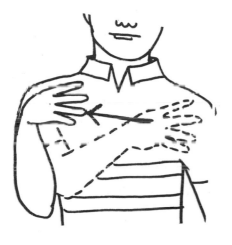

STRIPE

4-hand slides across chest to the right

STRONG ♔

Index finger draws muscle on upper left arm

STRENGTH = STRONG + -TH

STRUCTURE

S's build alternately upward on each other

(See "BUILD")

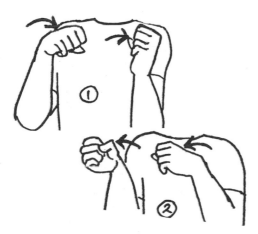

STRUGGLE

S's, palms-facing, rock back and forth toward each other

(See "WAR")

STUBBORN

Thumb touching temple, fingers flap forward together

(See "HORSE")

STUDY

Fingers wiggle above left palm

STUDENT = STUDY + -ENT

STUFF

Right palm-down S makes stuffing motions towards left C
(See "STORE")

STUNG

Sting + P. T.

STUPID

Back of V hits forehead

(See "DUMB")

STYLE

5 hand on torso, move upward on body fluttering fingers
(See "FANCY")

SUBJECT

Side of right S on left fingers, then on left heel of palm-up flat hand

(See "LESSON")

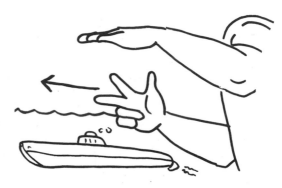

SUBMARINE

Thumb-up horizontal palm-left 3-hand glides under left palm

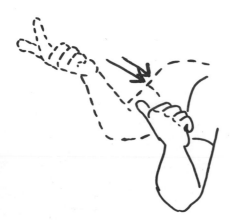

SUBSCRIBE

Palm up L-hand moves back toward body, closing to A; repeat

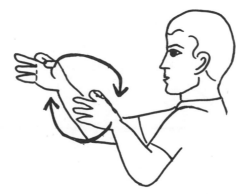

SUBSTITUTE

9-hands, right in front of left, circle each other vertically once (See "EXCHANGE")

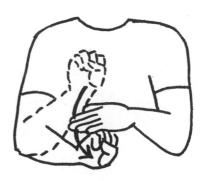

SUBTLE

Palm-out S moves from over left hand to under it

(See "HUMBLE")

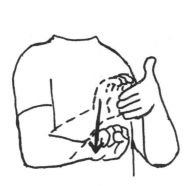

SUBTRACT

Fingertips of C scratch left palm downwards to S

(See "ADD")

SUBWAY

1-hand dives down under flat left hand

(See "ENTER")

SUCCEED

Index fingers at temples twist out to sides and up

(See "SUCCESS")

SUCCESS

Index fingers at temples twist out and up to sides, twisting twice

SUCH

S-hands together, arc up and apart

(See "MUCH")

SUCK

Flat hands draw inward sharply to grasp each other with thumbs

SUCKER

A-hand pulls an invisible sucker in and out of mouth

SUDDEN

Thumbs flip out from under index fingers

SUFFER

Thumb of A on chin, twist several times

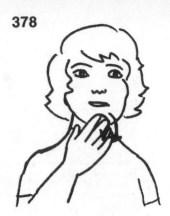

SUGAR

Fingertips brush downward off chin; repeat

(See "CUTE")

SUGGEST ♔

Palm-up hands arc up and forward

SUIT

Y-hands face each other, thumbs on chest, then arc down to little fingertips on body

SUM ★

Right 5, palm-down, over left 5, palm-up; move toward each other and meet as flat-O's

SUMMARY

5-hands face each other, approach, close to right S on left S

SUMMARIZE = SUMMARY + -IZE

SUMMER ♔

Palm-down X is dragged across forehead (wiping sweat)

SUN

C by eye swings up to side

SUNDAE

Extended-A thumb swirls up from C-hand in a narrowing spiral

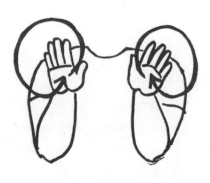

SUNDAY

Palm-out hands circle out to sides

SUNG

Sing + P. T.

SUNK

Sink + P.P.

SUPER

S circles over palm-down left hand

SUPERIOR = SUPER + -R

(See "OVER")

SUPERINTENDENT

Crossed C's at forehead separate and close to S's

(See "PRESIDENT")

SUPERVISE

Palm-out right S on side of left V; both circle horizontally

SUPERVISION = SUPERVISE + -TION

(See "CARE")

SUPPER

S circles forward near mouth (Sign may be made with P instead of S)

(See "EAT")

SUPPLEMENT

Palm-out right S arcs down and sideways to underside of palm-in horizontal left hand

(See "ADD")

SUPPORT

Support side of left S with top of right S; push up

(See "ALLEGIANCE")

SUPPOSE

Palm-in I-hand at temple moves out in two arcs

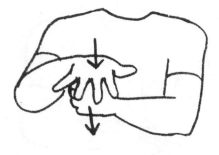

SUPPRESS

Right palm pushes down left S-hand

SURE

Index finger at chin arcs up and forward

(See "CERTAIN")

SURFACE

Right bent middle finger brushes back and forth on back of palm-down left hand

SURGERY

Thumb of extended-A cuts down open palm

(Can be done on body where surgery is done)

SURPRISE

S-hands, facing each other near eyes, snap open to L-hands

(See "AMAZE")

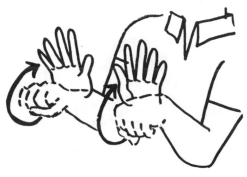

SURRENDER

Palm-down S's open and swing up to 5's

SURROUND

Horizontal 5-hand circles vertical index

SURVIVE

S-hands, palm-down, slide up chest

(See "ADDRESS")

SUSPECT

Scratch temple; repeat

SUSPICION = SUSPECT + -TION

(See "PARANOID")

SUSPEND

Right X hooks on horizontal left index and both move upward

SUSPENSION = SUSPEND + -ION

SWALLOW

Side of index of palm-left hand arcs down throat

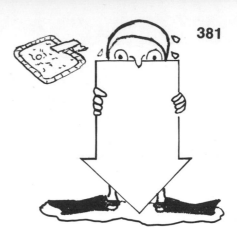

SWAM

Swim + P.T.

SWAN

Arm draws back to form S-shape with arm and hand

SWEAT

Palm-down 4 moves left over forehead, fluttering fingers

SWEATER

S-hands pull sweater down over head

SWEDE

(U.S. Sign)
S circles near forehead

SWEDEN = SWEDE + -N
SWEDISH = SWEDE + -ISH

(See "DENMARK")

SWEDEN

(Swedish Sign)
5-hand draws up from back of left hand and closes to flat-O; repeat

SWEDISH = SWEDE + -ISH

SWEEP

Side of hand sweeps up from left palm twice

SWEPT = SWEEP + P. T.

SWEET
Open hand rubs chin circularly
(See "HONEY")

SWEETHEART
Knuckles together, thumbs wiggle toward each other
(Can be Sweet + Heart)

SWELL ★
Claw-hands move forward from near eyes
SWOLLEN = SWELL + P. P.

SWIM
Palms-down, breast stroke forward
SWAM = SWIM + P. T.
SWUM = SWIM + P. P.

SWING
Bent-V sits on 2 fingers of left hand and swings forward and back
SWUNG = SWING + P. P.
(See "TRAPEZE")

SWITCH ★
1-hand index fingers, almost touching, reverse positions vertically
(See "CHANGE")

SWOLLEN
Swell + P. P.

SWORD
A-hand draws sword out of left C at side

SYLLABLE
G-hand brushes tip of left index several times
(See "WORD")

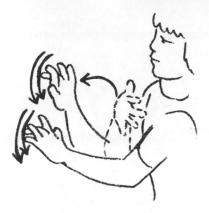

SYMBOL

Right S on vertical left palm, both move forward together

(See "SHOW")

SYMPATHY

Right bent middle finger touches heart, then both bent middle fingers stroke outwards

SYRUP

Palm-in I-little finger brushes side of mouth

SYSTEM

(Alt. 1)

S-hands move forward-left, back, then forward-right

(See "METHOD")

SYSTEM

(Alt. 2)

Palm-out S's together, separate sidoways and down; repeat lower down

(See "ANALYZE")

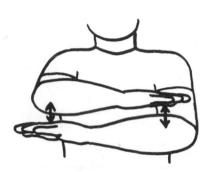

TABLE ♔

Right palm and elbow bounce on left arm

TACO

Flat hand slips into left "taco shell" like filling a taco

TAIL

Wrist rests on left index finger; wag hand with index extended

(See "WAG")

TAILOR

Right 9-hand sews near left T

(See "SEW")

TAKE

5-hand draws back toward body, closing to S

TOOK = TAKE + P. T.
TAKEN = TAKE + P. P.

TALE

Both T's together, palm-out, separate in a wiggling motion

(See "SENTENCE")

TALENT

Hand clasps side of left T and slides off to A

(See "EXPERT")

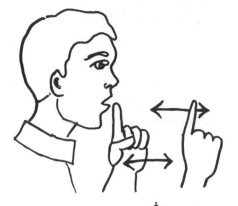

TALK

Index fingers move alternately to and from lips

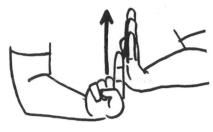

TALL

1-index finger slides up vertical palm-right palm

TAMBOURINE

A strikes on left flat vertical palm and shakes away from it to the right

TAME

T-hand strokes back of palm-down left hand

(See "PET")

TAN

Side of T moves down on cheek

(See "BROWN")

TANGERINE

T moves from in back of S to the front

(See "APRICOT")

TANK

I's touch, right behind left; right moves back, and both change to K's

(See "CAR")

TANTRUM

Palm-in T's near chest jerk up

(See "ANGER")

TAP ★

T taps left palm

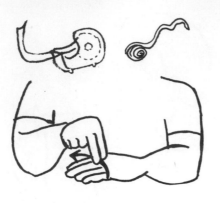

TAPE

U-fingers brush across backs
of left fingers

TARDY

Side of right T on left vertical
palm twists to palm-down

(See "MINUTE")

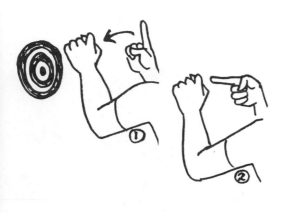

TARGET

Right index behind left T; index
jerks down to point at T

(See "AIM")

TART

T twists on chin

(See "SOUR")

TASK

Palm-down T arcs to left,
hitting back of left wrist

(See "JOB")

TASTE

Middle finger touches lower lip

TATTLE

Index under lips flicks out;
repeat

TAUGHT

Teach + P. T.

TAX

Thumb of T strikes straight down across left palm

(See "COST")

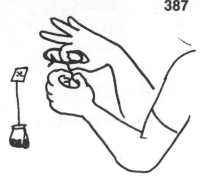

TAXI

X moves back from behind left X

(See "CAR")

TEA

Circle 9 above left O as if swishing a tea bag

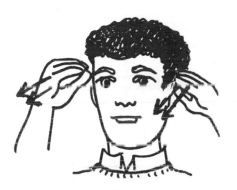

TEACH

Flat-O's pointing to temples move forward slightly; repeat

TAUGHT = TEACH + P. T.

TEACHER = TEACH + -ER

TEAM

Palm-out T's circle horizontally out to palm-in

(See "CLASS")

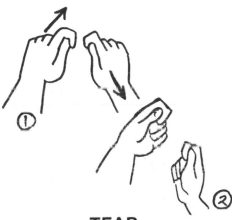

TEAR

(Rip)

Thumbs and indexes together grasp "material" in front of you; pull right back and left forward as if tearing something

TORE = TEAR + P. T.

TORN = TEAR + P. P.

TEAR

(Cry)

2 T's drag alternately down cheeks

(See "CRY")

TEASE

Right X on left, right brushes quickly forward on left; repeat

TEEN

T touches first at temple, then at cheek

TEENAGER = TEEN + AGE + -ER

(See "PARENT")

388

TEETER TOTTER

Palm-down T's move up and down alternately

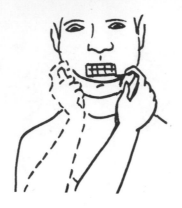

TEETH

X-hand crosses right to left in front of teeth

(See "TOOTH")

TELEGRAM

Palm-down X moves quickly along left index finger and off

TELEGRAPH

Palm-down X taps along left index finger

TELEPHONE

Thumb of Y near ear, little finger near mouth

TELESCOPE

Right O behind left O at eye, twist to focus telescope

TELETYPEWRITER
(TTY)
Spell T + T + Y

TELEVISION
T + V

TELL

Palm-down index under chin flips out to palm-up

TOLD = TELL + P. T.

TEMPER

Palm-out T slides up and down side of left index

TEMPERATURE = TEMPER + -URE

(See "THERMOMETER")

TEMPLE ★

Heel of T taps on back of S; repeat

(See "CHURCH")

TEMPORARY

Side of T slides back and forth a bit on side of left H

(See "SHORT")

TEMPT

X-index taps elbow

TEMPTATION = TEMPT + -TION

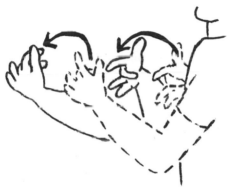

TEND ★

Bent middle fingers, right on chest and left ahead, move forward

TENDENCY = TEND + -ENCE + -Y

TENNIS

Right A-hand swings racket

TENT

V fingertips touch; separate down and out

(See "TEPEE")

TEPEE

T's together separate and fall in a tall inverted V

(See "TENT")

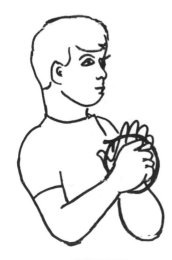

TERM

T on palm-right left hand; circles and touches palm again

(See "HOUR")

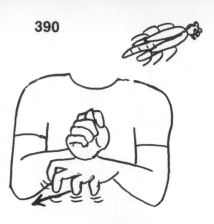

TERMITE

Right T rides forward on left wiggling fingers

(See "ANT")

TERRIFIC

Palm-out T's make small sideways circles; then flat palm-out hands push forward slightly

(See "FABULOUS")

TERRITORY

T's, palms facing, circle back to nearer body

(See "PLACE")

TERROR

Palm-out T-hands shake down and toward body

TERRIBLE = TERROR + -IBLE

(See "AFRAID")

TEST

Indexes change from 1 to X, moving downward

TESTIFY

Index touches lips and falls to palm-out T at back of left wrist

(See "PROMISE")

TEXAS

X moves down with a curve, palm-out

TEXTURE

Palm-in T rubs on chest near shoulder

(See "CLOTH")

THAN

Flat hand slaps down across left fingertips

THANK

Palm-in open hand at chin drops to palm-up

THANKSGIVING =

THANK + S + GIVE + -ING

THAT ♚

Palm-down I-L-hand on left palm

THE

(Alt. 1)
Palm-down Y drops slightly

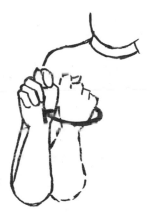

THE

(Alt. 2)
Palm-in T; twist to palm-out

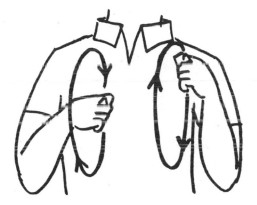

THEATER

T's brush alternately down chest

(See "ACT")

THEIR ♚

Palm-up hand at left of body sweeps right to palm-out R

THEIRS = THEIR + -S

THEM

Palm-up hand at left of body sweeps right to palm-out M

(See "THEIR")

THEME

Palm-out T circles beneath left hand

(See "BASE")

THEN ♚

Index moves from off left thumb to off tip of left index

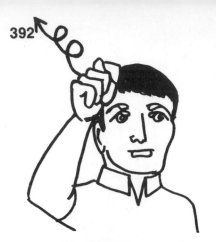

THEORY

T circles from forehead upward to right

(See "IDEA")

THERAPY

Left palm lifts right T

THERAPIST = THERAPY + -IST

(See "HELP")

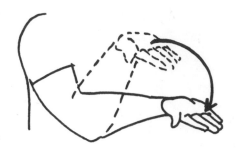

THERE

Palm-up hand arcs forward

THEREFORE

Index and thumb make 3 dots in the air in a triangle shape

THERMOMETER

Right index finger slides rapidly up and down side of left index finger

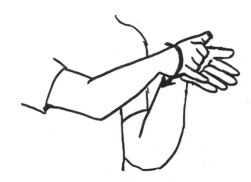

THESE

Palm-down Y on palm of left hand; twist or move Y across left fingers

(See "THAT")

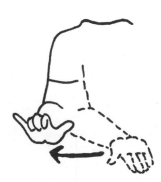

THEY

Palm-up hand at left of body; sweep right to palm-out Y

(See "THEIR")

THICK

C with thumb and index moves right along back of left hand

THICKEN = THICK + -EN

THIEF

Fingers of H slide from corner of nose to the right

THEFT = THIEF + -T

THIEVES = THIEF + -S

THIGH

T-hand pats thigh

THIMBLE

Put thimble on left middle finger

THIN

G-fingertips move down near face and body

THING

Palm-up, arc right hand slightly up and down to the right

THINK

Finger above brow on forehead (May circle slightly)
THOUGHT = THINK + P. T.

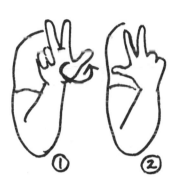

THIRD

Palm-out 3 twists to palm-in
(See "SECOND")

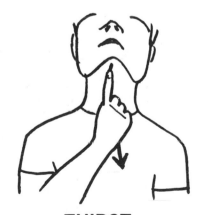

THIRST

Draw finger down throat
THIRSTY = THIRST + -Y
(See "THROAT")

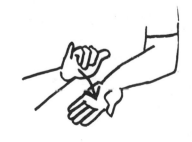

THIS

Palm-down Y drops on palm of left hand
(See "THAT")

THORN

Pull "thorn" out of vertical left index finger

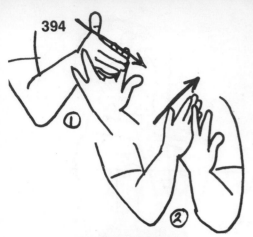

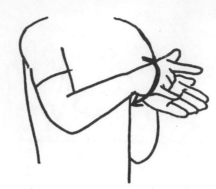

THOROUGH

Right hand slides through fingers of left; returns in the opposite direction

THOSE

Palm-down I-L-hand on palm of left hand; twist or move across left fingers

(See "THAT")

THOUGH

Slap hands forward and back against each other alternately

THOUGHT

(Noun)
T circles near temple
(See "REASON")

THOUGHT

(Verb)
Think + P. T.

THOUSAND

Fingertips of bent hand strike left palm

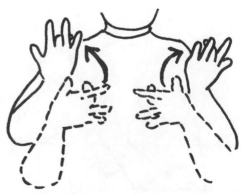

THREAD

I-fingertip shakes to side and slightly down from left T

(See "CORD")

THREAT

T arcs up, hitting back of left S; repeat

(See "DANGER")

THRILL

Middle fingers on chest flick up sides, palm-in

THROAT

Slide fingertips of palm-in G-hand down throat

(See "THIRST")

THROB

A bounces from heart to left horizontal palm, palms-in

THRONE

Bent 3's hold arms of "throne"

THROUGH

Open hand slides outward between fingers of left hand

THROW

Flat-O throws forward into 5-hand

THREW = THROW + P. T.
THROWN = THROW + P. P.

(See "PITCH")

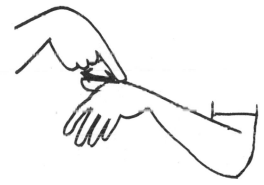

THUMB

Fingertip rubs thumb

THUNDER

Right index finger moves from ear to both S's jerking forward alternately

THURSDAY

T-hand to H-hand
(Can be done with H alone circling slightly)

(See "MONDAY")

TICKET

Bent-V fingers slide onto side of palm-in left hand (Punch ticket)

TICKLE

Bent index finger tickles near side

TIDE

Palm-down right T slides out and up onto back of left hand; slides back off

(See "SHORE")

TIE ★

Horizontal U-fingers circle around each other, then separate

TIGER

Both palm-in claw-hands, near cheeks, move outwards (drawing whiskers); repeat

(See "CAT")

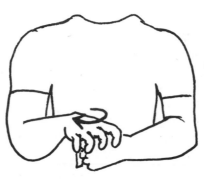

TIGHT

Right claw on left S; twist slightly right, as if to tighten cap

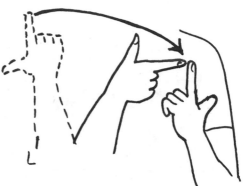

TILL ★

Right palm-in L index arcs over to touch index of palm-in left L

(See "TO")

TIMBER

Elbow resting on back of left hand, shake T

(See "TREE")

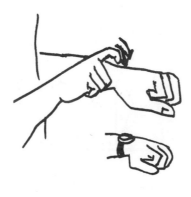

TIME

X-index finger taps wrist

TIMID

Palm-in T on cheek twists slightly upward

(See "SHY")

TIN

T arcs right, hitting side of left index

(See "METAL")

TINY

Palm-down right index bounces just above palm-up left index

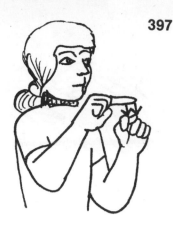

TIP ★

Index taps tip of left T-thumb

(See "CAP")

TIPTOE

Tiptoe with indexes pointing downward

TIRE ★

Palm-down T's near chest arc down to palm-up

TIRED = TIRE + P. T.

(See "WEARY")

TISSUE

Heel of right T strikes across left heel; repeat

(See "PAPER")

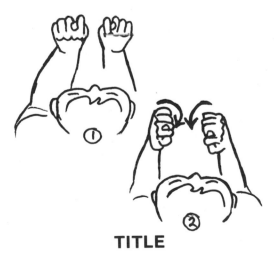

TITLE

Palm-out T's twist to face each other

(See "QUOTE")

TO

Horizontal index finger approaches and touches left vertical index finger

TOAD

S at left elbow flicks out to V when jumping; land with S; flick to V again, while moving down left arm

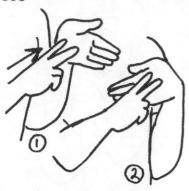

TOAST ★

V stabs on left palm and then on back of hand

TOBACCO

Fingertips of M twist back and forth on cheek

(See "GUM")

TOBOGGAN

Palm-up T rides forward on left palm

(See "SLED")

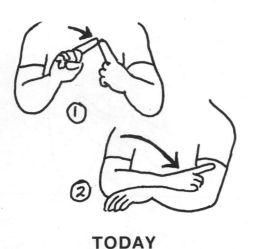

TODAY

Touch right index to left index and quickly drop right arm on left arm

TOE

T-hand passes around fingertips of flat hand

(See "EDGE")

TOGETHER

T-hands together; palms facing, circle together

(See "STANDARD")

TOIL

T bounces back and forth on left S

(See "BUSY")

TOILET

Palm-out T shakes

TOLD

Tell + P. T.

TOLERATE

T draws downward over chin

TOLERANT = TOLERATE + -ANT

(See "LONESOME")

TOMATO

1-finger from chin strikes past fingertips of left flat-O

TOMB

Palm-down T's arc back toward body

(See "BURY")

TOMORROW

Thumb on cheek, move forward and twist to point forward

TON

Side of T rocks on index of H-hand

(See "WEIGH")

TONGUE

Index points to tongue

TONSIL

Index finger touches each side of neck

TONSILLECTOMY

Palm-in V at side of neck moves forward to bent-V; repeat at other side of neck

TOO

O approaches and touches left index

(See "TO")

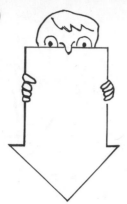

TOOK

Take + P. T.

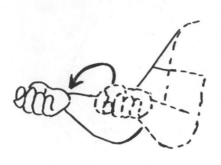

TOOL

Palm-up T arcs right

(See "THING")

TOOTH

Index points to a tooth

TOOTHACHE = TOOTH + ACHE

TOOTHBRUSH

Palm-down right index brushes back and forth in slight up and down wiggle at mouth

TOOTHPASTE

Right thumb and fist squeeze out toothpaste along horizontal left index

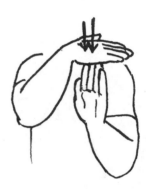

TOP ★

Flat hand tap tops of left palm-right fingers

(See "CAP")

TOPIC

Side of T touches left palm-up fingers then heel

(See "LESSON")

TORCH

O opens to 5; with fingers fluttering, rises above left T-hand

(See "FLARE")

TORNADO

T's facing each other, rotate around each other, rising to the right

(See "STORM")

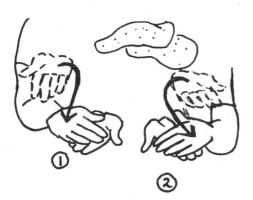

TORTILLA

Right hand on left, then left on right hand, press a tortilla

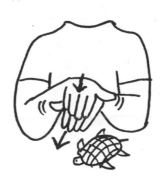

TORTOISE

Hands point forward, right on left; move forward, wiggling thumbs

TORTURE

Right T hits forward and off left T, then left off right

(See "PERSECUTE")

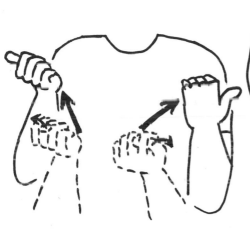

TOSS

T-thumbs snap out to sides

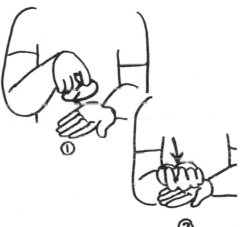

TOTAL

Palm-down T, over left palm, circles and inverts to palm-up T on palm

(See "WHOLE")

TOTAL COMMUNICATION

(T. C.)

Right T and left C move alternately forward and back, palms facing

(See "TALK")

TOUCH

Middle finger of right hand touches back of left hand

TOUGH

Bent-V hits back of left S in arc down to the right

(See "HARD")

TOUR

Bent-V circles jerkily, palm-down

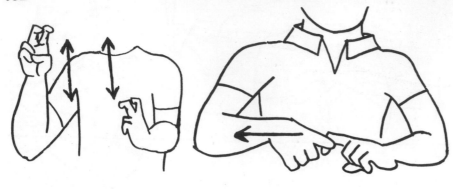

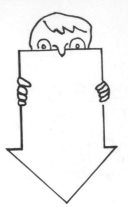

TOURNAMENT
Bent-V's face each other; move up and down alternately

TOW
Right X pulls left X toward the right

TOWARD
To + Ward

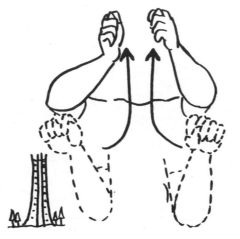

TOWEL
Open hands circle near cheeks; repeat

TOWER
Palm-out T's swing in and then up

(See "CHIMNEY")

TOWN
Fingertips touch at left, separate; touch at right

TOY
T-hands, one palm-out, one palm-in, swing back and forth, pivoting at wrists

(See "PLAY")

TRACE ★
Palm-down T draws wavy line on left palm, toward body

(See "ART")

TRACK ★
Palm-out T at side of palm-down left V; T moves forward

TRACTOR

T's steer large wheel
(See "DRIVE")

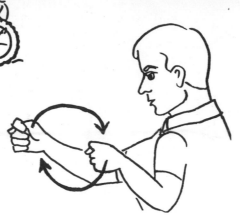

TRADE

T-hands, right in front of left, circle each other vertically once

(See "EXCHANGE")

TRADITION

Right T on left near right shoulder, both move forward and down

TRAFFIC

5-palms brush each other, moving rapidly forward and back

(See "FREEWAY")

TRAGIC

T's arc down from corners of mouth, outlining a sad mouth

TRAGEDY = TRAGIC + -Y

(See "GRIM")

TRAIL

Palm-down T weaves towards body

TRAILER = TRAIL + -ER

TRAIN ★

Palms down, right H rubs on back of left H

TRAIT

T circles near shoulder, then touches it

(See "CHARACTER")

TRANQUIL

T's near chin separate down and sideways

(See "QUIET")

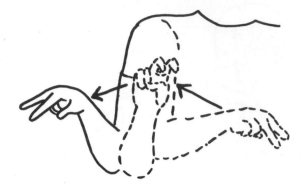

TRANSFER

Palm-down V lifts to bent-V and shoots to right to V again

(See "RELAY")

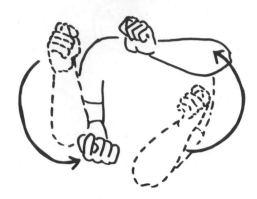

TRANSFORM

T-hands face each other right above left; reverse

TRANSLATE

Palms of T-hands touch, twist to reverse position; may repeat
(See "CHANGE")

TRANSPARENT

V, from eye, points between first and second fingers of left hand

TRANSPORT

Palm-up T.'s at left arc toward right

(See "BRING")

TRAP

Bent-V fingers drop to trap left index

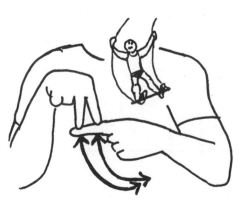

TRAPEZE

V-fingertips stand on left index; swing both hands together (See "SWING")

TRASH

Back of T on left palm, slide forward and throw off to palm-down 5 (See "DISPOSE")

TRAVEL

Index fingers circle each other; moving out, around, and slighty upward

(See "VOYAGE")

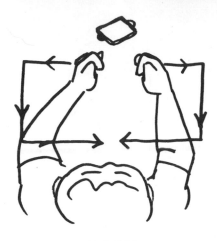

TRAY

T's draw shape of tray horizontally

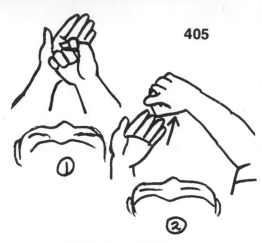

TREASURE

Palm-up T on left palm rises to palm-down T over palm

(See "RICH")

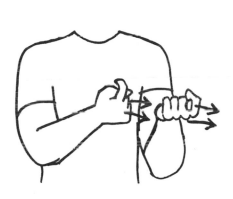

TREAT

Palm-up T's push forward; repeat

(See "URGE")

TREE

Elbow on back of left hand, shake 5

TREMENDOUS

X's face each other; pull apart in exaggerated gesture

(See "MUCH")

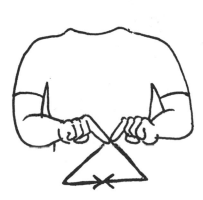

TRIANGLE

Indexes draw a triangle

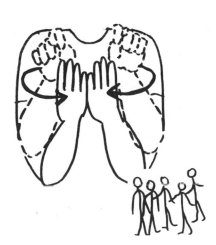

TRIBE

Palm-out T's circle out to palm-in B's touching

(See "BAND")

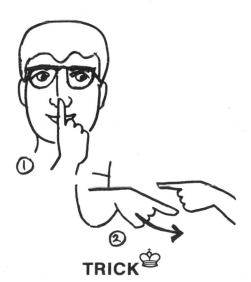

TRICK

Right index on nose quickly twists sideways under left hand, both palms inward

TRICYCLE

T-hands circle up and out alternately

(See "BICYCLE")

TRIED

Try + P. T.

TRILLION

Palm-down T arcs forward from left heel to hit fingertips

(See "BILLION")

TRIM ★

V-fingers scissor across tip of left T

(See "CUT")

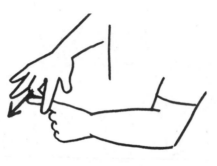

TRIP ★

Middle fingertip trips over left index

TRIPLE

Middle finger of 3 brushes up left palm

(See "ONCE")

TRIUMPH

T spirals up off left S

(See "WIN")

TROMBONE

Thumbs of both A-hands palms facing, at lips; right moves out and back several times

TROPHY

Palm-out T's outline cup

(See "SHAPE")

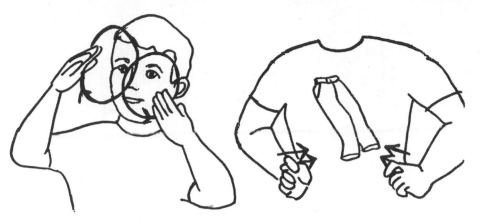

TROUBLE

Flat hands circle alternately before face

(See "WORRY")

TROUSER

T-hands tap waist

(See "PANT")

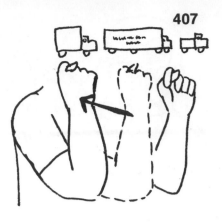

TRUCK

Right T behind left T; move right hand back

(See "CAR")

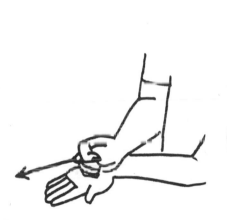

TRUE

Side of T on left palm; slide forward across palm and fingers

TRUTH = TRUE + -TH

(See "HONEST")

TRUMPET

Right fingers play outside left T at lips

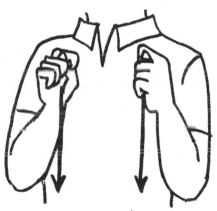

TRUNK ★

T's, palms facing, draw down, on chest

TRUST

5-hands pull out and close to S's near shoulder

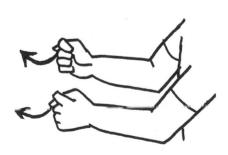

TRY

T-hands, palms facing, move forward with slight downward

TRIED = TRY + P. T.

(See "ATTEMPT")

TUB

T's swing upward to outline tub bottom

(See "JAR")

TUBA

Right T against left T at lips; right moves out and rises to 5

TUBE

Right G fingers on left G fingers; right moves up

(See "POLE")

TUESDAY

Palm-out T circles slightly

(See "MONDAY")

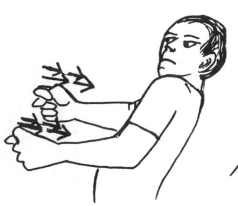

TUG★

T's tug diagonally inward; repeat

(See "PULL")

TULIP

T on each side of nose

(See "FLOWER")

TUMBLE

V-fingertips on left palm roll forward off palm

(See "SOMERSAULT")

TUNA

T swims forward

(See "FISH")

TUNE

Right T arcs from side to side behind left palm

(See "MUSIC")

TUNNEL

Right index spirals through left palm-down C

TURKEY

G-hand, pointing down at chin, shakes down

TURN

Right palm curves around left vertical index

TURNIP

Index finger slices side of T; repeat

(See "TOMATO")

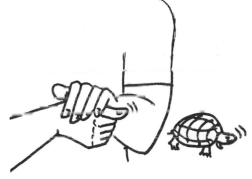

TURTLE

Left hand covers right palm—left A; wiggle right thumb

TUTOR

T's at temples move slightly forward; repeat

(See "TEACH")

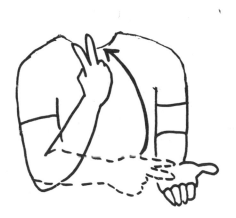

TWICE

Middle finger of 2 touches left palm, twist up to palm-in

(See "ONCE")

TWIN

Index of T touches left, then right corner of mouth

(See "BACHELOR")

TWIRL

Upside down T twirls

(See "SPIN")

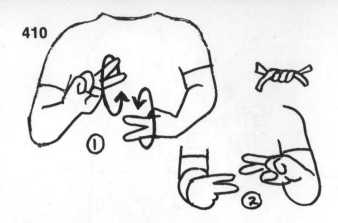

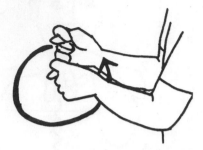

TWIST

Palm-down V above palm-up
V; reverse positions

(See "SPRAIN")

TYPE

Right T on left, then circle
vertically around each other

(See "KIND")

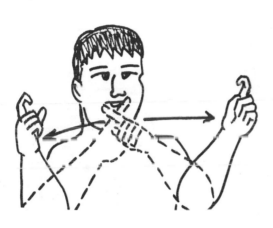

UGLY

Palm-down index fingers cross near nose; pull to X's at sides of face

UMBRELLA

Right S moves up once from left S

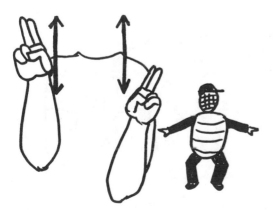

UMPIRE

Palm-out U's move up and down alternately

(See "BALANCE")

UNCLE

U shakes near temple

(See "AUNT")

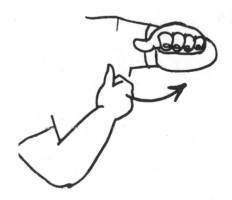

UNDER

Right A slides under left palm

(See "BRIBE")

UNDERNEATH

Under + Neath

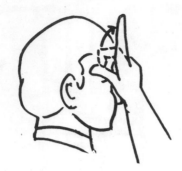

UNDERSTAND

Closed-X at temple snaps open to 1

UNDERSTOOD = UNDERSTAND + P. T.

(See "REALIZE")

UNIFORM

Palm-out U's move down body

(See "COAT")

UNION

Palm-out U's together; circle horizontally

(See "STANDARD")

UNITE

Right 9 grasps left U; both circle horizontally

(See "STANDARD")

UNIVERSE

Right H on left H; circle right H forward around left and rest on top

(See "WORLD")

UNIVERSITY

Horizontal U-palm circles up from left palm

(See "COLLEGE")

UNLESS

Right U, palm-down under left palm, drops slightly

(See "LESS")

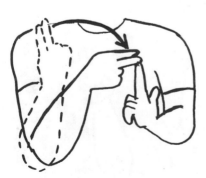

UNTIL

Right palm-in U arcs over to touch tip of palm-in left L

(See "TO")

UP ♔

Palm-out U moves up

UPON

Up + On

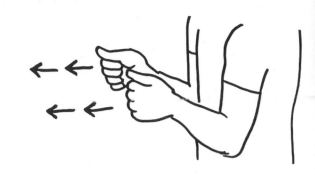

URGE ♔

A's jerk forward twice to the side

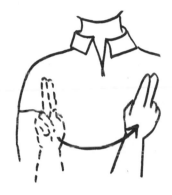

US

U at right side of chest circles to left side

(See "OUR")

USE

Heel of U-hand bounces on back of left hand

(See "BUSY")

USUAL

Use + -al

VACANT

V slides along back of left hand
VACANCY = VACANT + -Y
(See "BARE")

VACATION

Palm-in V's tap on sides of chest; repeat
(See "LEISURE")

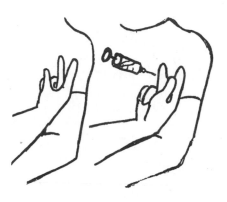

VACCINE

Back of V-fingers on upper left arm; thumb of V drops to index

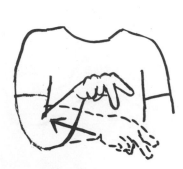

VACUUM

Palm-down V pulls back to the right

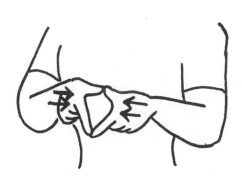

VAGINA

Thumbtips and index tips touch, indexes pointing downward

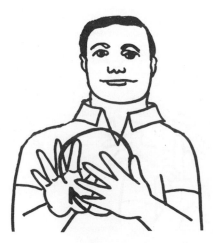

VAGUE

Left palm-in 5-hand in front of right palm-out 5-hand; circle alternately

VAIN

Palm-in V's near sides of head, drop fingers toward shoulders; hands remain stationary; repeat

VALENTINE

V's draw heart on heart

(See "HEART")

VALLEY

Beginning at sides, palms-down, draw valley

(See "CANYON")

VALUE

Palm-up V's circle vertically to touch palm-down

(See "IMPORTANT")

VAMPIRE

Bent V arcs to hit neck with fingertips

VAN

Palm-left V moves back from palm-right V

(See "CAR")

VANE

Back of right V hand rests on left index; rock back and forth like a vane

VANILLA

V circles on back of left hand

(See "CHOCOLATE")

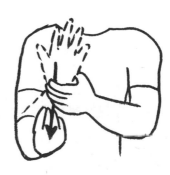

VANISH

Right open hand, palm-in, moves down through palm-in left C and closes to flat-O

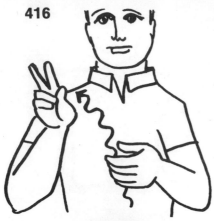

VAPOR

V wiggles up through left C-hand

(See "EVAPORATE")

VARY

1's, palms-down, move alternately up and down to each side

VARIOUS = VARY + -OUS
VARIETY = VARY + -ITY

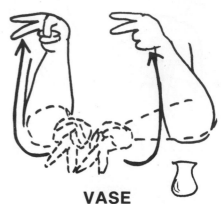

VASE

V's outline vase

(See "JAR")

VASELINE

Heel of V circles on left palm

(See "MEDICINE")

VEAL

Pinch side of left V and shake

(See "MEAT")

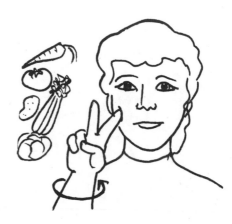

VEGETABLE

Index fingertip of V on cheek; twist

(See "APPLE")

VEHICLE

Palm-left V moves back from palm-right V; change to L's

(See "CAR")

VEIN

Fingertips of palm-down V draw up back of wrist

VERB

Side of palm-in V slides across chin below mouth

VERBAL = VERB + -AL

VERSE

Side of G finger and thumb slide across vertical left palm

VERTICAL

Palm-out V pulls downward

(See "DOWN")

VERY

Middle fingertips of V's touch and then arc apart

VEST

Palm-in V-hands arc inward on chest

(See "COAT")

VETERAN

Palm-out V brushes down side of head; repeat

(See "EXPERIENCE")

VETERINARIAN

Heel of V taps on left pulse

VETERINARY = VETERINARIAN + -Y

(See "DOCTOR")

VIBRATE

Palm-down 5-hands jerk forward and back alternately, quickly

VICE

Palm-out V index taps temple

VICTIM

Knuckles of palm-in A hit side of palm-out left V

(See "BUMP")

VICTOR

Right V on left S; V spirals
quickly upward

VICTORY = VICTOR + -Y

(See "WIN")

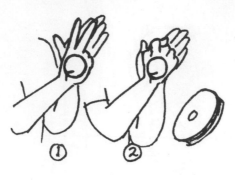

VIDEOTAPE

V and then T circle vertically
against left palm

VIEW

Palm-down V sweeps left
above left arm, "scanning"

VILLAGE

Index fingertip of V taps
fingertips of left palm-right
fingertips

(See "TOWN")

VINE

V grows and wiggles out and
down from left C

(See "GROW")

VINEGAR

Index finger of palm-left V on
chin; twist to palm-in

(See "SOUR")

VIOLET

V touches first one side of
nose, then the other

(See "FLOWER")

VIOLIN

9-hand plays violin

VIRGIN

V outlines face from left
temple, over head, to chin

(See "NUN")

VISION

Tip of index of V at corner of eye twists to palm-down V at right; sweeps left

VISUAL = VISION + -AL

VISIT

Palm-in V's circle vertically (May go in and out or out and in)

VISITOR = VISIT + -ER
(See "PEOPLE")

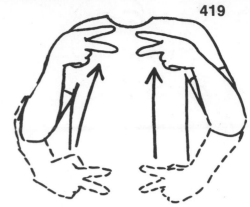

VITAL

Palm-in V's slide up body
(See "ADDRESS")

VITAMIN

Side of V throws toward mouth
(See "PILL")

VOCABULARY

Fingertips of V tap on side of left index; repeat
(See "WORD")

VOCATION

Palm-out V arcs side-to-side, hitting back of palm-down left S
(See "BUSY")

VOICE

Fingertips of palm-in V move up throat and out under chin

VOLCANO

From flat-O to 5, right arm repeatedly rises out of left C

VOLLEYBALL

Hands push up ball several times

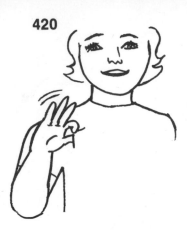

VOLUNTEER

At side of chest, right index and thumb of 9 tug material forward

VOMIT

5-hands arc out from throat (Can be done with one hand)

VOTE

Thumb and finger of 9 go into left O; repeat

VOW

Index on chin to heel of V on back of left hand
(See "PROMISE")

VOWEL

Palm-out V brushes across fingers of palm-in left 5
(See "ALPHABET")

VOYAGE

Right V pointing down, above left V pointing up; rotate alternately forward
(See "TRAVEL")

VULTURE

Draw palm-down V under nose, bending V-fingers

WADDLE

Inverted right Y rocks (waddles) forward on left horizontal palm

WAFFLE ★

Right W palm-down on left palm; lift again

WAG

Inverted W, hanging over left index, wags

(See "TAIL")

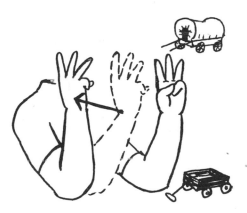

WAGON

Right W behind left W; right moves back

(See "CAR")

WAIL

Palm-in W shakes up and out from throat

(See "GROAN")

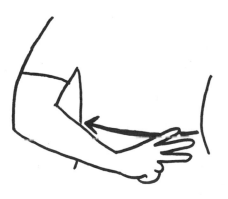

WAIST

W-hand drags across waistline

WAIT ♔

Palm-up right hand behind palm-up left, all fingers fluttering

WAKE

Closed G-hand at corner of eye opens to L

AWAKE = A + WAKE

WOKE = WAKE + P. T.

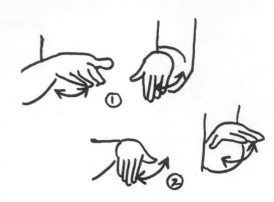

WALK

Wrists stationary, hands flip alternately

(See "HIKE")

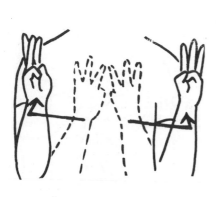

WALL

Palm-in W-hands together, separate, turn to face each other and move toward body

(See "DECK")

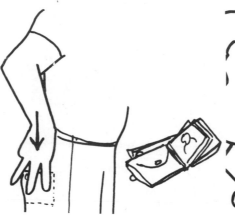

WALLET

Inverted W slides down hip as if into pocket

WALNUT

Index of palm-left W and then thumb of A jerk from under teeth

(See "NUT")

WALRUS

From mouth, C's curve out and down to S's

WANDER

Index pointing down moves forward on wavy path

(See "ROAM")

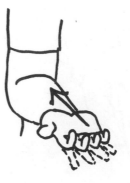

WANT

Palms-up 5's pull back to claws toward body

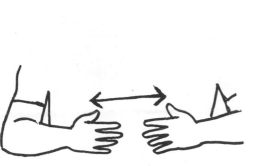

WAR

Palm-in 5's move side-to-side

WARD ★

Palm-out W moves forward

WARE

Palm-up W arcs slightly up and
down to right

(See "THING")

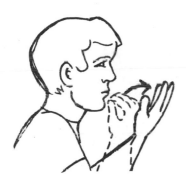

WARM

Flat-O at mouth opens slowly
to 5-hand while moving slightly
up and outward

WARMTH = WARM + -TH

WARN

Hand slaps back of left S-hand
sharply

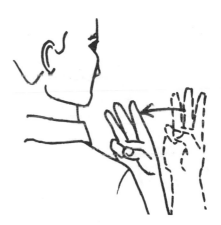

WAS

(Alt. 1)
Palm-in W moves back toward
right shoulder

(See "WERE")

WAS

(Alt. 2)
W passes to S back toward
right shoulder

(See "WERE")

WASH ♛

Palm-down A-hand scrubs
circularly in left palm

WASHINGTON

Palm-in W from shoulder
circles forward and right

WASP

W at cheek, then brush off wasp with open hand

(See "BEE")

WASTE

Flat-O, palm-up on left palm, slides off and opens to 5

WATCH ★

Palm-out V-index at eye; twist down to left wrist

WATER

Index finger of palm-left W taps chin

WAVE ★

Right hand waves

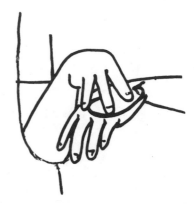

WAX

W waxes on back of left hand

(See "DUST")

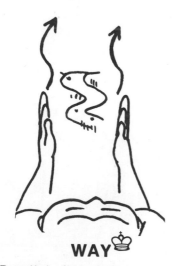

WAY ♔

Parallel flat hands move forward, weaving slightly side-to-side

(May be done with W's)

HIGHWAY = HIGH + WAY

FREEWAY = FREE + WAY

WE

W on right side of chest circles to left side

(See "OUR")

WEAK ♔

At right angle, fingertips on left palm; bend fingers; repeat

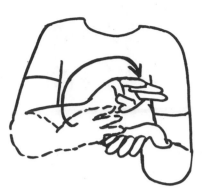

WEALTH

Back of W on palm-up left hand; arc up and over to palm-down

(See "RICH")

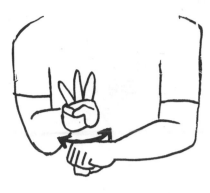

WEAR

Palm-out W arcs side-to-side, hitting back of left S

WORE = WEAR + P. T.

WORN = WEAR + P. P.

(See "BUSY")

WEARY

Fingertips of W's touch chest and drop downward to palm-up

(See "TIRE")

WEATHER

Palm-out W shakes downward

(See "SEASON")

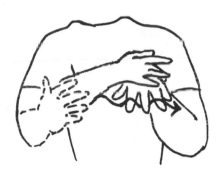

WEAVE

Right 5-hand makes weaving motion in and out of fingertips of palm-down 5-hand

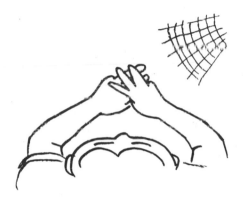

WEB

Palms-down, right W lies on back of left W

WED

Flat hands swing together and left clasps right

WEDDING = WED + -ING

WEDNESDAY

Palm-out circles slightly

(See "MONDAY")

WEE

Horizontal W's, palms facing close together, move slightly toward and away from each other (See "SMALL")

WEED

Flat-O grows rapidly through C, twisting to palm-out W

(See "GROW")

WEEK

1-hand brushes horizontally across palm

WEEP

2 palm-in W's drag alternately down cheeks

WEPT = WEEP + P. T.

(See "CRY")

WEIGH

Middle finger of right H rocks on side of left H-index

WEIGHT = WEIGH + -T

WEINER

S's and C's pull out of left W alternately

(See "BALONEY")

WEIRD

Fluttering W arcs past eyes

(See "FREAK")

WELCOME

Palm-up W curves horizontally toward body

(See "INVITE")

WELD

Thumb extended, point index at left palm; move back and forth

WELDING = WELD + -ING

(See "SOLDER")

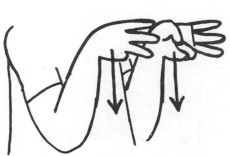

WELL

W-hands face each other; drop straight down

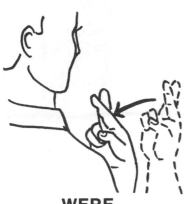

WERE

(Alt. 1)

Palm-in R moves back toward shoulder

(See "WAS")

WERE

(Alt. 2)

Pass W to R back toward right shoulder

(See "WAS")

WEST

Palm-out W moves left

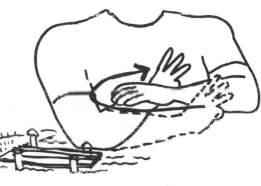

WET

Drop palm-in flat hand off chin, then open and close both flat-O's

WHALE

W makes 2 curves to the left, outside bent left arm

(See "DOLPHIN")

WHARF

W outlines left palm-down arm starting on outside

(See "DOCK")

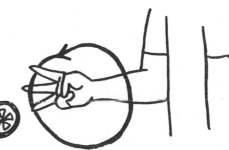

WHAT

Index fingertip brushes down across left fingers

WHEAT

Palm-out W brushes up through left C-hand

(See "GRAIN")

WHEEL

Palm-left W rotates vertically forward

WHEN

Indexes touch; make a circle with right index fingertip; return tip to tip

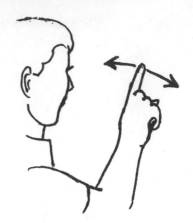

WHERE

Palm-out index shakes sideways

WHETHER

Palm-out W bounces off thumb, then off fingertip of left L   (See "THEN")

WHEW

Shake limp palm-down hand side to side

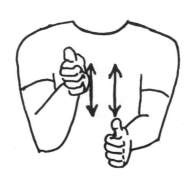

WHICH

A-hands, palms facing, alternately move up and down
(See "BALANCE")

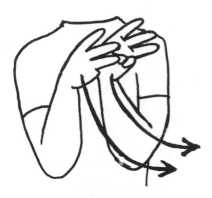

WHILE

W-hands face each other near right shoulder, arc down and forward
(See "DURING")

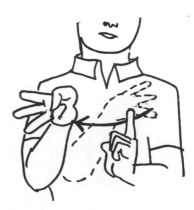

WHIP

Fingers of W whip past left index; may repeat
(See "BEAT")

WHIRL

Upside-down W circles rapidly
(See "SPIN")

WHISKEY

Side of W taps on side of I-1-hand; repeat
(See "LIQUOR")

WHISPER

Whisper behind hand

WHISTLE

Palm-in bent-V fingers near mouth

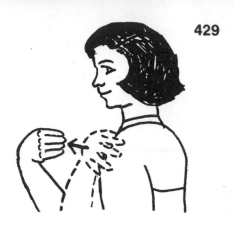

WHITE

5 on chest moves outward, closing to a flat-O

WHO

Thumb of L on chin; wiggle index finger

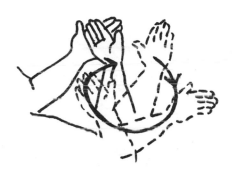

WHOLE ♔

Palm-down right flat hand circles and turns over, resting palm-up on left hand

WHOM

Who + palm-out M

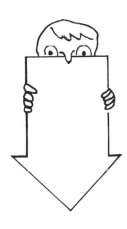

WHOSE

Who + palm-out S

WHY

Open hand, palm-in fingers on forehead, moves out to palm-in Y

WICKED

Palm-in W on chin; twist to palm-out and throw down
(See "BAD")

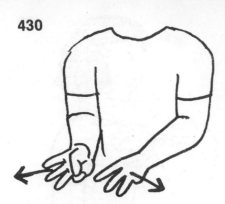

WIDE

W-hands, palms facing and thumbs touching, separate, moving slightly forward

WIDTH = WIDE + -TH

(See "BROAD")

WIFE

A at jaw to clasped C's

WIVES = WIFE + -S

(See "HUSBAND")

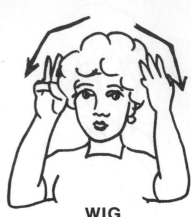

WIG

W-hands pull on wig

WIGGLE

Horizontal palm-left W wiggles forward

(See "FISH")

WILD

W twirls off temple

(See "IDEA")

WILL ♔

Flat-hand palm facing side of head; arc forward

(See "WOULD")

WIN ♔

Close right F on left S; spiral right S quickly upward.

WON = WIN + P. T.

WIND

(Verb)

Fingertips of W on wrist; circle W horizontally forward

WIND ♔

Horizontal hands swing back and forth, twisting at wrists, as wind "blows" them

WINDMILL

Palm-left W circles near left index

WINDOW

Sides of flat hands hit to open and close

WINE

Index finger of W circles on cheek, palm-out

(See "BEER")

WING

Left hand on right shoulder; flap right hand at the side

WINK

Thumb of L at eye, shut and open finger

WINTER

W's face each other; shake slightly (shivering)

(See "COLD")

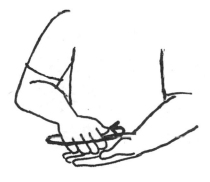

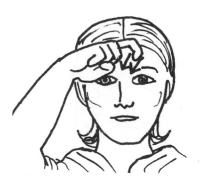

WIPE

Right palm wipes circularly on left palm

(See "WASH")

WIRE

I-fingertip shakes outward from left W and slightly down

(See "CORD")

WISE

Palm-down X nods near center of forehead; repeat

WISDOM = WISE + -DOM

(See "PHILOSOPHY")

WISH

Palm-in W slides down chest

(See "HUNGER")

WIT

Index of W on temple; W swings outward from wrist

WITNESS = WIT + -NESS

(See "SMART")

WITCH

Right X moves from nose to rest on left X, heels together

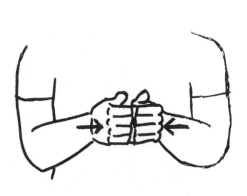

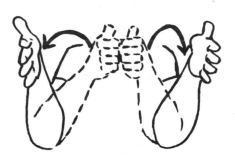

WITH

A-hands together, palm to palm

WITHIN = WITH + IN

WITHDRAW

Palm-out W moves back toward body, changing to D

WITHOUT

Knuckles together, A's move apart to 5's

WIVES

Wife + -S

WOLF

Hand at nose, pull out to flat-O

WOLVES = WOLF + -S

(See "BEAK")

WOMAN

A at jaw moves up to show height with bent hand

WOMEN

A at jaw; measure several
heights with bent hand

WON

Win + P. T.

WONDER

W circles near temple
WONDERFUL = WONDER + -FUL
(See "REASON")

WOOD

Elbow of W on back of left
hand; twist W slightly side to
side

(See "TREE")

WOOL

W slides up left arm
(See "FUR")

WORD

Right G-fingers rest against
left index

WORE

Wear + P. T.

WORK

Palm-out S taps back of left S;
repeat

WORKSHOP

Palm-out W's together; circle
out and meet as palm-in S's

WORLD

Right W on top of left W; circle right around left vertically

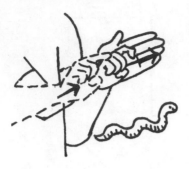

WORM

Side of right hand crawls across left palm, alternating 1 and X

WORRY

W-hands circle alternately before face

(See "TROUBLE")

WORSE

Palm-in V's arc from sides to cross wrists, palm-in

WORST = WORSE + -EST

WORSHIP

Left hand closed over right, move toward body in slight vertical circle

WORTH

Palm-up W's rise in vertical circle to meet, palm-down

(See "IMPORTANT")

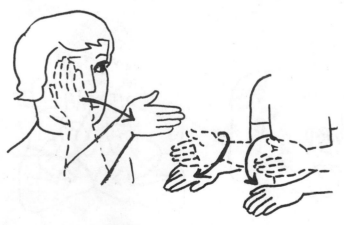

WOULD

(Alt. 1)

Palm facing side of head, arc forward; then flat hands, palms facing, drop to palms-down

WOULD

(Alt. 2)

Palm-out W-hand, at side of face, moves forward to D

WOW

W's on each side of O-mouth; push slightly forward

WRAP

Palm-in W's circle each other, separate

(See "TIE")

WREATH

Palm-out W's touch, circle vertically, and touch again

(See "BULB")

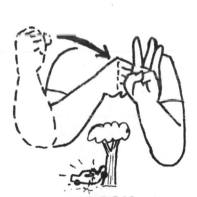

WRECK

S-fist hits side of left W

(See "BUMP")

WRENCH

Index and middle finger of W-hand "tighten" left index once

(See "MECHANIC")

WRESTLE

5-hands mesh fingers straight; shake forward and back slightly

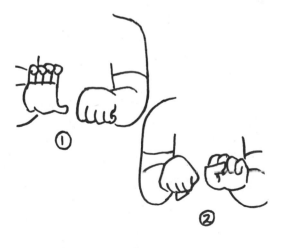

WRING

C's close to S's in a wringing motion

WRINKLE

W draws wavy wrinkles wherever they belong

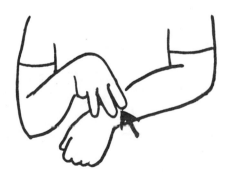

WRIST

Palm-down W draws across left wrist

WRITE

Thumb and finger of closed X
write on left palm

WROTE = WRITE + P. T.
WRITTEN = WRITE + P. P.

WRONG

Palm-in Y on chin

(See "MISTAKE")

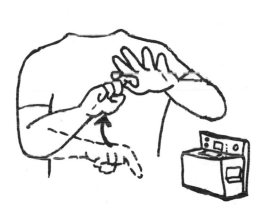

XEROX

Palm-down index rises to X
under left palm

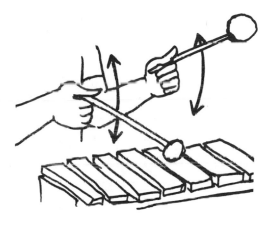

XYLOPHONE

A's alternately play from side to
side on xylophone

XRAY

X hand; then palm-in flat-O
opens, moving toward chest

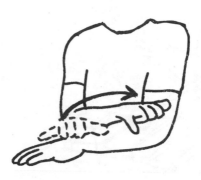

YARD

Palm-down Y on back of left hand moves up to inside of elbow

(See "MILE")

YARN

I-hand wiggles from left Y out and slightly down

(See "CORD")

YAWN

Palm-down Y under chin rises to palm-out; drops again

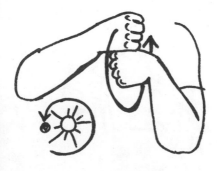

YEAR

S rests on left S; right circles vertically around left

YELL

Palm-in Y moves up and out from chin

(See "CALL")

YELLOW

Palm-left Y shakes

(See "BLUE")

YES

Y-hand nods
(Can be done with S-hand)

YESTERDAY

Thumbtip of Y touches near
chin, then near ear

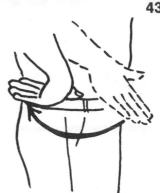

YET

Palm slaps gently backwards
near waist; may repeat

YIELD

Palm-in Y's arc forward to
palm-up

(See "GIVE")

YOGURT

Palm-up Y circles from left
palm to mouth

(See "SOUP")

YONDER

Y-palms face each other, right
slightly behind left; right
moves forward, thumb
brushing little finger of left, and
changes to palm-out R

(See "FAR")

YOU

Index points at person
addressed

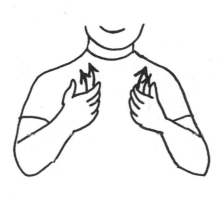

YOUNG

Tips of bent hands brush
upward twice off chest
YOUTH = YOUNG + -TH
(See "JUVENILE")

YOUR

Flat palm moves toward person
addressed
YOURS = YOUR + -S
YOU'RE = YOU + -'RE

ZEBRA
4-hands mark stripes on body

ZERO
Palm-out O circles once vertically

ZIP
Thumb and index-finger-knuckle zip up palm

ZIPPER = ZIP + -ER

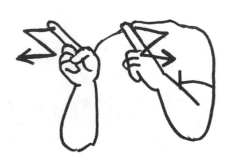

ZONE
Palms-out indexes outline two Z's in opposite directions

ZOO
Index finger draws Z on left 5-hand

SIGNS GROUPED BY FAMILIES

The following groups of signs are those which are similar in movement and belong together conceptually. We have found doing this has helped people to remember signs with greater ease. If a group of words originated from a traditional sign, we used that sign as the head of the family. If all the words are new, we merely alphabetize the list.

- The head if the family is shown with a ♔ after the word in the text.

- An asterisk (*) means look for a slight variation.

- Where we say see "_____", the "_____" will be the head of the family.

When there are only 2 words in a family, we cross-referenced them.

ACT	ADD	ADDRESS	ADVERTISE	ADVICE
drama	amend	biography	commercial	advise*
perform	divide'	exist	publicity	affect
theater	multiply*	inhabit		counsel
	subtract*	life		effect
	supplement	live		
		reside		
		survive		
		vital		

AFRAID	AGAINST	AIM	ALGAE	ALLOW
fear	con	goal	bacteria	grant
horror	prejudice	mission	cell	let
panic		object	fungus	opportune*
terror		target		permit

ALPHABET	AM	AMOUNT	ANGEL	ANGER
consonant	are	heap	elf	fury
vowel	be	mound	fairy	irritate
	is	pill	gremlin	rage
			leprechaun	tantrum
			pixie	

ANNOUNCE	ANT	APPLE	APPOINT	APRICOT
declare	beetle	fruit	engage	fig
proclaim	cricket	grapefruit	reserve	nectarine
	insect	pineapple		plum
	pest	vegetable		tangerine
	roach			
	scorpion			
	termite			

ARITHMETIC

algebra
calculus
figure
geometry
math

ART

architect
draw
etch
sketch*
trace

ASTRONAUT

eject
rocket

ATMOSPHERE

culture
environment
local
orient
region
social

ATTEMPT

effort
try

AUNT

cousin
niece
nephew
uncle

AVOID

dodge
evade

AXE

chop
hatchet

BACHELOR

single
twin

BAG

pouch
sack

BAD

evil
naughty
profane
rude
wicked

BAKE

casserole
roast

BALANCE

court
double
evaluate
judge
may
probable
referee
umpire
which

BALONEY

frankfurter*
sausage
weiner*

BAND

club
tribe

BANQUET

dine
feast
picnic

BAR

line
row

BARE

abort
empty
naked*
nude*
vacant

BASE

cellar
denominator*
element
fundamental
inferior
kindergarten
-neath
prime
sub-
theme

BASKET

April
hamper
purse

BAY

cove
gulf
harbor

BEAT

curse*
hit
lash
punch
slap
strike
whip

BED

hotel
motel
nap*
pillow

BELL

echo
jingle

BIG

grand*
great
huge
immense
large
tremendous

BICYCLE

bike
cycle
tricycle

BILLION

million
trillion

BIRD

chicken*
crow
duck
parakeet
parrot
robin

BLACK

coal
gray

BLUE	**BOARD**	**BODY**	**BONNET**	**BOOK**
green	panel	flesh	kerchief	album
purple	stage	health	scarf	bibliography
yellow		physical		

BORROW	**BOTHER**	**BOX**	**BROAD**	**BROOK**
credit	disturb	apartment	general	creek
rent	interfere	case	public	river
		den	wide	stream
		garden		
		kitchen		
		room		

BULB	**BUMP**	**BURY**	**BUSY**	**BUTTER**
globe	bang	grave	commerce	jam
wreath	crash	tomb	employ	lard
	damage*		function	margarine
	victim		industry	mayonnaise
	wreck		labor	oleo
			operate use	
			vacation	
			toil wear	

BUY	**CABBAGE**	**CALIFORNIA**	**CALL**	**CANCER**
cash	cauliflower	gold	shout	germ
invest	lettuce	silver	yell	infect
purchase				
shop				

CAP	**CAR**	**CARGO**	**CARPET**	**CAT**
lid*	bus	load	linoleum	kitten
lip*	jeep*	freight	mat	leopard*
top	tank*	stack	rug	panther*
	taxi			tiger*
	truck			
	vehicle			
	wagon			

CATERPILLAR	**CENT**	**CERTAIN**	**CHANGE**	**CHARACTER**
creep	dime	fact	adapt evolve	attitude
slug*	nickel	serious	adjust modify*	feature
snail*	penny	sure	alter reverse	moral
	quarter		amend revise*	noble
			convert switch*	personality
			distort translate	trait

CHICAGO	**CHILD**	**CHINA**	**CHIP**	**CHOCOLATE**
Detroit	dwarf	Asia	flake	caramel
Philadelphia	midget	Japan	piece	cocoa
		Korea		fudge
				vanilla

CHOOSE

choice
elect
option
select

CHRIST

duke
king
lord
majesty
prince
queen
royal

CHURCH

auditorium
temple

CIRCLE

ever
hoop
round

CLASS

bunch
department
family
group
herd
league
organize
team

CLEAR

bright*
obvious

CLOTH

fabric
rag
texture

COAT

blouse
jacket
robe
shirt
uniform
vest

COLD

chill
refrigerate
winter

COLLEGE

graduate
university

COMPLAIN

fuss
gripe
object

CONTINUE

constant
maintain
momemtum*
permanent
remain

COPY

duplicate
imitate
scissors

CORD

cable*
ribbon
string
thread
wire
yard

COST

charge
fee
price
tax

COUNTRY

county
foreign

COVER

frost
glaze
laminate

CRAB

lobster
shrimp

CRACKER

crackerjack*
matzo

CRY

tear
weep

CUT

scissors*
snip
trim

CYCLONE

hurricane
storm
tornado

DANGER

harm
threat

DARK

dim
fog
haze
shade
smog

DECK

porch
wall

DEER

antler
elk*
moose*
reindeer*

DENMARK

Finland
Norway
Swede

DEVIL

demon
mischief

DIAMOND

gem
jewel
ring

DIP

dye
rinse

DIRT

mud
pollute

DISPLAY

exhibit
model

DISPOSE

garbage
junk
trash

DO

behave
manner

DOCK

pier
wharf

DOCTOR	**DOLL**	**DOLPHIN**	**DOUGH**	**DOWN**
chiropractor	cartoon	porpoise	flour	low
medic	fun	whale	graham	vertical
nurse			pastry	south
paramedic*				
psychiatry				
veterinarian				

DRESS	**DRIFT**	**DUMB**	**EASE**	**EAT**
attire	float	idiot	convenient	breakfast
costume	glide	stupid	simple	dinner
gown	raft			lunch
pajama				meal
poncho*				supper

EDGE	**ELECTRIC**	**ENJOY**	**ENTER**	**EQUATOR**
crust	battery	amuse	invade	latitude
hoof	physics	entertain	infiltrate*	solar
lawn	socket		subway	
toe				

ESCAPE	**EVAPORATE**	**EXACT**	**EXCEPT**	**EXCHANGE**
evacuate	gas	perfect	especially	replace
flee	vapor	specific	particular	substitute
			special	

EXCUSE	**EXPERT**	**FABULOUS**	**FACE**	**FALSE**
apologize*	competent	elaborate	beauty	fake
pardon	excel	marvel	Hawaii	pretend
	skill	terrific	lovely	
	talent		pretty	

FANCY	**FAR**	**FAST**	**FEEL**	**FINE**
elegant	distant	rapid	emotion	courtesy
luxury	yonder	speed	mood	polite
style*			pride	
			proud	

FINISH	**FIRST**	**FISH**	**FIX**	**FLAG**
complete	January	shark*	mend	banner
end	prior	tuna	repair	pennant
expire		wiggle		
result				

FLOWER	**FORBID**	**FRACTION**	**FREE**	**FRESHMAN**
	ban			
daffodil	flunk	denominator	liberty	junior
pansy	prohibit	numerator	rescue	sophomore
rose				senior*
tulip				
violet				

FRIEND

acquaint
mate
neighbor
partner
relate

GALLON

pint
quart

GENERATE

heredity
inherit
legend

GHOST

goblin
haunt
spirit
spook

GIFT

award
dedicate
prize
reward

GIRL

female
her
Miss
Mrs*
she

GOD

admire
esteem
honor
respect

GOVERN

capitol
federal
mayor
politic

GRAIN

alfalfa
barley
crop
hay
oat
rye
straw
wheat

GRAVY

grease
oil

GROAN

growl*
howl*
moan
wail

GROUND

continent
-dom
ecology*
empire
field
land
meadow
plain
range

GROW

asparagus
broccoli
celery
ivy*
plant
rhubard
spring*
vine*

GUARD

defend
protect
prevent

HALL

lane
parallel

HAPPEN

chance
event
fate
incident
luck
occur
result

HAPPY

cheer
enjoy
glad
joy
merry

HARD

difficult
problem
tough

HE

fellow
guy
him
his
mister*
sir

HEART

February
valentine

HELP

aid
assist
rehabilitate
reinforce
therapy

HIDE

conceal
intrigue
mystery

HIND

behind
rear

HOLD

clutch
grasp
grip

HOLY

divine
pure
saint

HONEST

frank
genuine
real
true

HORSE

colt
mule*
pony
stubborn*

HOSPITAL

ambulance
clinic
infirmary

HOUR

age
century
decade
era
period
semester
term

HOUSE

barn
cabin
factory
garage
hut
museum
station

HUNGER

appetite
desire
passion*
starve
wish

HURT

ache
injure
pain

ICE CREAM

lollipop
popsicle

IDEA

abstract
concept
fantasy
fiction
hypothesis
myth
opinion
theory
wild

IGNORE

apathy
neglect

IMPORTANT

essence
main
precious
value
worth

INFLUENCE

contagious
infest

INSPECT

explore
investigate
pioneer
research

INVITE

guest
hire
welcome

JAIL

cage
prison

JAR

nest
net*
pot
tub
vase

JUICE

cider
lime
nectar

JUMP

hop
leap
skip

KILL

assassin
murder

KIND

breed
generous
type

LAW

constitute
curriculum*
doctrine
formula
ordinance
policy*
principle
rule
state

LECTURE

minister
preach

LEISURE

holiday
idle*
retire
vacation

LESSON

agenda
course
subject
topic

LIST

detail
ingredient

LONESOME

patient
tolerate

LOVE

dear
fond
hug

LUTHERAN

Presbyterian
Protestant

MAGAZINE

catalogue
journal
ledger
pamphlet

MAKE

create
manufacture
produce

MANAGE

control
dominate
handle
reign

MARK

notch
punctuate

MASK

Halloween
October

MEAN

define
intend*
purpose
rubella

MEASLES

freckle
pimple*
pox
pork

MEAT

beef
ham
liver
steak
veal

MEDICINE

alcohol
drug
vaseline

MELON

cantaloupe
jack-o-lantern*
pumpkin

MELT

cure
dissolve
remedy

MEMBER

committee
congress
delegate
faculty
legislate
parliament
senate

METAL	**MIDDLE**	**MINUTE**	**MONDAY**	**MONEY**
aluminum	center	instant	Friday	economy
brass	intermediate	late	Saturday	finance
copper	nucleus	moment	Thursday*	
iron		soon	Tuesday	
lead		tardy	Wednesday	
steel				
tin				

MONKEY	**MOUSE**	**MOUTH**	**MUCH**	**MUSIC**
ape	gerbil	oral	big	carol*
gorilla	hamster	speech	great	chorus
	rat		huge	hymn
			immense	lyric
			large	poem*
			quite	poetry*
			such	rhythm
			tremendous	song
				tune

NAME	**NATURE**	**NEAR**	**NEW**	**NOT**
identify	instinct	close	fresh	dis-
repute	litter	intimate	gospel	il-
			modern	im-
			raw	in-
				ir-
				mis-
				non-
				un-

NOTE	**NUT**	**OFFICE**	**OLD**	**ONCE**
detect	peanut*	boss	ancient*	double
memo	pecan	capital	elder	triple
recognize	walnut*	captain		twice

OPEN	**OPPOSE**	**OUR**	**OUT**	**OVEN**
expose	allergy	us	extract	broil
hatch	contrast	we	quit	grill
reveal	disagree*		resign	
	enemy			
	foe			

PANT	**PAPER**	**PARENT**	**PEOPLE**	**PERSON**
slack	kleenix	adult	folk	human
trouser	tissue	gender	visit	-ist
		neuter		
		orphan		
		sex		
		teen		

PICTURE

illustrate
photo

PLACE

area
district
island
lot
position*
situate
territory

PLAY

game
party
recess
sport
toy

POSITIVE

affirm
confirm
plus

POSTPONE

delay*
extend*
procrastinate

PRACTICE

coach
drill
intern
rehearse

PROMISE

guarantee
oath
pledge
testify
vow

PROVE

evident
proof

PULL

haul
tug

PUSH

buggy*
cart*

QUESTION

quiz*
riddle

QUIET

calm
gentle
peace
silent

QUOTE

idiom*
proverb*
slang*
title

REBEL

defy
revolt

READ

essay
prose

REASON

logic
meditate
ponder
thought
wonder

REQUIRE

condition
demand
impress
insist

RICH

fortune
treasure
wealth

SALT

cinnamon
spice

SATISFY

content
relieve

SAVE

conserve
reserve
safe

SCIENCE

biology
chemistry
experiment

SELL

peddle
sale*

SEND

deliver
export
refer

SENTENCE

fable*
grammar
language
linguistic
tale

SET

lay
occupy

SHAPE

contour
form
image
statue
trophy

SHINE

glow
polish

SHOE

boot
galoshes

SHORT

abbreviate
brief
temporary

SHOW

demonstrate
example
indicate
represent
symbol

SICK

disease
pervert

SIT

bench
chair
couch*
perch
roost
seat
sofa

SLICE

carve
pastrami

SMALL

compact
little
wee

SMELL	**SMILE**	**SOME**	**SOUND**	**SOUP**
fragrant	comic	factor	hear	broth
odor	giggle*	part	listen	cereal
	grin	section	noise*	dessert
	laugh*		radio*	pudding
				rice
				yogurt

SOUR	**SPAGHETTI**	**SPIN**	**STANDARD**	**START**
bitter	bacon	twirl	circumstance*	begin
sore	macaroni	whirl	common	commence
vinegar	noodle		company*	initiate
			together	origin
			union	
			unite	

STEAL	**STONE**	**STOP**	**STORE**	**STORM**
plagiarize	brick	cease	bank	cyclone
rob	concrete	halt	grocer	tornado
snatch*	gravel	interrupt	market	
	pebble		stuff	
	rock			

STRAIGHT	**STRANGE**	**STRONG**	**SUCCESS**	**SUGGEST**
career	fool	authority	accomplish	offer
direct	odd	energy	achieve*	present (v)
major	queer	intense	succeed*	recommend
minor*		might		
profess		power		

SUMMER	**TABLE**	**TALK**	**TALL**	**TEACH**
desert	counter	communicate	develop	educate
humid	desk	converse	erect	instruct
July		dialogue		tutor
		interview		

THAT	**THEIR**	**THEN**	**THERMOMETER**	**THING**
these	them	alternate	degree	component
this	they	either	meter	equip
those		neither*	temper	furnish
		nor*	barometer	item
		or	centigrade	material
		rather	fahrenheit	tool
		whether		ware

THINK

familiar
know
mind
remind

THOUGH

matter
spite

TIE

bind
wrap

TO

till
too
until

TOMATO

beet
cucumber
parsnip
turnip

TOWN

city
village

TREE

forest
grove
jungle
lumber
orchard
timber
wood

TRICK

irony
sarcasm

UP

elevate
high
north
rise

URGE

persuade
treat

WAIT

hesitate
pause

WAR

battle
crusade
quarrel
struggle

WASH

launder
wipe

WAY

path
road

WEAK

delicate
fragile

WEIGH

ounce
pound
ton

WHOLE

entire
include
total

WILL

destine
future

WIN

triumph
victor

WIND

air
breeze

WITH

accompany*
escort*

WORD

noun
syllable*
vocabulary

WORK

duty
obligate

WRITE

author
chalk
manuscript
pen
pencil
record (v)
secretary*

WORLD

civil
geography
international
universe

RESOURCES

This bibliography is purposely brief and necessarily incomplete. We offer it in hopes that it will offer a starting place for learning more.

I. General Language Acquisition.

Moskowitz, Breyne. Nov. 1978. "Acquisition of language." *Scientific American*. 239, 92-108.
A succinct, clearly stated article reviewing the basic findings in child language-acquisition as a general topic. Best place to start.

Dale, Philip. 1976. *Language Development: Structure and Function*. Holt, Rinehart, and Winston: New York.

DeVilliers, Jill and Peter DeVilliers. 1978 . *Language Acquisition*. Harvard University Press: Cambridge, Mass.

Both of these books are used as texts for classes in language acquisition. They *may* be a little difficult, but are the generally accepted texts for up-to-date information.

II. Language Acquisition by Deaf Children.

Bonvillian, John, Veda Charrow, and Keith Nelson. 1973. "Psycholinguistic and educational implications of deafness." *Human Development*. 16, 321-345.
A thoughtful display of evidence supporting the total communication approach in educating deaf children.

Reimer, Becky L. Dec. 1979. "A viable classroom model for using various communication modes." *American Annals of the Deaf*. 124:7, 838-846.
A clear, practical system for teaching English and speech through morphemic-based signs (S.E.E.) and meaning-based signs (ASL) in combination.

Spradley, Thomas and James Spradley. 1978. *Deaf Like Me*. Random House: New York.
An honest account of a hearing family's harrowing experience with their deaf child, and their final success through the use of signs. Highly readable and not at all sentimentalized.

III. Sign Language Research

Baker, Charlotte, and Carol Padden. 1978. *American Sign Language: A Look at its History, Structure and Community*. T.J. Publishers Inc. (order from 8805 Arliss St., Silver Spring, MD. 20901. $2.00). 22 pp.
A basic, simply stated review of current research on American Sign Language. Written for the interested lay person, it is well-organized and explains some of the recent discoveries linguists have made about ASL. Although there are a few minor inaccuracies, it is surely the best presentation of its type and is highly recommended.

Lane, Harlan. 1977. "Notes for a psycho-history of American Sign Language." *Deaf American*. 30:1, 3-7.
A very brief, elegantly stated history of ASL, emphasizing the importance of the historic cooperative efforts between deaf and hearing educators in the development and maintenance of ASL and the deaf community.

IV. The Use of Simultaneous Communication with *Non*-Hearing-Impaired Children. (These references are intended for the speech pathologist/language therapist who works with language-delayed children and language-impaired adults.)

Konstantareas, M., J. Oxman, and C.D. Webster. 1977. "Simultaneous communication: an alternative to speech training with autistic children." *Journal of Practical Approaches to Developmental Handicaps.* 1.1, 15-21.

Konstantareas, M., J. Oxman, and C.D. Webster. 1977. "Simultaneous communication with autistic and other severely dysfunctional nonverbal children." *Journal of Communications Disorders.* 10, 267-282.

Schaeffer, B. "Teaching spontaneous sign language to non-verbal children: Theory and Method." *Sign Language Studies.* 21, 289-316.

Schaeffer, B., A. Musil, G. Kollinzas, and P. McDowell. 1977. "Spontaneous language for autistic children through signed speech." *Sign Language Studies* 17, 287-328

Yamada, Jeni, Jack Kriendler, and Mardi Haimsohn. "The use of simultaneous communication in a language intervention program for an autistic child: A case study." To appear in *Working Papers in Cognitive Linguistics*, vol. 1. (will be published at UCLA, Department of Linguistics.

V. Other Resources

Modern Signs Press, 3131 Walker Lee Drive, Rossmoor, California 90720

SIGNING EXACT ENGLISH flashcard kit A (Sign on one side, drawing of the sign's meaning on the other, no words on the cards) Two-color cards are keyed to meaning: animals, food, clothes, home, people, places, shapes, vehicles, colors, verbs. 406 cards, 5 x 8, with a brief manual.
   Projected titles: States and Cities, Creative Signing, Sports, Holidays, SEE Teachers' Manuals.

Alinda Press (Frank Caccamise and Carolyn Norris, P.O. Box 553, Eureka, California 95501).

Large-picture primers of signs for ages 2 and up, booklets for hospital signing, police signs, guide to deafness for hearing children, novel: ISLAND OF SILENCE.

National Association of the Deaf, 814 Thayer Avenue, Silver Spring, MD. 20910.

Free catalogue lists scholarly texts on deafness, sign language books, fiction for and about the deaf, children's sign and story books, parents' guides, rehabilitation literature, films, cassettes, games, electronic aids. The DEAF AMERICAN magazine, published monthly.

International Association of Parents of the Deaf, 814 Thayer Avenue, Silver Spring, MD 20910.

Assists parents with education and communication; offers public information.
Bi-monthly newsletter, THE ENDEAVOR.

Gallaudet College, 7th and Florida Avenues, N.E., Washington, DC., 20002.

Sign language programs and public service, pre-primary through college and graduate-level courses. Gallaudet Bookstore carries materials parallel to those of the NAD.

NOTES

NOTES